String Methods for Beginne

String Methods for Beginners is designed for students to receive the essential playing and teaching skills on all orchestral string instruments. The goal of this textbook is to be truly methodical in its approach, and to assist the instructor, completely eliminating the need to do additional research, or reorganization in preparation to teach this class. Students will gain the basic knowledge and experience to teach bowed stringed instruments in public schools. *String Methods for Beginners* covers the necessary topics to learn and teach the violin, viola, cello, and string bass. It explores the fundamentals of those instruments and teaching considerations, utilizing a heterogeneous approach.

As the primary resource to any college- and university-level String Techniques, String Methods, or Instrumental Methods class, this course book fits into a standard semester, comprised of 25 lessons, which correspond with two hourly classes per week for the term. It provides the instructor with the tools to teach a classroom of non-majors or string education majors, or a mixed classroom of both.

FEATURES

- Offers a blueprint for a semester long string methods course.
- For beginning students, and also comprehensive for more in-depth study or for reference.
- Logical, step-by-step "recipe-like" approach.

Selim Giray is Director of Orchestral Studies at the University of Mississippi.

String Methods for Beginners

Selim Giray

Routledge
Taylor & Francis Group

NEW YORK AND LONDON

First published 2020
by Routledge
52 Vanderbilt Avenue, New York, NY 10017

and by Routledge
2 Park Square, Milton Park, Abingdon, Oxon, OX14 4RN

Routledge is an imprint of the Taylor & Francis Group, an informa business

© 2020 Taylor & Francis

Library of Congress Cataloging-in-Publication Data
Names: Giray, Selim, author.
Title: String methods for beginners / Selim Giray.
Description: [1.] | New York : Routledge, 2020. | Includes bibliographical references and index.
Identifiers: LCCN 2019050809 (print) | LCCN 2019050810 (ebook) | ISBN 9780367226831 (hardback) | ISBN 9780367226862 (paperback) | ISBN 9780429276347 (ebook)
Subjects: LCSH: Bowed stringed instruments–Methods. | Bowed stringed instruments–Instruction and study.
Classification: LCC MT259 .G54 2020 (print) | LCC MT259 (ebook) | DDC 787/.193071–dc23
LC record available at https://lccn.loc.gov/2019050809
LC ebook record available at https://lccn.loc.gov/2019050810

ISBN: 978-0-367-22683-1 (hbk)
ISBN: 978-0-367-22686-2 (pbk)
ISBN: 978-0-429-27634-7 (ebk)

Typeset in Baskerville
by Swales & Willis, Exeter, Devon, UK

Visit the eResource: www.routledge.com/9780367226862

Contents

Illustrations

Preface

Music teachers are often assigned to teach string instruments in their workplace. To assure competence in this area, college and university-level String Techniques, String Methods, or Instrumental Methods classes are an essential component of Bachelor of Music Education degrees and satisfy course requirements of a course in a NASM accredited music program. *String Methods for Beginners* is designed to serve as a primary text and resource book. It presents 25 lessons that correspond with two hourly classes per week for a semester and can be used in full without any chapter omission. *String Methods for Beginners* and its accompanying supplemental materials are designed for the instructor to achieve an efficient and readily organized class. Music students, majors, non-majors, or a class of both string majors and non-majors are taught essential, fundamental playing and teaching skills on all orchestral string instruments.

This course has been prepared with 20 years of string orchestra, techniques, methods, and pedagogy experience at the secondary and higher education levels, and was used in class at University of Mississippi before it was published. This book provides the instructor with the tools and aids required to face all eventualities of the student body: from a classroom of non-majors to string education majors.

Notes for the Instructor

You may use any string method book or graded repertoire to accompany this textbook. As you prepare the student instruments for this class, please mark all of your classroom instruments with tape. You may affix four strips of 1/16 inch white striping tape on fingerboards for this class (upper strings: whole, whole, 1/2, whole; cello: whole, whole, 1/2; bass: whole, whole, whole, 1/2). For the violin and viola thumb alignment, you may place a hole punch reinforcement label on the side of the neck. Lastly, behind the neck, you may place a hole punch reinforcement label to help position the thumb for all low strings (for detailed instructions on taping, please refer to Chapter 17).

Prepare the bows with white striping tape by marking the stick with two tapes roughly 8 inches apart at its middle 1/3 section, effectively partitioning the bow into three equal playing sections. This reference gives students an exact visual cue in picturing the middle-third portion, which is the first section of bow they will learn to play.

This textbook and its lessons have been planned to rotate among tasks to allow students to build their stamina without causing tension or possible injury. Theoretical and practical aspects of the course and rotating tasks between left-hand and right-hand techniques are arranged with that interest in mind. Since playing string instruments involves breathing and uses the entire body, it is highly recommended to begin classes with breathing and stretching exercises (see Instructor's Packet for specifics), as it is helpful for students to stand up and stretch to alleviate any possible tension during the rotation of tasks. In addition to those exercises, the Instructor's Packet (available at www.routledge.com/9780367226862), provides additional resources as guided in-class exercises, exams and quizzes, and a sample course schedule.

Notes for the Student

Be determined yet patient with your own progress in this course. After all, this is a survey course that covers all four orchestral string instruments within a semester. Your instructor will present this course much like it is in secondary-school teaching. Therefore, both the terminology and choice of words are reasonably applicable to the age groups that you will likely teach. For that reason, you need to start contemplating how to translate the knowledge and activities we cover in this class to a specific age group. Toward that end, imagine and treat your classmates as your future class, and start building your peer-teaching and presentation language accordingly.

It is expected that in the earlier stages of this class you may not have much endurance in holding and playing a string instrument. In this class you will acquire the necessary stamina and comfort level to play for a prolonged period of time. Be observant of your body and communicate with the instructor if you notice any discomfort with holding or playing an instrument during class or outside of class. Lack of tension is of the utmost priority of this text to introduce string instruments.

Acknowledgements

My special thanks go to my editor, Constance Ditzel, and editorial assistant Pete Sheehy; production editor Lauren Ellis; project manager Natalie Thompson, and copy editor Emma Lockley; for her help at National Music Museum, Ms Arian Sheets, for the help with excerpt copyrights, Erin Dickenson; Dr Rodney Schmidt, Susan Gaston for their invaluable editorial help; Senior Catalog Librarian Prof John Leslie, for his expert help with the index; Prof Amanda Johnston for her encouragement and inspiration throughout the process; Dr Robert Riggs and Prof Nancy Maria Balach Schuesselin, for their unwavering administrative support; Master Luthiers Anton Krutz, Dustin Williams and Yücel Açın, for sharing their wisdom; and Dr Mark Foley, Dr Jacob Dakon, Dr Kasia Bugaj, Frances Oare, Dr Steve Oare, Starkey Morgan, Dr Christine Kralik, Dr Andrew Paney, Dr Ayşegül Giray, and Necati Giray for making this book possible. I would like to express my gratitude to my former violin professors Fritz Gearhart and Eliot Chapo for their encouragement, inspiration, and mentorship in realizing this project. I thank my wife Wendy C. Giray and daughter Sara Pelin Giray for their support and help through the long process of research and writing, and for realizing the photography.

Lesson 1

Contents

The first lesson will introduce the following:

- The discipline of string instruments.
- Some qualities of a string teacher.
- A quick overview of string teaching fundamentals.
- How to build string practice skills.
- A course outline and its requirements.
- A detailed list of string-instrument parts and the bow.
- Items to research and possibly purchase.

Introduction

Welcome! This class will cover topics necessary for teaching and learning string instruments: the violin, viola, cello, and double bass—also known as the violin family. This is a survey course exploring the fundamentals of those instruments and teaching considerations, using a heterogeneous approach. This course will prepare students with the fundamental knowledge and experience to teach bowed stringed instruments in secondary schools. The students will gain an understanding and ability to play string instruments at a rudimentary proficiency level, teaching string instruments in a heterogeneous setting in a secondary school, learning pedagogical strategies to address common mistakes at this level, and learning to produce good tone and left- and right-hand techniques on string instruments. Because these lessons will encompass multiple string instruments at various proficiency levels, some techniques covered may be above the student's current playing capabilities, nevertheless, students will have an understanding of how to teach and what strategies to follow for those necessary techniques.

It is necessary to use string instruments in a variety of settings, such as recruiting, building school and community support for the music program, and collaborating with the band and choral programs. Whether in due course students will assume the role of a string teacher at a secondary school or not, a good understanding of string instruments is essential for any well-rounded musician.

The skills presented in this class must be practiced daily regardless of previous experience. It is an expectation of this course for students to practice their assigned instruments outside class, in addition to their major instruments or voice. The goal of this class is to provide students with pedagogical strategies to gain new string-related experiences, and therefore increase their comfort level as string teachers. The students may, however, incorporate prior experiences from their disciplines in the daily string practice regimen.

When it comes to string-specific issues, students may not have an understanding and an appreciation for the complexities they will face in recruiting for their future program. Generally speaking, both choir and band programs are more numerous and more readily accepted than strings, therefore, promoting strings is more challenging. Even though strings make up the majority of a full orchestra, which is a familiar sounding ensemble, only 8.8% of US adults have attended a classical music concert.

In addition to traditional methods, some secondary-school teachers foster their string programs by seeking answers in alternative styles such as strolling strings, rock, and non-Western genres. Through our course we will study the issue of recruiting, promoting for strings, and consider possible solutions for those challenges.

Address to Non-Majors

If you think this is just another routine methods or techniques course, I urge you to consider the following: even though your current primary career goals might be completely different, there is a real possibility you will become a string teacher at a secondary school. Those of you with a non-string background make up anywhere from 25% to 30% of public school string teachers in the US. "How so?" you may ask. It just might be that the path to your dream job of Director of Bands or Director of Choirs at such-and-such high school comes with the caveat of 50% string teaching. It is the reality and distinct possibility that your efforts this semester may very well make up the contents of your toolbox, and be the first steps toward string teaching. Furthermore, it may very well lead to a change in your career goals, and *you might become a string teacher!*

Address to Majors

Regardless of your major instrument, your instructor may call upon your skills as a string major, where you will be expected to help with peer-teaching. The initial, or the setup phase is the time where most hands-on teaching is necessary. Therefore, your instructor may ask for your help in physically molding your classmates into the perfect stance, and instrument hold. Furthermore, your instructor may ask for you to share your earliest experiences as a string student—as in reservations, fears, and memorable discoveries—and why those memories made a lasting impression on you.

Some Qualities of an Accomplished String Teacher

A gifted string player, and an accomplished string teacher are not necessarily one and the same. With talent, education, and much practice, one can acquire the knowledge and facilities of a superlative string performer. Although it is a major accomplishment and arguably an advantage, performance ability alone does not spontaneously make said performer a competent teacher. Furthermore, as we have discussed earlier, some of the finest string teachers are of non-string background. Among the required qualities of a string teacher are: a discriminating ear and unrelenting demand for intonation and tone quality, a thorough understanding of—and instantaneous solutions to—the technical demands of all string instruments, an in-depth knowledge of the string repertoire, and an inexorable enthusiasm for music and teaching.

Fundamentals of String Instruments

In this course, we will accomplish the following list of fundamental elements of string instrument playing, strategies in teaching those rudiments in the secondary-school setting, and all relevant competencies required of a string teacher:

1. Instrument hold.
2. Bow hold.
3. Sound production: bow weight, speed, and placement (contact point).
4. Left-hand and bow-arm techniques.
5. Music reading skills and rhythm exercises.
6. Common technical problems and their remedies.
7. Teaching individual instruments: violin, viola, cello, and double bass.
8. Discussion on various teaching approaches.
9. Instrument selection and maintenance.
10. Developing knowledge of string library and graded repertoire.
11. Programming appropriate repertoire for a string ensemble.

Building Practice Skills

As music students understand and appreciate the necessity of continuous practice on any major instrument, each string instrument requires the same dedication to daily practice. Furthermore, it is imperative to learn how to practice these particular string instruments. The ability to play string instruments requires two separate and seemingly unrelated activities: the left hand, and the bow arm. It takes perseverance and focused practice to undertake both techniques separately, and eventually combine them. If students devote the required outside-class time, their comfort level will allow the required attention during class, and they will be able to focus on other essential elements. Also, performing in front of the class on a string instrument might be an uncomfortable prospect—given that students of this class are accomplished performers in their major area. Therefore, a regular and attentive practice regimen is the only way for students to acquire the ability to perform on all members of the string family.

Course Outline

Reading, theory, and applied approaches to string instrument teaching will be discussed during class. Students do not possess much stamina at the earliest stages of string playing regardless of age. Correct playing position cannot be sustained for a prolonged time. During class we will switch between tasks to build endurance. All string instruments will be taught concurrently for maximum learning opportunities through observing other instruments in action.

Students will gain the knowledge and ability to demonstrate the items below:

1. Awareness of diverse string class teaching strategies.
2. Knowledge of the history and development of string instruments.
3. Parts of the instruments.
4. Care, maintenance, and recognition of quality brands.
5. The importance of working with local violin shops for lease, purchase, and repair needs.
6. Demonstrate correct posture, instrument hold, and bow hold.
7. Gain an understanding of, and ability to perform with desirable tone production and intonation.
8. Ability to perform at Grades I to II.
9. Ability to recognize and fix common bad habits in beginning-level string students.
10. Gain knowledge of the basic finger patterns on all four string instruments and play scales and arpeggios in D major, G major, and C major from one to two octaves.
11. A thorough understanding of first position and shifting to higher positions, playing ability in first position.
12. Ability to demonstrate the basic bow strokes *détaché*, *martelé*, staccato, and spiccato, and their appropriate application to basic period styles. In addition, gain an understanding of bowings and bow distribution.
13. The student will be able to demonstrate and teach vibrato on the assigned instrument and will have an understanding of particular vibrato approaches on *all* string instruments. The student will have knowledge of those teaching strategies of vibrato as well as common vibrato problems and appropriate solutions.
14. The student will know the knowledge base for Grades I through to VI, and published recommended lists for school orchestra music.
15. Good recruitment and retention strategies for string classes and knowledge of successful string and orchestra scheduling in schools.

Course Requirements

1. Attendance.
2. Completing the assignments at the end of each lesson.
3. Reviewing the previous lesson.
4. Reading the following lesson prior to class.
5. Active involvement in class is expected, and furthermore, you will assist the instructor in actual teaching when called upon and demonstrate good peer teaching habits throughout the class.
6. All string instruments demand daily practice. Students are expected to practice *every* day of the week, throughout the semester. There is no other way to acquire the necessary

motor skills required by those instruments. Thirty minutes of practice a day is the preferred method, but not three hours of practice crammed into one weekend.

7. Visit an area secondary school: the instructor will modify this component by the local access to a competent string program, and availability of participating string teacher(s).
8. Four playing tests: the student will receive a grade on proper posture, and instrument hold. Correct left- and right-hand positions, intonation, tone production, correct style and bowing, and overall facility (please see Playing Test Rubric for the exact criteria).
9. Written work: write a report on a secondary-school string or orchestra class visit at the discretion of the instructor.
10. Midterm, written exam, final exam.

Parts of String Instruments

All four instruments in the violin family are bowed chordophones, featuring a wooden resonator or soundbox, and a neck. The members of the violin family, violin, viola, cello, and double bass, are purpose-built instruments for their acoustical properties: the strings under tension are excited and engage the bridge, which rocks back and forth on top of the bass bar and sound post. The sound post is what engages the back plate, which behaves like a trampoline to move up and down. This pulls air in and out of the f-holes, thereby producing an amplified sound. All orchestral string instruments use three different kinds of wood selected for the density, flexibility, and resonance ability required for that particular portion of the instrument.

Most commonly used wood are:

1. **Maple:** the hardwood used to make the back, neck, ribs, and bridge.
2. **Spruce:** the softwood used to make the rest of the instrument. Specifically, the top plate, bass bar, sound post, linings, corner blocks, neck block, and end block.
3. **Ebony:** a dense wood used to make the pegs, string nut, fingerboard, saddle, and end button. It is black, or very dark brown in color. Ebony is always used for the fingerboard. Rosewood or boxwood may be used instead of ebony for other areas. The ebony, or its substitutes, are not varnished but left in their natural state.

Let's identify parts of string instruments students will need to know at this point. All must memorize these parts, as the instructor will refer to them for all of the following class activities (Figures 1.1 and 1.2):

External Features

1. **Scroll:** the scroll at the top of all string instruments is an ornate yoke. Some earlier instruments would have carvings of a human head, a lion head, etc. Some contemporary makers and factories leave out the ornamentation and terminate the top of the pegbox without a scroll. However, the student instruments will exclusively have the scroll, giving the player reliability in weight and length reference points.
2. **Pegbox:** this is the carved portion of the yoke with four pegs holes drilled, two on each side. In some older instruments, there may be signs of repair on the peg holes due to wear over time.
3. **Pegs or Tuning Pegs:** the four pegs are made of ebony, boxwood, or rosewood. They are conical in shape, and are only held in place by friction. The pegs are fitted by

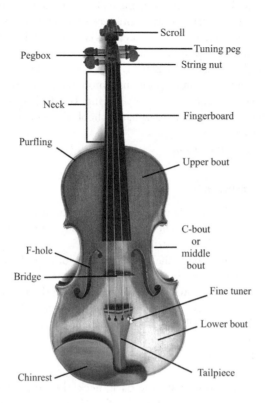

Figure 1.1 The violin, front

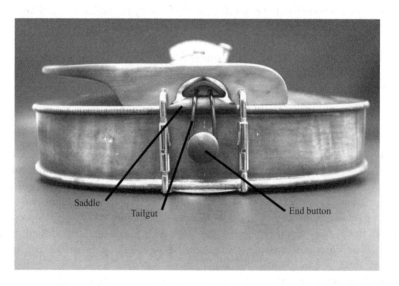

Figure 1.2 The violin, bottom

shaping the pegbox with a peg reamer, shaping the pegs with a peg shaper, cutting the ends with a hand saw to eliminate the extra overhang, and by drilling holes on the peg for the string to go through. The two pegs of the lower strings are attached on the corresponding side, and the two upper string pegs on the opposite side. The outmost string peg is always located on the bottom on each side. Roth-Caspari mechanical pegs are discussed in Lesson 9.

4. **Machine Head:** the double bass is furnished with a machine head or individual machine head pegs to ease tuning. A machine head is a set of streamlined metal gears located on a plate, allowing the player to tune with great precision and little effort, and individual machine heads perform the same function without the need of a plate.

5. **C-String Extension:** on the double bass, this is an option for the low E string (E1) to be extended down to a C-natural (C1). It is a requirement for an orchestral bassist, and only an advanced student would need this option.

6. **Nut or String Nut:** the ebony string nut is at the beginning of the fingerboard and the resonating portion of the string. The length of the string nut is aligned with the neck and fingerboard, but it is cut slightly higher than the fingerboard to allow the string to resonate freely. The string nut has four rounded corresponding channels to allow the individual strings to be routed, and be able to slide back-and-forth during tuning without causing any chafing.

7. **Fingerboard:** most well-made instruments use a fingerboard made of ebony.

8. **Neck:** carved of maple matching the back and ribs. It is secured onto the instrument by gluing it to the neck block. Neck thickness, width, and smoothness are all essential elements for ease of playing. Traditionally, the length of neck is not treated with colored varnish.

9. **Back or Back Plate:** the back is cut in the book-matched fashion, and those two pieces of spruce are glued in the center, known as a two-piece back plate (found in student-grade instruments), or is made of single cut maple, known as one-piece.

10. **Ribs or Sides:** made of maple, ribs are six pieces of grain-matching wood, curved to the instrument mold and glued to the internal blocks. Also, internally, they are fortified by linings. The violin maker soaks the pre-cut and planed pieces of ribs then uses a bending iron to bend those pieces to match the instrument mold.

11. **Top Plate or Belly:** this portion of the instrument is spruce, cut in the book-matched fashion and glued at the center. It is either a two-piece top plate (found in student-grade instruments) or a single-cut spruce one-piece top plate.

12. **F-holes:** the two mirroring soundholes or f-holes are positioned both on the bass and treble side of the bridge and are shaped like a lower-case script letter *f.* They allow resonant air to escape the resonator or soundbox. This enhances the amplitude and tone quality of the instrument. The inside notch of the letter F marks the alignment of the bridge. The label may be seen through the f-hole on the bass side. Furthermore, these soundholes allow the installing and adjusting of the sound post, among other luthierie functions, as mundane as removing dust balls, called "dust bunny".

13. **Bridge:** an unvarnished cut of maple. The ornate cut of the bridge is mostly standard, however, some subtle differences from maker to maker can be observed. Its two feet on the treble and bass sides—or treble foot or bass foot—are fitted to the particular shape of each instrument. Also, the crown must follow a template and it should match the profile of the fingerboard. The bridge must be fitted within perfect measurements, what is called a shop setup. A quick guide for bridge placement is that the inner notches of the f-hole line up with the top of the bridge. However, on older instruments, this practice may not

produce the desired standard measurement. Therefore, it is best to measure the top of the bridge from the string nut, ensuring perfect resonating string length.

14. **Purfling:** predominantly a decorative item, is three sandwiched pieces of pearwood with two outer layers dyed in black, inlaid into a channel carved near the edges of the top and back plates. Aside from pearwood, other types and combinations of wood or even other materials may be used to make purfling. Those include: maple, poplar, ebony, boxwood, and plastic or synthetic materials. Some inexpensive instruments are painted to look like purfling. However, those instruments lack the function of purfling: to stop cracks or knocks at corners and bouts (especially the C-bout where unintentional bow contact may occur) from advancing further. This line of defense is especially helpful for the top plate that is made of softwood, in contrast of the hardwood back.

15. **Tailpiece:** usually a piece of ebony, it supports four holes with a wedged end atop, one for each string, or a fine tuner (or string adjuster) to be installed. On its bottom, tapered end are two holes, where the tailgut is attached. Some tailpieces come with four built-in fine tuners. A few makers for tailpieces are Wittner, Thomastik-Infeld, and GEWA. Tailpieces may be wood (ebony, boxwood, rosewood, or pernambuco), composite graphite, plastic, aluminum alloy, or carbon fiber.

16. **Tailgut:** historically catgut, or twisted cattle intestine, has been used until the invention of nylon tailgut. Fernando Sacconi's (1895–1973) adjustable nylon with brass adjusters, known as Sacconi tailpiece adjuster, revolutionized tailgut with its safety, reliability, and for being impervious to all weather and barometric pressure changes. Recently, the Kevlar tail cord came to the market as a viable option or aircraft-rated steel wire rope assembly for a double bass. Student instruments often use a nylon tailgut, or Sacconi-style tailpiece adjuster, although it is possible to come across a catgut on an older instrument, or a solid wire hanger on a double bass.

17. **Saddle:** the ebony piece that fits at the end of the top plate, where the tailgut rests and bends at a 90° angle before looping onto endpin or end button.

18. **Strings:** historically, strings have been made with gut or silk. Currently, the violin family instruments use synthetic, wound, or steel strings. Strings need to be evenly strung onto the fingerboard, properly shop adjusted to resonate freely without buzzing when plucked or played with the bow. The bridge should not raise the strings too high for comfort when playing.

19. **End button:** located at the tailpiece end of the violin or viola. It is a peg inserted through a hole into the rib and the end block and secures the strings onto the instrument. It must withstand pressures in excess of 55 pounds on a violin.

20. **Endpin or spike:** located at the bottom of the cello or double bass, the endpin is a retractable metal rod inserted into a conical ebony plug (or fitting). It is secured and adjusted by a metal sleeve and a tightening screw. Some performers insert a non-adjustable endpin, made of ebony, rosewood, or boxwood, but all student instruments are furnished with adjustable endpins.

21. **Varnish:** one of the violin maker's signs of mastery and personalization, varnish has been subject to extensive discussions. For our purposes, we will mention that there are two varnish bases: oil and alcohol (spirit). Violin makers apply multiple coats of varnish, both colored and clear, depending on the type of varnish, and the vision of end product. Some mass-produced student instruments, however, may not have any sealer ground applied before the varnish, or a spray varnish may be applied, or paint in some cases.

22. **Chinrest:** most likely made of a piece of ebony grooved to fit the violin or viola player's jawbone or underneath the side of the mandible. There are two holes where the chinrest

clamp screws are attached. Some chinrests attach to the left of the tailpiece, some rest across it. Most inexpensive student instruments have a plastic chinrest. The chinrest must fit the student without the clenching of teeth or other signs of tension. Companies do make adjustable chinrests that can fit an individual player, leaving the left hand free to move without the weight of the instrument.

23. **Shoulder Rest:** the shoulder rest is an accessory attached below the lower bout of the instrument, where it is placed roughly below the chinrest and rests on top of the collarbone (or the clavicle) of the player. Shoulder rests vary in shape, size, and material. Shoulder rests can be a thin piece of fabric or foam, suede, metal, wood, or carbon fiber. Students should be fitted with a properly sized chinrest *and* shoulder rest or pad.

Internal Parts

1. **Bass bar:** is a piece of spruce, cut, fitted, and glued underneath the top plate. It is on the lower pitched side of the instrument just inside the f-hole and below the bass foot of the bridge. It is approximately 3/4 the length of the top plate and it tapers at both ends. The thickest point is the middle conforming to the inside curvature of the top plate. Some student instruments may not have a separate bass bar, but it may be formed during the shaping of the top plate.

2. **Sound post:** is a spruce dowel, cut, fitted, and friction wedged with a sound post setter on the treble side of the instrument just beyond the treble foot of the bridge. To avoid the sound post moving or falling, the instrument cannot be subjected to forceful knocks or jolts. Also, when changing strings, a single string should be replaced at a time, in order not to take a chance with the sound post falling.

3. **Blocks:** made of spruce, the neck, end, and corner blocks are glued and shaped into the mold, and after the mold is removed, remain as structural stiffeners, and foothold points of string instruments.

4. **Linings:** these are thinly cut edge pieces of spruce—much like the ribs—bent into shape with an iron, and glued on both top and back edges of the ribs. They help with the structure of the instrument, and extend the gluing surface of both the top and back of the instrument.

5. **Glue:** a water-soluble bone and hide glue, traditionally from horses, known as "cologne" glue is used in making and repairing string instruments. The beige-colored glue pearls are melted in a double-boiler, and applied while warm. The gluing surfaces are cured under pressure by way of clamping overnight, or up to 24 hours for larger surfaces. The use of proper water-soluble glue allows for the instrument to be maintained and repaired, allowing the top plate or any other part to be removed without damage. Student-grade instruments may make this practice impossible by using permanent, furniture-grade wood glue in the manufacturing process.

6. **Label:** affixed inside of the instrument on the bass side of back plate, the label identifies the maker, year, and city. Historically it is written in Latin, regardless of the country of origin, indicating *fecit*, the maker, (or *faciebat*, he made) and *anno* year. More-or-less this tradition continues to date. In student instruments the label specifies which instrument was modeled after in production of the instrument, along with its manufacturing specifics as model and serial numbers. The label in an older instrument is never to be taken at face value by a layperson, as fake, unreliable, and missing labels are commonplace.

Parts of the Bow

Let's look at the bow and its parts and how these parts function (Figures 1.3, 1.4 and 1.5).

- **The Stick:** the bow shaft, called the stick, is made of dense wood such as pernambuco, brazilwood,[1] rosewood, or snakewood—mostly on Baroque or gamba bows. Pernambuco (*caesalpinia echinata*) comes from the eastern pacific-coast region of Brazil—the country's namesake—has been the most desirable material for finest bows, and is currently an endangered species. There are, however, synthetic materials which respond much like their biological counterparts. Most student bows are made of fiberglass, and select carbon fiber bows are becoming more accepted among professional string players.
- **Frog:** made of ebony (sometimes ivory, tortoiseshell, or plastic), the frog anchors the hair. Sometimes a completely decorative inlaid mother of pearl dot adorns either side of the frog, and can be used for pedagogical reasons, as to placement of the middle or the ring finger. Sometimes another decorative shape such as a flower embellishes the frog, or this inlaid dot is omitted altogether.

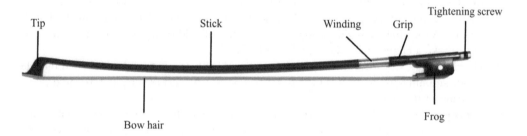

Figure 1.3 The bow

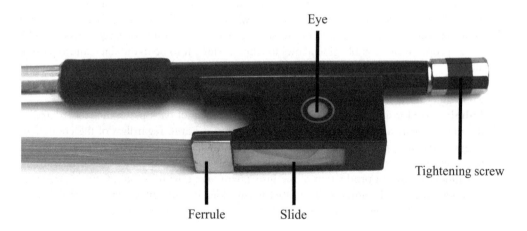

Figure 1.4 The bow, frog detail

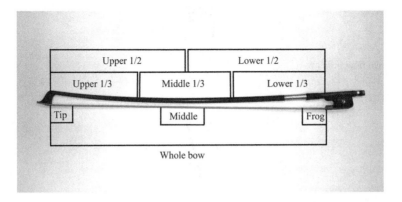

Figure 1.5 The playing partitions of bow

- **Button or Adjuster:** on top of the frog and inside the shaft mortise, the button, or adjuster is a threaded brass piece offering a shank and an adjustable eyelet, which accommodates the tightening screw.
- **Bow Hair or Hair:** bow hair is perhaps among the most important elements of sound production. With the help of applied rosin, which creates friction, the bundle of bow hair makes the string vibrate. The horse hair comes from the tail of a male cold climate horse such as a Siberian or Mongolian. For most string instruments, white horse hair is used, however, bass bows may use a "peppered" black-and-white combination, or all black horse hair for the coarse qualities of the black hair, arguably allowing for a better "bite". Inexpensive student bows, however, may have synthetic hair, which is inferior to real horse hair.
- **Tightening Screw:** the tightening screw is inserted into the shaft right above the frog and attaches onto the button or adjuster.
- **Slide:** a decorative piece of mother of pearl is attached onto the bottom of the frog, which disguises the hair, where it is anchored onto the frog with a maple tenon (or plastic in the case of inexpensive student bows), called a frog plug.
- **Ferrule:** [/ˈfɛrəl/] a metal piece attached onto the frog by friction with the help of a spread wedge, keeps the slide in place, shaped with a rounded top and flat bottom perfectly fitted to the contours of the frog.
- **Grip:** the grip is a piece of leather that wraps onto the stick, adjacent to the frog.
- **Winding:** a Silver wire wound onto the stick where the index finger rests, placed right at the end of the grip. Sometimes winding is omitted—as in the case of some student bows.
- **Tip:** the terminating end of the bow, referred to as the "head" within the context of bow making, is shaped like a hatchet in which the hair is secured. The hair bundle is wedged into the mortise cavity and secured with a tapering piece of maple tenon (or plastic in the case of inexpensive student bows), called a tip plug. Under the hatchet is an ivory piece, which extends further than the shaft, protecting it from knocks, or drops.

Motions of the Bow

Playing with the bow, referred to as arco playing, will require the down-bow and up-bow motions (Figures 1.6, 1.7, 1.8, and 1.9). The down bow direction is from frog to tip, and

Figure 1.6 Down bow indication

Figure 1.7 Up bow indication

Figure 1.8 Frog, down bow indication superimposed

conversely, up bow from tip to frog. Down and up bow, however, merely refer to the bow direction only, but not its placement. For instance, it does not necessarily mean for the bow to be placed at the frog for down bow motion to take place, for it can occur anywhere in the bow. Generally speaking, down bow occurs on strong beats, and up bow on weak beats. The reason for this preference is the weight distribution of the bow and the natural arm movement for starting every bow stroke.

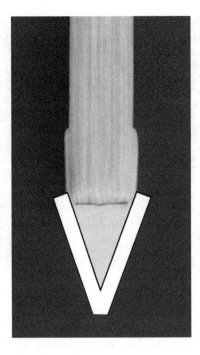

Figure 1.9 Tip, up bow indication superimposed

Course Timeline for Bow Application

In this course, we will learn fundamentals of string playing as separate components before combining them all. As far as the bow technique is concerned, we will first:

- Become familiar with the bow hold.
- Learn preparatory bow exercises.
- Learn all motions associated with the bow.
- Apply the above to open strings.
- Lastly, combine the fingered playing with the bow (Figure 1.10).

Items to Receive a Quote, and if Necessary, Purchase

- A complete string instrument outfit: 4/4-size violin, 15 1/2"–16" viola, 4/4 cello, and 3/4-size double bass.
- Shoulder rest for upper strings.
- Endpin stop for low strings.
- Rosin.
- Mute.
- Dust towel.
- A set of student-grade strings such as D'Addario Prelude.

Although the assigned string instrument should come with all furnishings, it is prudent to receive a quote on every replaceable and personalized item. A shoulder rest or an endpin stop

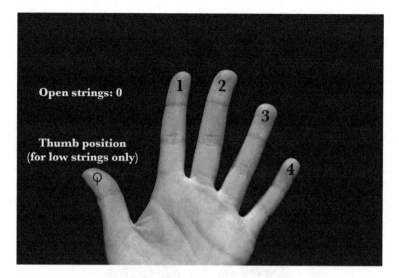

Figure 1.10 The left-hand finger numbers

for a string player is akin to a mouthpiece or a reed for a wind player. If feasible, students should go to a local specialized violin shop, rather than a general music shop.

Assignment

1) Purchase the textbook and other items as requested by the instructor.
2) Prepare the quote list for the assigned instrument, and be ready to share it with the class.
3) Prepare a typed, one-page, double-spaced essay that answers the following questions, to be turned in at next class:

   - Why did you enroll in this course?
   - What do you hope to learn in this course?
   - What secondary instrumental experiences do you have, if any?
   - What string experience do you have, if any?
   - Which particular string instrument interests you, and why?
   - Do you have any pre-existing condition that the course instructor should be aware of when assigning your instrument?
   - In a perfect world, what ensemble and grade-level would you teach?

4) As per the syllabus mark the videotaping and playing dates in your calendar.
5) Fill out the student's portion of the Instrument Rental and Check-Out Contract (see Lesson 2).
6) Memorize parts of string instruments and the bow.
7) Review today's lesson and read Lesson 2.

Note

1 Sometimes used interchangeably with pernambuco, here it encompasses all subspecies of this family of trees.

Lesson 2

Contents

This lesson's objectives are:

- Learn how to care for the assigned string instrument.
- Become familiar with seating arrangements in a heterogeneous string class.
- Learn the string instrument assignment process.
- Become familiar with, and be able to point to parts of the newly-assigned string instrument.
- Learn string playing posture and how to hold the instrument.
- Learn to play pizzicato.
- Learn preparatory bow exercises.

Theory: Instrument Overview and Care

Before we discuss playing and teaching we must first address instrument precaution and protection considerations. It is most likely that the instructor has assigned mass-produced student-grade instruments in this class, which are known to be durable and rather forgiving. However, no student instrument can be expected to survive when it is stepped on. Thus, it is best to learn how to respect instruments and treat them as best as we can and set a good example for our future students. Toward that end it is imperative that we establish a classroom procedure for each task and abide by that routine. Many successful string teachers have strict rules and expectations for every routine task in their classes.

While under our care we should never expose any of the string instruments to the following situations:

- Extreme heat or cold.
- Direct sunlight.
- Close to a heat source.
- In a wet and damp environment.
- To be dropped, jarred, or shaken.

The following maintenance rules apply to the bow:

- The bow hair must be loosened after each playing session, otherwise constant tension will cause the bow to warp.
- Never touch the bow hair, since oil from your hand will impede the bow's ability to retain rosin, and will cause gunk to build.

The students may already be familiar with carrying an instrument case, however, string instruments may require a bit more care due to their construction materials and their particular structure, as we briefly discussed in Lesson 1. For instance, all members of the violin family contain a dowel made of spruce, called a sound post. This custom-cut piece of wood is not glued, but is held in place by snugly fitting it with a sound post setter, and is further secured by string tension on the instrument—more on this as we discuss changing strings. The bridge is also held in place by string tension, and is the highest point on top of all string instruments, therefore, it should be guarded against all knocks, furthermore, it may not be well protected in the case, if the instrument is not tied down to the case by any internal ligature. Hard cases provide an exceedingly wide range of protection. Where a well-made case can take the greatest torment imagined by commercial airline carriers, another may suddenly open when one least expects it and drop the instrument. However unlikely, metal strap clips (lobster claw hooks, clasps, or snap hooks), and their plastic cousins are known to fail, and the instrument may fall onto the floor from as high as the shoulder height. At the time of instrument assignment, it is advisable to become familiar with the instrument case.

How to Carry an Upper-Strings Hard Instrument Case

- Upper string cases should be carried with the top bulge away from the person carrying the case.
- The case may be placed on its side, or flat, but not on its bulged top, as it will put weight onto the bridge.

How to Carry a Low-Strings Soft Instrument Case:

- Cello soft cases do not protect the bridge of the instrument so use caution when passing other objects and moving through doorways, or carrying it up and down the stairs (see Figure 2.1).
- The same concern pertains to the double bass scroll while carrying inside its soft case, and without it. The person carrying the instrument must beware of the height of the doorjamb, and be cautious that the retracted endpin will not get caught over a threshold, and remain clear and behind the carrying person while carrying the bass up or down the stairs (see Figures 2.2 and 2.3).

Figure 2.1 Carrying a cello up the stairs in a soft case

How to Open and Close an Upper-strings Instrument Case

Place the hard case on a chair where it is secure and open it. Momentarily, for example, while rosining the bow, the violin or viola may be placed in the case while the case is open. Once out of its case, *never* place an upper-string instrument on the floor, or on a chair! Similarly, *never* hang an instrument on a music stand by its scroll. Such careless practices must be avoided at all times. When putting an instrument away, remove the shoulder rest or shoulder pad, wipe off any rosin from the belly of the instrument and strings by the bridge and the bow stick with a dust towel and loosen the bow hair.

How to Open and Close a Low-strings Soft Case

First, remove the bow from the soft case's front pocket, and place the soft case on its side on the floor. Unzip the case from the bottom, hold the instrument by the neck, and remove from the case. Conversely, when putting instrument away, reverse the entire process and place the bow in the case as the last item.

Heterogeneous String Classroom Setup

The instructor of this class most likely follows a seating system most consistent with the particular classroom and class setting that allows quick access to each student.

Figure 2.2 Carrying a bass up the stairs

Therefore, it is imperative that all belongings, including backpacks and instrument cases, be placed well away from the playing area of the classroom. Once the assigned seating is established per the instructor's directions, it is the responsibility of students to follow this established procedure to maintain a safe and functional classroom setup. A well-organized string classroom is imperative to teach effectively and maintain a safe environment.

Instrument Assignment

The instructor will be assigning instruments by fitting them as they are assigned. Generic features of hands best fitted for particular instruments are as follows:

Violin: medium-size hands with equal spacing between fingers.
Viola: medium-size hands with longer fingers and equal spacing between fingers.
Cello: larger and stronger hands with wide spacing between fingers.
Bass: larger, stronger, and stout hands with wide spacing between first and second, and second and fourth fingers[1].

These rather generalized preferences must be broached with care and discussed with students during instrument assignment, providing a logical justification why it is best to start with a particular instrument based on the student's physical features. The

Figure 2.3 Carrying a bass down the stairs

assignment may be a tender subject and some students may have their hearts set on an instrument in advance. It is imperative that the teacher takes care to explain in detail and exercise judgment in this process. At the time of recruitment it is best to have a small ensemble to present a musical selection for prospective students to hear each instrument. It is likely that this is the first time they will have heard a string instrument played live.

First, all students should get their arm measurements from the side of the neck to mid-palm: extend the arm straight out, palm up, and measure. See Appendices for further measurement information. To determine each student's correct size, the instructor will place the violin or viola in the playing position on the collarbone, and the student will reach around the scroll with their left hand (Figure 2.4). If the hand cannot reach the scroll comfortably with a relaxed elbow, the instrument size is too large. If the scroll can be reached with a relaxed elbow, the instructor will help the student place their first, second, third, and fourth fingers on the first position tapes that are marked on the neck, and keep the thumb aligned with first finger (Figure 2.5). It is imperative for a teacher *never* to assign an instrument too large for a student, as playing on an ill-fitted instrument may cause intonation, technical, and most importantly, permanent physical issues.

Figure 2.4 Upper strings sizing: left hand placed on scroll

Figure 2.5 Upper strings sizing: left fingers placed on tapes

For the cello, the instrument size can be determined with the following method: student's overall height vs the instrument scroll, C peg behind student's left ear (Figure 2.6), and left-hand fingers placed on proper tapes on the fingerboard without having to over extend. To fit the cello, locate an orchestral chair at the proper height for each student: heels should make full contact with the floor, and knees should be at a 90° angle. If students need to find a different chair, they must do so before attempting to fit the cello. To fit the left hand, place the first, third, and fourth fingers on the first position tapes that are marked, and keep the thumb opposing the second finger under the neck. The fingers should be in the proper left-hand position (C shape) to remain rounded while they reach proper placement, and should not be straightened (Figure 2.7).

To fit the double bass, adjust the endpin length to bring the first tape of the fingerboard to the eye-level of the student (Figure 2.8). To fit the left hand, place the first, second, and fourth fingers on the tapes that are marked on the neck, and keep the thumb behind the second finger. Just like the cello, the fingers should be in the proper left-hand position (K shape) to remain rounded while they reach proper placement, and should not be straightened (Figure 2.9). Once the students have fitted for the proper size and been assigned an instrument, all students need to fill out the proper sections and return the Instrument Rental and Check-Out Contract to the instructor (Figure 2.10). The necessary information for the instrument is either in the label inside the instrument by the maker or the factory, outside the instrument affixed by a particular institution (e.g. the university), or occasionally, both.

Figure 2.6 Cello sizing: C peg relative height behind student's left ear

Figure 2.7 Cello sizing: left fingers placed on tapes

Figure 2.8 Bass sizing: first finger is at eye level when placed on first tape

Figure 2.9 Bass sizing: left fingers placed on tapes

A Review of Parts of String Instruments

Now that students have been assigned their new string instruments, we will go over the parts of string instruments that were introduced in Lesson 1, by touching each part named by the instructor, and name the kind of wood or material used to make that particular item.

1. **Scroll**
2. **Pegbox**
3. **Pegs or Tuning Pegs:** touch the pegs one by one from the lowest to the highest tuning (violin: G, D, A, E; viola: C, G, D, A; cello: C, G, D, A; double bass: E, A, D, G).
4. **Nut or String Nut**
5. **Fingerboard**
6. **Neck**
7. **Back or Back Plate**
8. **Ribs or Sides**
9. **Top Plate or Belly**
10. **F-holes**
11. **Bridge**
12. **Purfling**
13. **Tailpiece**
14. **Tailgut**
15. **Saddle**

Sample Instrument Rental and Check-Out Contract

This institution hereby makes a loan and grants temporary custody of the musical instrument listed below to _____, hereinafter "the Student".
(*PRINT full name*)

1. If Student notices that repair is needed, he/she must notify his/her area director immediately.
2. The Student shall replace or repair the instrument if lost or damaged.
3. The instrument listed below shall be returned to the School of Music by the last day of finals of the semester for which it is checked out. **Failure to return instrument** by deadline will result in student being placed on Academic Hold with the University, a report will be made to the University Police Dept., and appropriate legal action will be taken as necessary.

Instrument Shared with:_____

Instrument		Brand Name		Student ID No
Serial No.			Equipment/ Accessories	
			Case No	

Instrument to be used in which class, ensemble: MUS _____ Ensemble_____

In signing this contract, the student agrees to all of the above conditions and acknowledges receipt of the above instrument with any equipment and accessories listed.

_____   _____

Student Signature   Date

Student Information

My Student ID: _____

Local Address: _____   *Local Phone:* _____

Home Address: _____   *Home Phone:* _____

Email Address: _____   *Cell Phone:* _____

Office Use Only

Person Issuing Instrument: _____ Date Instrument Issued: _____

Person Checking Instrument In: _____ Date Instrument Returned: _____

Copy of Driver's License/State ID Card attached: __ **Copy of Student ID Card attached:** __

Figure 2.10 Instrument Rental and Check-Out Contract

16. **Strings:** touch the strings one by one from the lowest to the highest, naming the string you are touching (violin: G, D, A, E; viola: C, G, D, A; cello: C, G, D, A; double bass: E, A, D, G).
17. **End button**
18. **Endpin or spike**
19. **Chinrest**
20. **Shoulder Rest**

Point at the exact spot on your instrument as the instructor names the internal part, and name the sort of wood used to make it:

1. **Bass bar**
2. **Sound post**
3. **Neck Block**
4. **End Block**
5. **Corner Blocks**
6. **Linings**
7. **Label**

Applied: Posture and Instrument Hold

When it comes to an instrument hold there are multiple schools of thought, and below is one way of teaching proper posture on all string instruments. Chinrest and shoulder rest height decisions with the upper strings, and height and angle decisions with the low strings are among those varying choices. If the student has an established posture and setup, whether it follows the below guidelines perfectly or not, it does not need to be changed. However, if the student demonstrates engrained bad habits, evident by tension and other visible signs, it is necessary to intervene and address those posture and setup issues.

Eminent pedagogue Rolland prefers well-balanced weight shifting between both feet, Suzuki favors the left foot,[2] as does Joachim,[3] while Havas prefers the "third leg" theory, where the balance is maintained at the base of the spine.[4] When it comes to the sitting position both Rolland and Havas promote a well-balanced weight distribution, complete with the "third leg" expression of Havas, while Suzuki promotes a forward-sitting position and left-leg preferred balance.

Posture and Instrument Positioning

Upper Strings Standing Position

The definition of good posture for the upper strings is standing tall, shoulders back (*never* raised), feet shoulder-width apart, in a straight line to allow one heel to come off the floor, allowing a sway motion. A good analogy for this posture is as follows: the student must stand much like riding in public transportation, as in a bus, subway car, etc. Therefore, the upper strings students can keep their balance and will be able to sway without feeling "boxed in".[5]

Once proper posture is achieved, upper string students turn their heads 45° to the left and place the violin or viola on the collarbone. The instrument should be at a slight angle to its right, but not too steep. Also, the positioning on collarbone should not allow the instrument to droop onto the chest, or be raised onto the shoulder. It is impossible to overstress how critical it is not to tilt the head onto the instrument, or clinch the jaw. The scroll will be high enough to allow the strings to be perfectly horizontal, or parallel to the floor, and "nose, scroll, elbow, toe" adage is helpful in remembering this positioning (Figures 2.11 and 2.12). Additionally, Rolland's Balancing a Ball exercise (or Holding Game) is an effective way to keep the instrument from drooping: place a ping pong ball or rubber ball in-between the low two strings between the bridge and the end of the finger board, and keep it from rolling away from the bridge (ensuring proper instrument height), and falling off from the side (ensuring proper instrument angle) (Figure 2.13).[6] Upper strings instruments that are properly fitted to the student with shoulder rest and chinrest, should be held in place without the help of the left hand. In other words, lifting or keeping the instrument in place is never the left hand's job: the sole responsibility of the left hand is to play. At this early stage it is common for students to experience the instrument to droop onto chest, or struggle with other issues in holding the instrument, therefore, constant attentiveness is necessary. The instructor may have to make adjustments with the shoulder rest or chinrest, until a comfortable and reliable instrument hold is attained.

Upper Strings Sitting Position

In this class we will sit tall in the front four inches of the chair (*never* leaning back), shoulders back (*never* raised), feet shoulder-width apart, with the left heel planted and the right knee low enough to

Figure 2.11 Correct upper strings setup

Figure 2.12 Correct upper strings instrument hold and posture

allow free bowing. While sitting down in an ensemble, upper string players must maintain the exact healthy foundation for their instrument as they have established while standing. This involves balancing the weight between the hips and feet and sitting straight but not rigid. The instrument positioning should remain exactly the same as the standing position.

Cello Sitting Position

The cello player sits tall (*never* leaning forward, or torso rotated), shoulders back (*never* raised), using only the front four inches of the chair with their feet open at shoulder-width apart. The cello will be placed in front of the body and endpin placement should create a triangle between the feet and the endpin. The following reference points will decide the cello's tilt angle: the student will extend the endpin to about 6 inch by placing the cello in the guitar position (longer endpin length for a taller

Figure 2.13 Balancing a ball between G and D strings on a violin

student, and shorter one for the opposite), scroll pointing left, left hand holding the neck. Once the endpin is extended, points of the backside lower bout will be in contact just in front of, and slightly above the knee bone, the top of the upper rib (or upper edge behind the neck) will be right on top of the breastbone, C peg behind the left ear, and the neck is one fist-width above the left shoulder. The cello will be slightly tilted toward the left knee, but will not poke into the side of either knee and the right knee should remain low enough to allow free bowing. The fingerboard and endpin should be aligned with the student's centerline and the instrument should not be crooked. Lastly, the left hand should be able to reach the entire span of the fingerboard, and the left fingers will be able to stretch on the corresponding tapes or notes (on D string: first finger on E-natural, third finger on F-sharp, and fourth finger on G-natural) in their proper position, and without any discomfort. "Hugging" the instrument is a good way for proper instrument angle and endpin length to be confirmed.

Double Bass Sitting Position

The string-bass players may use a 24-inch metal shop stool, or a 24-inch wooden bar stool. Depending on the student's height, some adjustment may be needed with the stool selection. The student will extend the endpin to about 6 inch. The player will sit tall (*never* leaning forward or torso rotated), shoulders back (*never* raised), the instrument will be slightly leaning back with the right corner of the instrument in front of the sternum, the instrument should be positioned diagonally in front of the player (the student should not sit on the side or behind the instrument) with f-holes facing the conductor. The left knee will be behind the double bass, while the right foot should be planted firmly on the floor. The first finger will be at eye level when placed on the first tape (A-natural on the G string). The right-hand palm must be able to make contact with the bridge without leaning forward. If the bridge is too low to make contact with the palm, extend the endpin, even though the first finger of the left hand will be above eye level.

Double Bass Standing Position

The student will extend the endpin to about 6 inches. The player will stand tall (*never* leaning forward or torso rotated), shoulders back, feet shoulder-width apart. The right corner of the instrument will be in front of the sternum, the instrument should be positioned diagonally in front of the player (the student should not stand on the side or behind the instrument) with f-holes facing the conductor. The instrument will lean slightly into the player, and be balanced without any weight on the left hand. Remember, the left hand's responsibility is to never carry the instrument, but to play. Just like in the sitting position, the first finger will be at eye level when placed on the first tape (A-natural on the G string). The right-hand palm should be able to make contact with the bridge without leaning forward. If the bridge is too low to make contact with the palm, extend the endpin, even if the first finger of the left hand is above eye level.

Left Hand and Left Arm Shape

The left hand and arm must be free of tension and completely pliable so that the student may play comfortably, remain free of injury, and so that solid technique can be built upon it. To accomplish a tension-free foundation, relax the shoulder and the entire left arm. In the initial phase of learning string instruments, it is crucial to rotate between tasks (as in left arm, bow hold, bow arm, and instrument hold), so that students do not get tense while building their stamina.

Upper Strings

The left hand will be positioned on the right side of the neck, the third crease of the index finger (right above index knuckle) forming an imaginary line following the natural curve of the finger-board. The base of the thumb nail should be about across the third index crease (Figures 2.14 and 2.15). Left thumb naturally opposes the rest of the hand on the left of the neck, touching lightly but never clamping down on it. The height of the thumb depends of the individual, however, the neck should never rest on the bottom of this first interdigital space (between thumb and index), but there must be enough space to push a pencil under the neck (Figure 2.16). Thumb should be able to move back and forth and be removed from the neck at will. If not, the thumb is too tight. The upper arm will be supinated slightly to allow the tips of curved four fingers to hover right above their assigned tapes and the elbow would be under the instrument, pointing at the floor but never pointing behind the student. It is imperative this rounded position for left fingers remains so, even when playing open strings: do not allow the left fingers to pop up but keep them in their curved position. The wrist will be straight from *all* angles but not collapsed, flexed, or radially deviated at the beginning-level of playing covered in this course. It is expected that students will reinforce these good habits throughout the open-string stage.[7]

Cello

Left hand will be positioned on the left side of neck with a C-shaped hand allowing the first, third, and fourth fingers to hover right above their assigned first position tapes. Place the

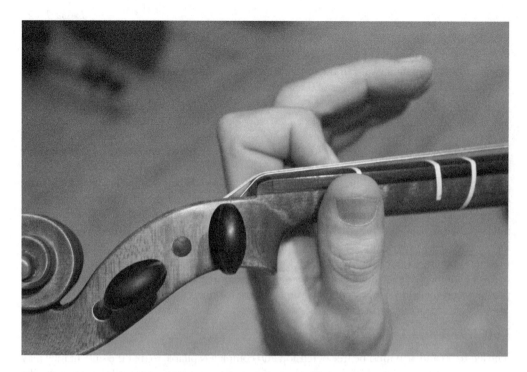

Figure 2.14 Upper strings left thumb's proper height

Figure 2.15 Upper strings left index finger and thumb alignment

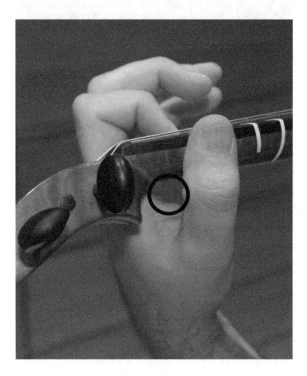

Figure 2.16 Upper strings proper space under neck between left index finger and thumb

rounded thumb opposite the second finger under the neck, letting only the tip of the thumb make light contact with it. The wrist *must* be perfectly straight, not collapsed, or radially deviated. The arm will have a natural slope where the arm is raised at about 30° to 45° with the shoulder in its ordinary position, but not raised (Figure 2.17).

Double Bass

Left hand will be positioned on the left side of neck with a K-shaped hand allowing the first, second, and fourth fingers to hover right above their assigned first position tapes. Place the rounded thumb opposite the second finger under the neck, letting only the tip of the thumb make light contact with it. The wrist must be perfectly straight but not collapsed, or radially deviated. The arm will have a natural slope where the arm is raised at about 30° to 45° with the shoulder in its ordinary position, but not raised (Figure 2.18).

Five Steps to Instrument Posture

As the optimum posture and instrument hold have been discussed, the below is a pedagogical strategy to achieve the same in a secondary-school classroom. In this course the following Five Steps to Instrument Posture will be employed to consolidate the foundations of posture and instrument hold, however, students are encouraged to start pondering their own classroom friendly terminology (Figure 2.19).[8]

Figure 2.17 Cello: proper left arm slope with left hand in first position

Figure 2.18 Bass: proper left arm slope with left hand in first position

	Violin/viola	*Cello*	*Bass*
Preparation	Shoulder rest on	Endpin out	Endpin out
1	Stand, feet in "V" position, instrument in rest position, arms by your side.	Stand four inches in front of chair, left hand holding the cello by its neck with the instrument placed on your left side.	Stand, left hand holding the bass by its neck with the instrument on your left side.
2	Move left foot slightly out, to 9 o'clock position, place left hand on shoulder of instrument (underneath the neck) with thumb on backside of instrument.	Sit on front four inches of chair and place feet in open position. Cello remains supported by left hand on your left side.	Take one step back and slightly to the side with the left foot, so that you are now just behind the left upper bout of instrument.
3	Move instrument with left hand in front of your stomach with the arm stretched out, bring right hand index finger to the end button.	Move cello in front of body. Endpin placement should create a triangle between feet and endpin.	Twist bass slightly so that the right back upper bout is angled towards your stomach.
4	Lift violin/viola with both hands directly overhead.	Tilt cello back towards body. Points of backside lower bout contact just inside knee bone, top of upper rib contacts breast bone, C peg behind ear, neck is one fist width above your shoulder. You will have to play with the angle of the instrument and endpin height to fit to individual student.	Tilt bass back towards body, corner of back upper right bout rests between hip bone and stomach. Endpin height is correct if knuckles of extended bow arm contact bridge.
5	Bring instrument down to left shoulder and turn head to the left (45°), *without* tilting it, place jawbone inside chinrest making sure tip of jawbone contacts chinrest. Left elbow should be able to come under instrument and be over left toe.	Wrap arms around cello neck to "hug" without lifting shoulders.	Wrap arms around bass neck to "hug" without lifting shoulders.

Common Errors

Violin/viola not high enough on shoulder	*Reposition*
Neck of cello too low on shoulder. Cello not high enough on chest. Cello held inside legs. Violin/viola: chin in chinrest instead of jaw.	Check angle of instrument to body and endpin length. Lengthen strap and endpin. Touch jaw bone, check height of instrument on shoulder, have student look straight at you, then turn head to look down fingerboard.

Left-Hand Position

	Violin/viola	Cello/bass
1	Instrument in playing position. Left hand on shoulder, thumb under.	Instrument in playing position, drop relaxed left hand by side.
2	Make a "stop sign" (thumb at first tape, aligned with the first finger), point thumb at ceiling, neck of instrument rests just above first finger's knuckle and at first joint of thumb.	Reach straight out to left to hold onto an imaginary soda can.
3	Walk fingers down on tapes "one, two, and three".	Reach across neck of instrument to your right shoulder, then slowly slide back to the fingerboard.
4	Align your nose with scroll, and elbow with toes, reciting the following reminder: "nose, scroll, elbow, toe".	Place fingers at tapes, check thumb position.
5	Correct positioning will allow fingers to contact string from above string at tip of finger. Finger nails pointing down at an angle. The angle will be flatter from the first to the fourth fingers.	Maintain "C" shape of hand—thumb directly behind second finger, curved on neck—do not allow to collapse. Bass place second finger equal distance between first and fourth finger.

Common left-hand errors:	Remedy
Collapsed wrist.	Concentrate on pointing thumb to ceiling—make sure it is not too high above fingerboard. Physically move students' hands, and have them wiggle the wrist to relax, and come to a rest at straight position.
Squeezing with first finger.	Do pre-shifting and vibrato exercises. Sirens, polishing strings and keeping the squirrel hole with the left thumb.
Fingers collapsing as you cross string.	Walking finger exercise.
Upper string elbow too far to left.	Pinky strums: focus on finger angle to string.
Bass/cello thumb position: thumb comes too far around neck.	Pad or sticker at back of neck, or tape line.
Bass/cello elbow collapse.	Remind daily that there is an invisible beach ball under left elbow.

Figure 2.19 Five Steps to Instrument Posture

Proper Right-Arm Positioning for Pizzicato

The right-arm position for pizzicato is essentially the same as the regular bow-hold position. The proper right arm slope must be maintained throughout pizzicato playing for the particular string. To play pizzicato notes the player will forego the bow hold and grasp the frog in the hand, allowing a particular finger to pluck the string. Exact thumb anchoring and plucking finger angles vary depending on the individual instrument, however, the regular plucking point is three to four inches inward on the fingerboard.

Much like with the bow, tonal adjustment while playing pizzicato is possible by way of contact point and the point in which the finger plucks the strings. The closer to the bridge, the more metallic and present the sound, the further onto the fingerboard the more subtle. Similarly, the more pulpous portion of the first joint, the fuller, the further to the tip of the first joint, the more metallic the tone quality of note.[9]

Upper Strings

The tip of the right thumb will be anchored at the right bottom corner of the fingerboard. Bow will be secured in the hand by the middle, ring, and pinky fingers, and will be pointing up. The first joint of the index finger will pluck the string (Figures 2.20 and 2.21). When playing a pizzicato chord, the index finger will strum from the lowest string to the highest.

Figure 2.20 Upper strings pizzicato with a bow

Figure 2.21 Upper strings pizzicato without a bow

Cello

The tip of the right thumb will be anchored on the side, at the last three to four inches of the fingerboard. Bow will be secured in the hand by the middle, ring, and pinky fingers, and will be pointing up. The first joint of the index finger will pluck the string at an angle (Figure 2.22). When playing a pizzicato chord, the thumb will strum from the lowest string to the highest (Figure 2.23).

Figure 2.22 Cello pizzicato with a bow

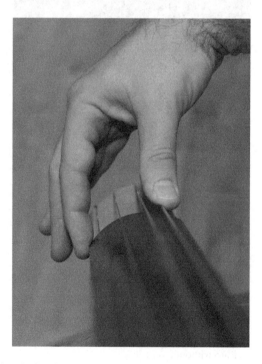

Figure 2.23 Low strings thumb chord strum

Double Bass

The tip of the right thumb will be anchored on the side, at the last three to four inches of the fingerboard. Bow will be secured in the hand by the middle, ring, and pinky fingers, and will be pointing up if French, pointing down if German (Figures 2.24, 2.25 and 2.26). The first joint of the index finger will pluck the string at an angle. When playing a pizzicato chord, the thumb will strum from the lowest string to the highest.

Preparatory Bow Exercises

In order to produce a reliable and pleasing tone, the bow hold must be free of tension, and the arm movement associated with bowing should be fluid. The combined use of weight of the bow arm, and fluid motion of the bow make up the foundation of tone production.

Three-Step Low-String, and Four-Step Upper-String Pencil Bow Holds

This is the preliminary introduction to the bow grip, which we will accomplish later. The reason for the pencil exercise is to learn the bow hold without having to carry the weight of a bow, which can cause tension. Initially, we will use a regular hexagonal pencil to describe a bow hold, or bow grip, in five steps:

Figure 2.24 Bass pizzicato with a French bow

Figure 2.25 Bass pizzicato with a German bow

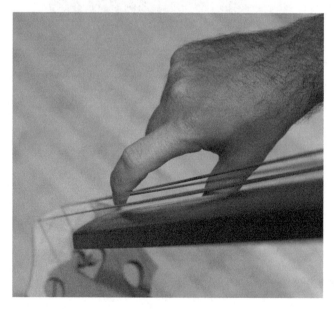

Figure 2.26 Low strings pizzicato without a bow

Step one: the basis of upper- and low-string bow holds is unified, tip of right thumb's first joint has a natural inward curl at about a 120° obtuse angle, and its tip touches the first-joint of the middle finger (Figure 2.27).

Step two: the pencil will be captured in-between the tip of the thumb and behind the first joint of the middle finger (Figure 2.28).

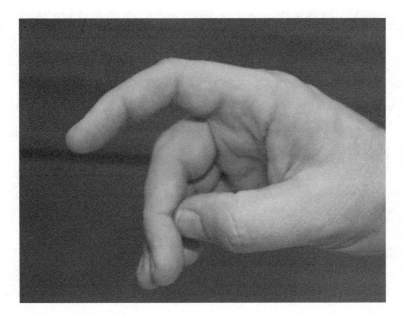

Figure 2.27 The Basis for Upper-Strings Bow Hold

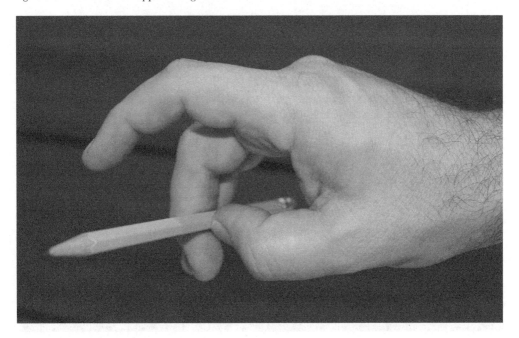

Figure 2.28 Two-Finger Pencil Bow Hold

Step three: allow the index, ring and pinky fingers to rest on the pencil (Figure 2.29). We now have the low-string bow hold.

Step four: place the tip of the pinky on top of the pencil. We now have the upper-strings bow hold (Figure 2.30). Lastly, rotate the bow hold to double-check on thumb, so that it remains slightly bent (Figure 2.31).

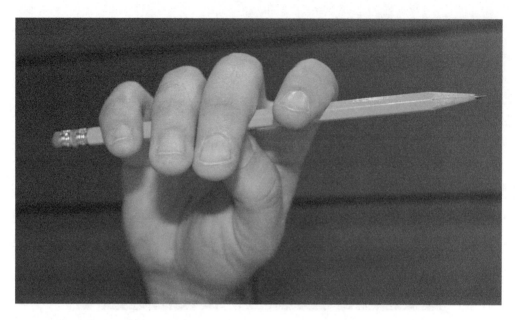

Figure 2.29 Low-Strings Pencil Bow Hold

Figure 2.30 Upper-Strings Pencil Bow Hold

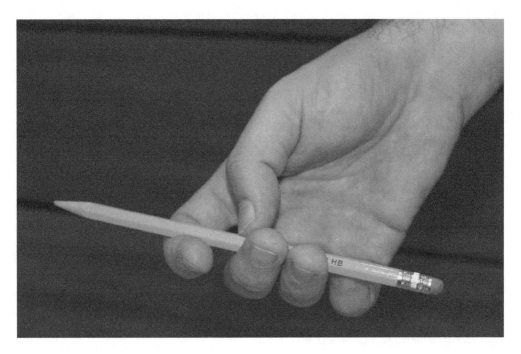

Figure 2.31 Pencil Bow Hold Rotated

Ultimately, all bow holds will have the middle finger resting on the ferrule. On the upper-string bow hold, the tip of the finger will make contact with the ferrule, where, with the low strings, the finger will extend below it. The ring finger, however, may rest on the ferrule in the French double bass bow hold due to school of bowing. The thumb positioning may also be different (bow holds will be discussed again in Lesson 13).

German Bow Hold Exercise

In the case of the German double bass bow hold, the pencil exercise is different. This is a bow grip that resembles a chop-stick hold.

Step one: the basis is the thumb, index and middle fingers are joined at the tips (Figure 2.32).
Step two: the pencil will be captured in-between the tip of the thumb, middle and ring fingers (Figure 2.33).
The ring and pinky fingers float, and are not pasted onto the middle finger. Ultimately, the ring finger will support the grip underneath the ferrule.

All through these exercises, it is absolutely *critical* to keep the thumb slightly bent and not allow it to collapse, keep all other fingers rounded, and do not raise your knuckles. The bow grip must remain pliable and relaxed, and never become rigid and tense (Figure 2.34). Unlike the straightened pinky and elevated knuckles, the straightened thumb is unobservable from the student's point of view, therefore, it is a good idea to rotate the bow hold to observe the

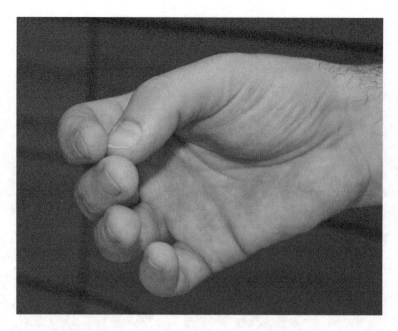

Figure 2.32 Basis for the German Bow Hold

Figure 2.33 Pencil German Bow Hold, the "Chop-Stick Hold"

Figure 2.34 Incorrectly Straightened Pinky in Pencil Bow Hold

straightened first joint (Figure 2.35), or incorrectly positioned thumb (Figure 2.36). Repeat this exercise and get comfortable with it. At this stage it is common that students start with a perfect bow grip, and lose it subsequently. Therefore, it is imperative to stay determined, yet patient with oneself and join the instructor in offering constant encouragement and help to classmates.

Assignment

1) Write a typed, one-page, double-spaced essay that answers the following, to be turned in at next class:

   • How, where, and when did the standardization of the violin family take place?
   • What are some differences between the viol and violin families?

2) Listen to 16th century consort music, provide the name of the work and its instrumentation.
3) Notate the open strings of all four members of the violin family on staff paper in the correct clef and pitch.
4) Repeat Five Steps to Instrument Hold, Left Hand Three-Step Low-String, and Four-Step Upper-String Pencil Bow Hold exercises.
5) Practice pizzicato exercises.
6) Review today's lesson and read Lesson 3.

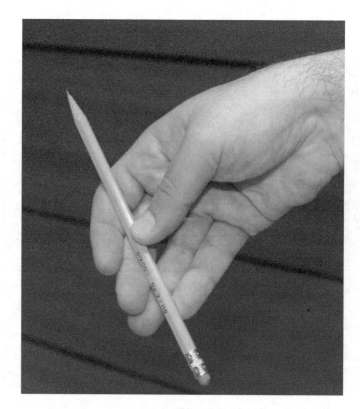

Figure 2.35 Incorrectly Straightened Thumb in Pencil Bow Hold

Figure 2.36 Incorrectly Positioned Thumb in Pencil Bow Hold

Notes

1 Dillon-Krass and Straub, *Establishing a String and Orchestra Program*, 20.
2 Shin'ichi Suzuki (1898–1998) was a Japanese string pedagogue, and founder of the Suzuki method.
3 Joseph Joachim (1831–1907) was an influential Austro-Hungarian violinist and pedagogue.
4 Kató Havas OBE (1920–2018) was British violinist and pedagogue of Hungarian birth known for her work in injury prevention and stage fright.
5 It is preferable to teach upper strings in the standing position during the first stages of string playing. Likewise in this class until good posture is achieved, the instructor will always require the upper strings students to play in standing position.
6 Rolland and Mutschler, *The Teaching of Action in String Playing: Developmental and Remedial Techniques [for] Violin and Viola*, 71.
7 Playing in higher positions, as the 5th, 6th and up, the wrist will bend slightly forward to allow left hand's reach.
8 Five Steps to Instrument Posture follows variations of Paul Rolland's feet positioning and "Statue of Liberty" (Rolland and Mutschler, *The Teaching of Action in String Playing: Developmental and Remedial Techniques [for] Violin and Viola*, 70.), and is based on Frances Oare's same-titled list with minor changes.
9 The extended techniques of snap pizzicato and left-hand pizzicato will be discussed later.

Lesson 3

Contents

This lesson will introduce:

- A quick review of the Five Steps of Instrument Posture and Left-Hand Position.
- Tuning.
- Pizzicato: "Pendulum" exercise.
- Preparatory bow exercises.
- A historical overview of string instruments.
- A discussion of tone production.

Applied: Review of Five Steps to Instrument Posture and Left-Hand Position

We will go over the Five Steps to Instrument Posture and Left-Hand Position procedures until those skills become second nature. At this juncture, it is necessary for the instructor to take a hands-on approach. Any advanced members of the class, and if available, assistants will help the instructor by physically correcting any posture and setup issues. This phase may be characterized as the "molding period", where it shapes the fundamental setup and determines the ultimate technical ability on the instrument. It is difficult to overstate the significance of good setup and the necessity for tension-free playing. After this lesson students are expected to memorize these steps on their assigned instruments.

Tuning

Efficient and proper tuning of string instruments is a formidable challenge for any string teacher, as the task and quality control of tuning falls squarely on the shoulders of the teacher. There are numerous successful strategies for tuning and it is the string teacher's responsibility to decide which strategy to employ to achieve a desirable accuracy. Proper tuning of instruments is critical to allow students to play in tune, promote conscientious approach to intonation, and help improve their aural skills.

In professional orchestras the standard concert a' is given (with the help of an electronic tuner) from the first oboist to the Concertmaster, then it is moved onto the string, woodwind, and brass sections of the ensemble. The number of times an A is played to tune different sections, the order in which those sections are tuned, and how many sub-sections of the ensemble are tuned separately depends on the particular ensemble. Even the exact Hertz (or cycle per second) an orchestra tunes depends on variables such as the ensemble's artistic choice and established traditions.

In a string ensemble the Concertmaster plays concert a' to which all sections are tuned. Those sections can be tuned separately by members of the violin family to ensure that healthy tuning occurs: violins, violas, cellos, and double basses. Contingent on the number and playing level of students in each section, this division may be altered at the discretion of the teacher.

This course will examine tuning in three different segments:

1) Scholastic ensemble tuning sequence.
2) Tuning by way of adjacent strings.
3) Tuning by way of natural harmonics.

Scholastic Ensemble Tuning Sequence

In this lesson we will discuss scholastic ensemble tuning sequences preferred by many secondary string teachers: A, D, G, C, and E. To accomplish this method of tuning, at first, the standard A (A or A_2, a or A_3, and a' or A_4) is produced and sustained by a tuner, CD player, or an instrument. The drone pitch should be at an amplitude that allows students to hear their instruments in meticulous tuning of their strings. Then the same procedure is repeated on the following pitches on corresponding octaves for each open string: D, G, C, E. Only one pitch at a time is tuned, albeit multiple octaves may be tuned concurrently if tuning multiple sections at once.

How to Tune

In the beginning stages students require the teacher's help in tuning their instruments, however, they *must* become self-sufficient without delay. Tuning is a significant part of every string player's education, as it is a fundamental proficiency to develop. The ability to tune impeccably is vital; not only for the ensemble's intonation, but also for student's unimpeded development in aural skills. To attain tuning experience rapidly, students will first start using fine tuners (tuning with pegs will be introduced later in Lesson 5). The following pizzicato tuning method is not ideal as far as pitch accuracy is concerned, nonetheless, it will let students gain valuable tuning experience with fine tuners at this early stage of instruction.

1) **Upper Strings:** proceed through the Five Steps to Instrument Posture. Once in position, reach for the A-string fine tuner with your left index finger and thumb and pluck the string continuously with your right index finger to tune it. This is an excellent way of getting used to tuning with the left hand in preparation to arco tuning (Figures 3.1 and 3.2). Fine tuners

Figure 3.1 Upper strings tuning with fine tuners using left hand

Figure 3.2 Upper strings tuning with fine tuners using right hand

are manufactured to tighten clockwise for a higher pitch "righty tighty" and loosen anticlockwise for a lower pitch "lefty loosey".

2) **Cello:** proceed through the Five Steps to Instrument Posture. Once in position, reach around the cello for the A-string fine tuner with your right index finger and thumb and pluck the A-string continuously with your left third finger to tune it (Figure 3.3). Fine tuners are manufactured to tighten clockwise for a higher pitch "righty tighty" and loosen anticlockwise for a lower pitch "lefty loosey".

3) **Double Bass:** proceed through the Five Steps to Instrument Posture. Once in position, reach for the A-string metal peg with your left index finger and thumb and pluck the A-string continuously with your right index finger to tune it (Figure 3.4). Machine heads are manufactured to tighten clockwise for a higher pitch "righty tighty" and loosen anticlockwise for a lower pitch "lefty loosey".

"Pendulum" Exercise

Follow the Left-Hand Position procedure. Once in position, move your left arm from the lowest to the highest string hovering position, and repeat it back and forth. Once comfortable with this motion, play the following "Pendulum" exercise with the guidance of the instructor. The fourth finger will pizz. all four strings, starting from the lowest to the highest. To accomplish the exercise's intended goal, students must keep their wrists straight from *all* angles but not allow them to collapse, flex, or radially deviate. It is imperative that the *entire*

Figure 3.3 Cello tuning with fine tuners using right hand

Figure 3.4 Bass pizzicato tuning using left hand

arm moves with a pendulum motion to pluck the strings, but not the finger and the wrist (Figure 3.5).

Preparatory Bow Exercises (Continued)

First, repeat Three-Step Low-String, and Four-Step Upper-String Pencil Bow Hold exercises, all the while making sure to keep the thumb bent at a natural angle (roughly 120° obtuse angle) and not allowing it to collapse, keeping all other fingers rounded, and not raising the knuckles.

Second, we will start the Air Drawing exercises by wiggling our fingers to draw imaginary shapes as circles, horizontal and vertical straight lines, and crosses in the air with our pencil, all the while not losing the basis of bow grip. In other words, students will *never* allow the pencil to roll between the tip of the thumb and first joint of the middle finger while performing these exercises, and allow the first joint of thumb to collapse but always keep its natural inward curl.

Third, the Swimming Octopus exercise will be imitating the bow motion in air. The forearm and wrist will be pronated, and both wrist and all five fingers will act as the swimming octopus as graceful and smooth as the animal itself (Figure 3.6).

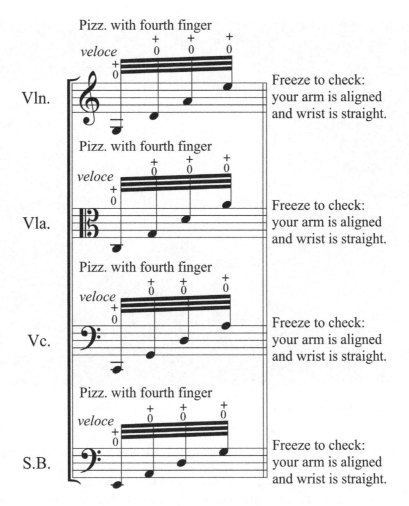

Figure 3.5 "Pendulum" exercise

Theory: A Brief History of the String Instruments

Early History of Bowed String Instruments

All four instruments of the violin family can be classified as composite chordophone,[1] a variant of bowed lute, featuring a wooden resonator, or soundbox, and a neck. It is believed that bowed chordophones originated in Central Asia, and by the 10th century it was common throughout Islam and the Byzantine Empire. The Mongolian and Turkic spike fiddles of *ikil, huur, khuur, qobuz,* or *hugur,* and their Chinese counterpart *huqin*—"barbarian string instrument"—is said to have become common in China in the mid-8th century, however, it is believed to have arrived from Mongolia centuries earlier.[2] Mongolian traditions label and shape parts of instruments with equine references as *morin khuur* (khuur with a horse head), as well as mare or stallion horse hair used in bows, and two horse hairs for strings, one thin *nariin* and one thick *büdüün.*[3] Most likely the first chordophones, spike fiddles share the common dowel shaped long yoke that goes through

Figure 3.6 Swimming Octopus exercise

the sound resonator, and as the name *ikil* indicates, the instrument has two strings. It is likely that the table, or the top resonator is made of stretched membrane, such as snakeskin. The earliest depiction of a bowed string instrument, between the 9th and 10th centuries, was on a wall painting of a *rubāb* in the Palace of the governor of Khulbuk, located in the Kurban Shaid settlement of the Vose region, in southern Tajikistan. In the 10th and 11th centuries, there have been Byzantine depictions of bowed string instruments. The mention of *rabāb*, a common name for a bowed lute, is made in medieval texts in Arabic, dating back to the 9th and 10th centuries, and slight variations of the same instrument are found in North Africa, the Middle East, Central Asia, and throughout Asia. In literature, however, al-Fârâbī's indication of drawing [bow] strings over the instrument's strings is the first mention of a bowed chordophone. (The word for bow hair and instrument string has been used interchangeably.)

European rebec, originated from *rabāb* and Byzantine *lūrā*, appeared in the continent in the late 10th to 11th centuries. One of two of the earliest common shapes of rebec were the pair-shaped version as the Greek *lira* (or Greek *kemençe*), and the more narrow version with a top resonator made of stretched skin. In addition to the copious variations of lyra and rebec, other instruments as *gigue*, fiddle, Welsh *crwth*, and viol have all helped make the rich and varied tapestry of bowed string traditions throughout the following centuries—both in term and in instrument shape—before the advent of the modern violin. The instrument shape of rebab and rebec is exceedingly close. One significant difference between the playing positions of the two instruments is the European tradition of placing the instrument on the arm, where

Figure 3.7 Kemangeh a'gouz (Turkish)
Illustration by Edward Heron-Allen (1884)

Figure 3.8 Viol of the 10th century
Illustration by Edward Heron-Allen (1884)

Figure 3.9 Gigue or rebec of 11th century
Illustration by Edward Heron-Allen (1884)

Far Eastern, Central Asian, Middle and Near Eastern instruments are vertically placed, whether on the ground, in front of the torso or placed on the knee (Figures 3.7–3.11). When we discuss viols, as in viola da gamba [leg viol], *lira da braccio* [arm lyre] and viola da braccio [arm viol], all refer to instruments labeled so by virtue of their playing position and range.

Emergence of the Modern Violin: the Brescian and Cremonese Schools

Before the emergence of the modern violin, much of the range distribution, number of strings and their tuning, among many other aspects of the abundance of string instruments were not standard. Depending on region, country, and musical traditions, an array of string instruments were abound. By the 16th century, several prominent makers, or luthiers, were perfecting and standardizing the modern violin, and its family members. In northern Italy, Brescia was a leading school in early violins. The earliest violin maker with surviving instruments of the Brescian school is Zanetto da

Figure 3.10 Crwth of 13th century from Worcester Cathedral
Illustration by Edward Heron-Allen (1884)

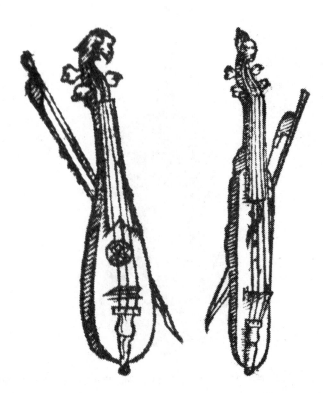

Figure 3.11 Two kits from *Syntagma musicum* 2/1619

Montichiaro (1489/90–1560/61). Zanetto's son Peregrino, and grandsons were all violin makers—as the violin-making tradition was founded upon apprenticeship practices and family shops. Another early, and among the best representatives of the Brescian school is Gasparo da Salò (1540–1609). Gasparo was also born to a family of musicians and makers, and is known particularly for his violas. Gasparo passed his craft onto his son and pupils, among whom is Gio[vanni] Paolo Maggini (1580–1630/31?). Maggini was specially known for his more than 60 violins and is said to be a source of inspiration for notable luthiers as Guarneri and Stradivari.

The founder of the Cremona school of violin makers was Andrea Amati (*b* before 1511–1577) (Figure 3.12). Credited as not only the patriarch of the Amati family of makers, but of the modern violin, his form of the instrument is widely accepted as standard to date. Andrea Guarneri has apprenticed with the grandson Nicolò Amati (1596–1684), with whom he learned the Amati's style of violin making. His grandson, Giuseppe "del Gesù" (1698–1744),[4] however, is considered one of the two most influential violin makers in the history of the instrument. Italian virtuoso violinist and composer Nicolò Paganini's (1782–1840) favorite violin, the fabled 1742 "del Gesù", he nicknamed *Il Cannone*, is one of many fine examples of existing instruments of Giuseppe "del Gesù".[5]

Figure 3.12 Amati violin (ca. 1559), National Music Museum, The University of South Dakota, Byron Pillow, Photographer

Figure 3.13 Stradivari violin "the Harrison" (1693), National Music Museum, The University of South Dakota, Bill Willroth, Sr., Photographer

Undoubtedly, the most awe-inspiring name in violin making is Antonio Stradivari (1644/9–1737) (Figure 3.13). Not much is known of his education, however, his possible apprenticeship with Amati may be deduced from a label, dated 1666, where he signed as "pupil of Nicolò Amati". In addition to the aforementioned, there have been numerous noteworthy Italian makers and families: Bergonzi, Gagliano, Guadagnini, and Rugeri to name a few. Throughout Europe, there have been many international makers of historical prominence who produced notable instruments, such as Jacob Stainer (1617–1683) in Austria, Mathias Klotz (1653–1743) and the Klotz family in Germany,[6] and Jean-Baptiste Vuillaume (1798–1875) in Mirecourt, France.

The Current State of Violin Making

Although the great influence of the 17th- to 18th-century Italian violin makers continues to date, many international makers have been experimenting new techniques of all aspects of violin making to great success, and have arguably surpassed the work of old masters.[78] Changing taste and contemporary demands placed on string instruments may all have played a role in this gradual but deliberate transformation. Today's playing field in the string instrument making is level, where makers from Southeast Asia, to Russia, to the Americas, all have equal say in the future of violin making, in hand with technological advancements, changing playing styles, and audiences.

Hand-made vs. Factory-made Instruments

It is almost certain that all assigned string instruments in this class are "factory-made", or more precisely, have been mass produced. This in itself is not a sign of a lesser instrument, but a more appropriate one, given the demands of the job it will have to endure in the hands of young students. The purpose-built student string instruments are expected to endure some physical challenges a two-hundred-year-old instrument may not withstand. It is also important to take into account, that overall value of instrument vs. cost of repair is the deciding factor when making a decision on any major repair, not part of routine maintenance. For instance, a broken neck may be the end of a cello; since the cost of repair is greater than the instrument's current value, and greater than the acquisition cost a new outfit.

"Factory-made" or mass produced instruments are widely available through string instrument vendors, and are critical in continuation of string programs in the US and around the world. The demand for mass production of student-grade string instruments were met in Mirecourt, France, Markneukirchen and Mittenwald Germany in the 19th century. Today, in addition to Eastern European instruments, China has become perhaps the strongest provider of factory-made student instruments.

The mechanized stage in production of instruments, however, must not be mistaken for lesser quality and lack of care in the hands of master luthiers. The best analogy of modern mechanization can be made with early known violin shops' use of less experienced craftsmen, as that of Amati's, and their work in preparing and shaping the wood in preparation for the master's finer work. Similarly, today's master luthiers' practice of employing such production methods cannot take away from the final product. The level of attention and time the master luthier devotes to each instrument determines the final success and value of the instrument. Even though the members of the violin family instruments are wooden soundboxes with synthetic strings, they produce sound extremely close to the human voice.

Tone Production

The discussion of tone production of string instruments may be likened to that of wind instruments—or any instrument for which the student has formed an understanding. On all string instruments, we must be able to produce a well-supported and rounded tone. Furthermore, we must begin each tone with a proper attack, and sustain it without wavering or diminishing. What embouchure and breath support are to winds, and what breath management is to vocal technique, bow control and bow management are to string players.

Good tone production on all string instruments is a direct result of an understanding of their construction and function. Personal taste and school of bow technique, however, play a substantial role in what constitutes "good tone production", and may differ significantly from one string teacher to another. This personal ideal of tone production will have an influence on a variety of decisions a string teacher makes, from instrument and string selection, to fingering choices. Most importantly, the greatest influence will always be attaining and maintaining a solid technique for all students and modeling it in achieving good tone production habits. Successful string teachers frequently encourage their students, and make constant corrections to maintain a good setup and produce a consistently substantive and pure tone.

Laws of physics dictate how sound is produced on string instruments and are the decisive factor in the pedagogical approach to the bow technique. Performers and teachers are instinctively aware of these laws and abide by them. There are certain key acoustical terms relating to tone production that need to be clarified before we discuss pedagogy of tone production. The first term is stick-and-slip cycle. It refers to the perpetual action of rosined hair pulling the string (stick), and letting it go (slip). It is also called Helmholtz motion, in respect to German physicist Hermann von Helmholtz (1821–1894). The stick-and-slip cycle can only occur with the resistance of the hair—created by the application of rosin—weight of the bow as in the pressure applied by the player, and the bow movement on the string. Those variables attributed to the bowing have an influence on this cycle. In the acoustical scientific literature, bow speed is referred to as "velocity", and bow weight as "bow force". Another scientific term is "slipping attacks". This term refers to the inadequate attack at the beginning of a bow stroke—as opposed to a "clean attack". Also, there may be different concurrent "stick" tendencies across the entire width, or the cross section of bow hair, as in "secondary backward slips" and "secondary backward partial slips". These tendencies become much more pronounced as the string circumference is increased. For instance, the highest and lowest strings in the violin family, the violin's E string, versus the double bass's E string are completely different in the way they respond to input from the player. The violin's highest string is much more forgiving to a player's faulty inputs and is not prone to slipping, in contrast the double bass requires each bow stroke to start with a clean "bite", or a "clean attack" to draw solid tone free from slipping.

Bow distance from the bridge must remain constant in order to produce a reliable and solid tone. Similarly, bow weight distribution requires continuous adjustments for tone to remain constant—both in amplitude and color. The bow weighs the most at the frog, and the further toward the tip the bow is drawn, progressively more and more index-finger weight must be applied to compensate this differential. Conversely, the player will have to apply counter weight with the right pinky finger to allow the bow to produce a piano dynamic at the frog. This combination is expressed as the "recipe", or "WS&P recipe" by Fritz Gearhart.[9] "WS&P" stands for weight, speed, and placement (contact point) of bow and "recipe" denotes the ever-changing percentages of each constituent to draw constant tone. The listener must remain blissfully unaware of this smooth and continuous process of a balancing act. Moreover, sound production is not comprised of just these three fundamental components but there are secondary elements, also critical in producing a solid and reliable tone. Among those parameters are the amount of bow tilt, bow hair tightness, total bow weight and its distribution, and degree of concave curvature of the stick.

In his treatise titled *Problems of Tone Production in Violin Playing* (1934), among the 20th century's most influential violin pedagogues, Carl Flesch (1873–1944) summarizes the teacher's responsibility in tone production as follows:

> Faulty sound conditions are created, first of all, through a mechanism based upon incorrect fundamental principles of tone production. It is the teacher's duty to explain clearly the apparent reasons for tonal shortcomings to the pupil and to find the remedy for their removal.
>
> Flesch, *Problems of Tone Production in Violin Playing*, 6

Flesch expresses how easy it is to determine the left-hand related issues, i.e. intonation problems that are caused by simply a "finger touch[ing] the string at too high or too low a point." He contends that tonal issues, along with ancillary noises, are wrongly attributed to such elements as weather phenomena, strings, bow hair, and rosin. He further conveys: "In reality tone-production is governed by equally restricted, though infinitely more complicated mechanical laws, than those of pitch, in which a mathematically established number of vibrations constitutes the only deciding fact." In Flesch's description, main flaws in tone are caused "when a physiologically wrong method of guiding or holding the bow is accompanied by a defective *point of contact* between bow and string." He further lists backward tilt of bow, excessively tilted bow, deficiencies in bow changes, and improper pressure of the bow or bow arm as the main causes of unsatisfactory tone production. He offers the conclusion that the contact point (or point of contact) is more directly responsible for tone production than bow technique itself.

The scope of this textbook and associated efforts of the instructor will first establish a reliable instrument hold that allows for a solid platform, on which the bowing can take place. A proper bridge alignment in relation to the bow is a critical step in accomplishing the straight bow motion. For instance, a misaligned low string instrument or drooping upper string instrument will make it impossible for a bow to remain parallel to the bridge. A drooping upper string instrument will cause the strings to slope away from the player, therefore, keeping the bow close to the bridge is a constant struggle. Particularly on upper strings, a vertically unstable platform will take away from the continuous bow weight, therefore, making sound production uneven.

The bow hold and right arm functions will be initially established by way of pre-bowing exercises, then applied with the bow on the instrument. The complexity of bow technique necessitates that this process be taken with circumspection. Rushing into a haphazard bow hold for the sake of achieving quick results is unadvisable, as it will result in long-lasting deficiencies in the student's bow technique. The teacher must implement the pre-bowing exercises separately in a several-week-long process and must continue those along with bowing exercises after the left hand and bow arm are merged. Bow technique encompasses both the ability to produce a long sustained tone and a multitude of different strokes (for a complete list, please refer to Lesson 13).

In summary, tone production solely relates to the bow hand and bow arm, while vibrato, provided by the left hand only offers an aesthetical aspect to the perceived quality of tone, but accomplishes nothing for the sound production itself. After all, the entire bow technique is a means to an end of physically providing the proper combination of weight, speed, and placement (contact point) of the bow, in the pursuit of pure and reliable tone production.

Assignment

1) Write a typed, one-page, double-spaced essay that answers the following, to be turned in at the next class: discuss tone production fundamentals of string instruments and compare those with other musical instruments, including voice.
2) Memorize Five Steps to Instrument Posture and Left-Hand Position, and practice applying those steps on the assigned instrument.
3) Practice pizzicato tuning in the scholastic ensemble tuning sequence.
4) Practice "Pendulum" exercise.
5) Practice pizzicato exercises.
6) Practice Preparatory Bow exercises.
7) Bring an empty paper towel roll for next lesson's preparatory bowing exercises.
8) Review today's lesson, and read Lesson 4.

Notes

1 Hornbostel-Sachs system.
2 Although derogatorily translated as "barbarian," in Chinese "*Hu*" refers to Mongolic peoples and numerous Chinese spike fiddles with the derivative of the same word: as in *jinghu*, *erhu*, and *gaohu*.

3 Horses had great influence in inception of the earliest chordophones in Central Asia, as every part of the animal was commonly used by nomadic peoples.

4 Giuseppe is known as "of Jesus" due to his "IHS" inscription below a cross he drew on his labels.

5 Paganini nicknamed his beloved "del Gesù" "the cannon" because of its powerful tone.

6 Most prominent in the 18th century, credited as founders of Mittenwald school of violin making in Bavaria, Germany.

7 www.thestrad.com/blind-tested-soloists-unable-to-tell-stradivarius-violins-from-modern-instruments/994.article (accessed February 2, 2020).

8 www.npr.org/sections/health-shots/2017/05/08/527057108/is-a-stradivarius-violin-easier-to-hear-science-says-nope (accessed February 2, 2020).

9 Gearhart, "The Use of 'Tartini Tones' in Teaching," 33.

Lesson 4

Contents

This lesson's objectives are:

- A quick review of the five steps of instrument posture and left-hand position.
- Continued work on pizzicato: "Pendulum" exercise.
- Continued preparation of our right hand and arm for the bow.
- An introduction of left-hand finger patterns.
- A discussion of bow hold and arco playing.

Applied: Review of Five Steps to Instrument Posture and Left-Hand Position (Continued)

As the class remains in the "molding period" we will continue to go over the Five Steps to Instrument Posture and Left-Hand Position procedures until it becomes second nature. It is expected that the class is able to go through these procedures by memory. The instructor may still need to take a hands-on approach, however, at this point mostly if not all verbal corrections will be used. The advanced members of the class may help the instructor.

Tune

As discussed in Lesson 3, tune by way of pizzicato with the scholastic ensemble tuning sequence that your instructor follows.

"Pendulum" Exercise (Continued)

As discussed in Lesson 3, students will play the "Pendulum" exercise. The fourth finger will pizz. all four strings, starting from the lowest to the highest. Students will remember to keep their wrists straight from *all* angles but not allow them to collapse, flex, or radially deviate, while the *entire* arm moves as a unit to pluck the strings.

Preparatory Bow Exercises (Continued)

First, repeat Three-Step Low-String, and Four-Step Upper-String Pencil Bow Hold exercises, all the while making sure to keep the thumb bent at roughly 120° obtuse angle and not allowing it to collapse, keeping all other fingers rounded, and not raising the knuckles.

Second, we will start wiggling our fingers to draw imaginary shapes as circles, horizontal and vertical straight lines, and crosses in the air with our pencil, all the while not losing the basis of the bow grip. In other words, students will *never* allow the pencil to roll between the tip of the thumb and first joint of the middle finger while performing these exercises (refer back to pencil exercises in Lesson 2).

Third, we will commence the Swimming Octopus motion: raise right hand in the air with the forearm slightly pronated, motion the wrist as an octopus and get the fingers to act like its tentacles while swimming. This motion mimics the down-bow and up-bow motions. In string playing, before the bow change occurs, forearm, wrist, and fingers anticipate the bow change. The anticipated motion is a more subdued version of this Swimming Octopus motion. Once comfortable with the Swimming Octopus exercises in the air, we will apply it to the pencil bow hold. We will expand the bow motion exercises to the entire arm. This exercise is called the Opening and Closing the Imaginary File Cabinet. To do this exercise, all students in class will pair up with a partner facing each other an arm's length apart, placing their right palms flat against one another's, and motion their arms back-and-forth, all the while, not losing full palm contact (Figure 4.1). This is the full motion of the bow: down bow, hand moving away from the player, up bow, hand moving toward the player.

Fourth, we will add a new exercise with an empty paper towel roll. We will first hold the cardboard paper towel roll with the left hand placed at the same angle and height as the imaginary bridge of the assigned instrument, and start the following exercise with the paper towel roll (Figures 4.2 and 4.3). Once comfortable, install the roll on the instrument with a rubber band, insert the bow into the roll and repeat the following exercise in the middle 1/3 section of the bow (Figures 4.4 and 4.5). After each repetition stop to check the bow grip, making sure that it is not collapsed. If collapsed, correct it and continue with the exercise.[1]

Fifth, pick up the assigned instruments and a pencil as a stand-in for the bow. The class will air bow, or pretend to bow in air, with pencils providing bow grip. First go to the D string and place the pencil on the string perfectly parallel to bridge, and halfway in-between bridge and end of fingerboard. Notice the natural arm slope with the right wrist being the highest point, or holding the arm up in the air as if by an invisible string. This is the D-string height for the bow arm. The overall slope within the hand and arm will remain the same regardless of the string. Once comfortable, lower the entire arm without changing the angles within the arm, as if there is an invisible cast to keep all parts of the arm and hand in perfect position. Next step is to lift the arm for the lower-string positions. It is imperative to keep the entire arm as a single unit when moving from one string elevation to another. Remember: *never* allow the right shoulder to lift when elevating the arm for lower strings.

When comfortable with the arm elevation for all four strings, repeat the paper towel roll exercise with the pencil: draw the pencil silently on the string with the exercise's rhythm.

Figure 4.1 Opening and Closing the Imaginary File Cabinet exercise

Figure 4.2 Paper towel roll exercise while holding the roll

Figure 4.3 Paper towel roll exercise no. 1

Figure 4.4 Paper towel roll installed on a violin

- Repeat it on the highest string (I), then the second string (II), third string (III), and the lowest string (IV), all the while keeping the pencil parallel to the bridge.
- Reverse the order, and repeat it on the lowest string (IV), then the third string (III), second string (II), and the highest string (I). Make sure to keep your shoulder from lifting when moving your arm from the lowest to the highest string elevation.

Lastly, set aside pencils and instruments and assume a good sitting or standing position. Place your left hand on your right shoulder and repeat the bowing exercises with air bowing. Make sure not to allow the shoulder to lift as arm elevation is raised for low strings. This exercise is to ensure tension-free playing for the right shoulder.

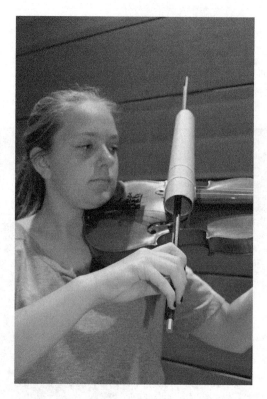

Figure 4.5 Paper towel roll exercise with upper strings

Finger Patterns

As the violin family does not feature frets, it is up to the player to locate the correct pitches for all stopped notes on the fingerboard. Left-hand finger patterns are the building blocks of different keys in string instruments, thus we can liken those to tetrachords that makeup scales in the eight-note diatonic system. Regardless of which classroom method book a string teacher uses (*Strictly Strings, Essential Elements, Sound Innovations, et al.*), all method books introduce specific elements of finger patterns in a logical system—notwithstanding relatively minor differences in their variable procedures.

In teaching these finger patterns, we will start with the D major scale. Since we are in a heterogeneous classroom, D major is the best scale for this setting. We will start with the D tetrachord: D–E–F-sharp–G. For the upper strings, the second and third fingers are close, and the first and fourth are separated (Figures 4.6 and 4.7). This is the first finger pattern we will learn in this class. The thumb will be lined up with the first finger, as in "A-OK!" For the cello, four separated fingers with enough room to allow each finger to fit the opposite hand's fingers in-between, and finger numbers are 1–3–4 (with the thumb behind the second finger) (Figure 4.8). Lastly, for the double bass, the first finger pointing up, and the first to second and second and fourth fingers are equidistant, the finger numbers are 1–4 (with the thumb behind the second finger) (Figure 4.9). On all four string instruments, the first finger placement from the string nut is a major second (or whole step), and all instruments start from an open D string. Much like the bow hand, the thumb and all other fingers will be slightly curved, as straightened fingers are a clear sign of tension.

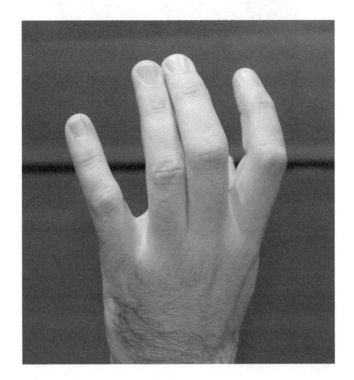

Figure 4.6 Upper strings first finger pattern

Figure 4.7 Upper strings first finger pattern on the instrument

Figure 4.8 Cello left-hand finger placement on the instrument

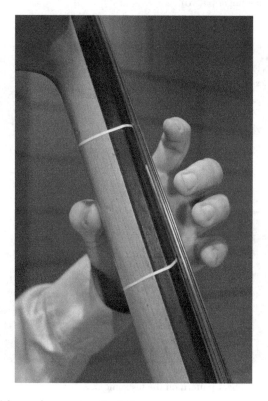

Figure 4.9 Bass left-hand finger placement on the instrument

Tightening the Bow and Rosining

Among the first questions a student may have is "how tight does the bow need to be?" There is not a single right answer. Since some players like to tighten their bows more than others, and due to permutations involved as the natural curvature of the bow, overall tightness and shape of the bow may vary. In any case we can clearly discern if a bow is under- or over-tightened. An under-tightened bow will cause the stick to make contact with the string, particularly in the middle section of the bow, resulting in scraping noises and rendering springing bowings becoming difficult, if not impossible. Conversely an over-tightened bow will wobble and shake uncontrollably.

To be able to rosin a bow without taking a chance of breaking or chipping the rosin cake, it is necessary to acquire good habits for this routine procedure. Hold the bow at frog with your right hand, place your thumb under the ferrule, overlapping it slightly so that the rosin cannot hit it (Figure 4.10). Start applying rosin onto the hair with short and quick back-and-forth motions. Gradually start drifting away from the frog with this continuous motion, making sure that the entire bow, including the upper third and tip, get an equal amount of rosin.

The Bow Hold and Arco Playing

The "WS&P" Recipe

As was mentioned in the Tone Production section of Lesson 3, Fritz Gearhart's "WS&P" recipe weight, speed, and placement (contact point) of bow accounts for this ever-changing weight, speed and contact point system for an even tone.

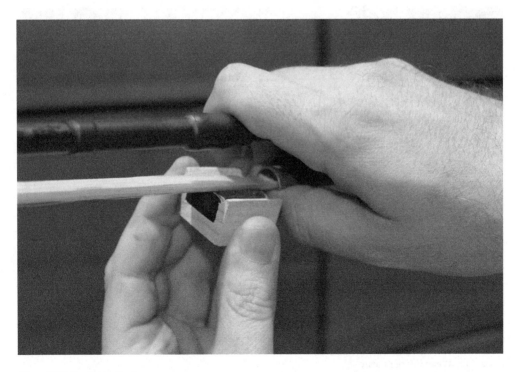

Figure 4.10 Rosining the bow

- To address the weight portion of the equation, index-finger weight must be used to draw an even tone. If no index finger weight is applied, the loudness will simply dissipate as the bow moves away from the frog in down bow, and it will increase as the bow approaches the frog on an up bow. Therefore, for a consistent dynamic, index finger weight is incrementally added from frog to tip, and it is incrementally decreased from tip to frog. As opposed to the index finger's weight, the pinky finger accounts for the counterweight. In other words, when a piano dynamic level is required, the pinky finger provides the required counterweight to lessen the combined weight of the bow and bow arm—which is maximum at frog and minimum at tip.
- At the early stages of string instruction speed is not altered significantly, as it is a complicated element of the recipe. At first only two simple bow speeds will be used (slow and fast) and as a variation of dynamics, note values and uneven slurs are introduced, multiple speeds of bow and acceleration and deceleration will be further studied.
- At the beginning stages only a constant contact point of halfway between the end of the fingerboard and bridge will be used and the third portion of the "WS&P" recipe will be fully addressed later.

To appreciate the right arm weight that is available for use of the bow, let's weigh our right arm by holding the right forearm with the left hand, and letting the right arm be completely lifeless, as if it were numb. This exercise illustrates that the arm has considerable weight that we often fail to appreciate. In fact, a person's arm weight is about from 5% to 6% of the total body weight (Figure 4.11).

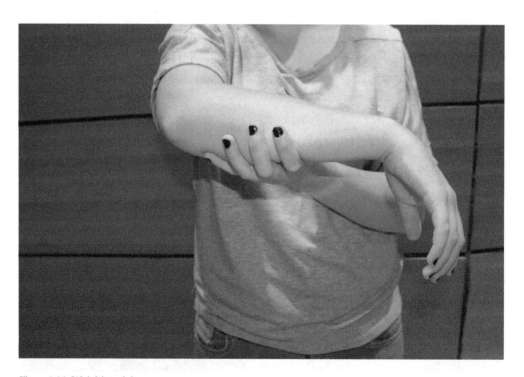

Figure 4.11 Weighing right arm

We will now transfer our preparatory bow hold onto the bow itself. First of all, we will hold the bow at its balance point, so that our newly-achieved bow grip will not collapse due to the weight. This is the point where the bow can be balanced, and it will be somewhere in the lower-third of the bow. To find the balance point, place the stick onto the left index finger and adjust if necessary (Figure 4.12). Hold the bow just as we have been practicing with the pencil. Notice the weight difference between the pencil and the bow. We will do our Air Drawing exercises by drawing imaginary shapes in the air: pluses, circles, any geometric shape or letter one can imagine. As with the pencil, watch not to lose the grip and do not allow the bow to roll. Remember: first joint of the thumb should *never* collapse, but keep its natural inward curl during these exercises. Lastly, we will do our Swimming Octopus exercises with the pencil.

Once comfortable with the preparatory bowing exercises, we will pick up the bow from its midpoint with the left hand, and place the thumb between the grip and the frog on the exposed portion of the stick (Figure 4.13). Place the bow on the D string at an equal distance from the end of the fingerboard and the bridge, perfectly parallel to both (Figure 4.14). Play the following exercise arco, in the middle third, with a constant contact point of bow and flat hair on the string (Figure 4.15). Make sure not to stop the bow between down and up bows, but play with a connected articulation.

Once comfortable with this short exercise, apply the paper towel roll exercises on the D string (refer back to Figure 4.3). Make sure to connect all notes and do not allow them to decay. After each repetition, stop and check yourself for bow grip, bow alignment, and instrument hold.

Figure 4.12 Finding the balance point of bow

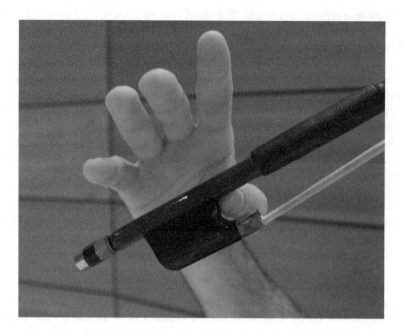

Figure 4.13 Correct thumb position on bow

Figure 4.14 Correct bow placement on the instrument

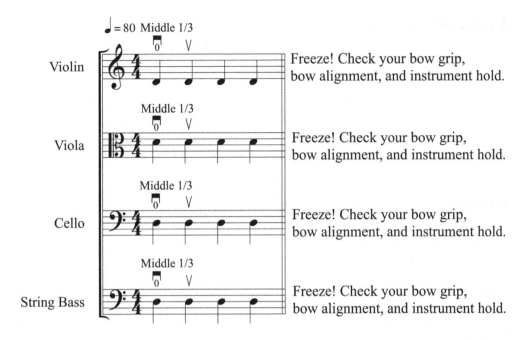

Figure 4.15 D string arco exercise no. 1

Assignment

1) Write a typed, one-page, double-spaced essay that answers the following, to be turned in at next class: discuss the repertoire of the violin family in the 16th century.
2) Continue to repeat Five Steps to Instrument Posture and Left-Hand Position and practice applying those steps on the assigned instrument.
3) Practice pizzicato tuning in the scholastic ensemble tuning sequence.
4) Practice "Pendulum" exercise.
5) Practice pizzicato exercises.
6) Practice Preparatory Bow Exercises.
7) Review today's lesson and read Lesson 5.

Note

1 It is also possible to apply this exercise on a spring tension window curtain rod (7/16" diameter, 18").

Lesson 5

Contents

This lesson's objectives are:

- Continued work on preparatory bow exercises.
- Continued work on the bow hold and arco playing.
- A historical overview of the bow.
- A discussion on tuning strategies.
- Work on use of pegs in tuning.

Preparatory Bow Exercises (Continued)

First, repeat Three-Step Low-String, and Four-Step Upper-String Pencil Bow Hold exercises, all the while making sure to keep the thumb bent at a natural angle (roughly 120° obtuse angle) and not allowing it to collapse, keeping all other fingers rounded, and not raising the knuckles. Second, we will start the Air Drawing exercises by wiggling our fingers to draw imaginary shapes as circles, horizontal and vertical straight lines, and crosses in the air with our pencil, all the while not losing the basis of the bow grip. In other words, students will *never* allow the pencil to roll between the tip of the thumb and first joint of the middle finger while performing these exercises, and allow the first joint of the thumb to collapse but always keep its natural inward curl (Figure 5.1). Third, the Swimming Octopus exercise will be imitating the bow motion in air. The forearm and wrist will be pronated, and both the wrist and five fingers will act as the swimming octopus, as graceful and smooth as the animal itself.

After the bow hold is established, practice a three-finger bow balance exercise with the middle, ring, and pinky fingers: hold the bow in front of the body and balance it by way of wrapping the middle finger around the stick, place your ring finger next to it, and counter-balance it with the pinky finger (Figure 5.2). This exercise makes an effective point of how light the bow is (from two to three ounces) and with a well-balanced bow hold there is no possibility of tension.

The Bow Hold and Arco Playing

Hold the bow at its balance point just like with the pencil. Perform the Air Drawing exercises by drawing imaginary shapes in the air: pluses, circles, any geometric shape or letter one can imagine. As with the pencil, watch not to lose the grip and do not allow the bow to roll. Remember: first joint of the thumb should *never* collapse, but keep its natural inward curl during these exercises. Lastly, we will do our Swimming Octopus exercises with the pencil.

Once comfortable with the preparatory bowing exercises, pick up the bow from its midpoint with the left hand, and place your thumb between the grip and the frog on the exposed portion of the stick. Place the bow on the D string at an equal distance from the end of the fingerboard and the bridge, perfectly parallel to both. Play the following exercise arco, in the middle third of the bow, with a constant contact point and flat hair on the string. Make sure to check your posture, instrument hold, and bow hold at the end of each two-measure figure (Figure 5.3). Once comfortable move onto the A string and repeat the same exercise (Figure 5.4). As students move onto other strings, the same arm angle and arm slope *must* be preserved. Once comfortable move onto the G string and repeat it (Figure 5.5), and lastly move onto the E and C string exercise (Figure 5.6).

Theory: A Brief History of the Bow

The bow's roots go back to pre-8th century Mongolia. Both equine and archery being an intricate part of the nomadic Mongol way of life, it is only natural to conceive to produce sound from a spike fiddle with the use of a bow. Later, we find references to bowed chordophones, in Arabic literature of philosophers Al-Fârâbî and Ibn Sînâ, among others. The bow's earliest known illustration is on a mural in a palace located in Kurban Shaid, Tajikistan, tracing it back to the 9th and 10th centuries (Lesson 3). The bow arrived in Europe in the 11th century through two points of entry: Byzantium with rebec and Moorish Spain with rabāb. We may describe these instruments as bowed lutes, as in Byzantine lūrā (derivative of the lyre family). The earliest bows were about one third of the size of modern bows (about 8 inch hair length), convex, with a pike head.

We will, however, discuss both the bow and bowings in relation to the modern bow's inventor, "Stradivari of the bow" François Xavier Tourte [*le jeune*, the young] (1747–1835). François Xavier belonged to a family of bowmakers (archetiers). His father Pierre Tourte's [*père*, the father] violin (luthierie) and bow making shop was a place for the apprenticeship-style education both brothers Nicolas Léonard and François Xavier received, much like the violin makers. François Xavier Tourte is credited for making the first example of the modern bow circa 1785 in Paris, featuring a heavier hatchet head—as opposed to pike. In his 1832 violin treatise, titled *Violinschule*, influential German violinist, composer, and educator Louis Spohr (1784–1859)

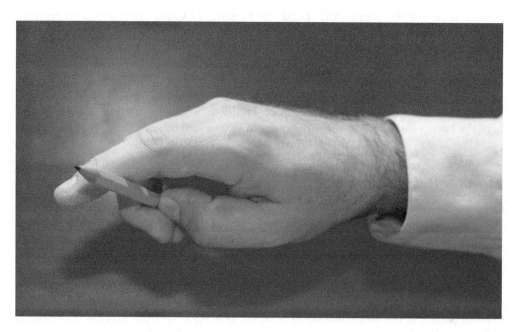

Figure 5.1 Air Drawing exercise

Figure 5.2 Balancing the bow with three fingers

Figure 5.3 D string arco exercise no. 2

Figure 5.4 A string arco exercise

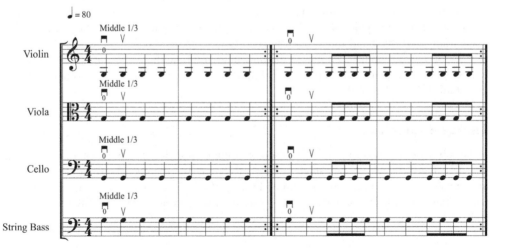

Figure 5.5 G string arco exercise

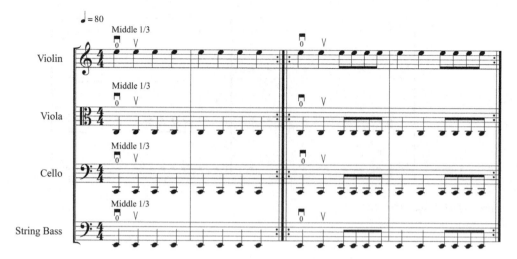

Figure 5.6 E and C string arco exercise

extolled Tourte's bows for their elasticity, light weight, for their exacting "beautiful, uniform bending", of concave shape "by which the nearest approach to the hair is exactly in the middle".

Tourte's violin bows are two to four centimeters longer than their contemporaries (at 74 to 75 cm), octagonal or round sticks, weighing around 56 grams and balanced in a manner that allows players to execute bow strokes which were previously impossible. To compensate the heavier hatchet head complete with a mother-of-pearl plate, at frog is a metal ferrule—made of silver or gold in better examples—and a mother-of-pearl slide. Tourte and other bow-makers have also used tortoiseshell for the frog, as opposed to the more common ebony. Another early bowmaker known as the "English Tourte" is John (Kew) Dodd (1752–1839) of the Dodd family of bowmakers, whose bows were exemplary, though, not just at quite the same level as of Tourte's.

There are two versions of double bass bows: French (also known as Bottesini), and German (also known as Simandl or Butler). Both versions feature hatchet heads, concave stick shapes, and similar stick lengths—German stick's concave curvature is more pronounced because of a taller frog, and an overall bow length is greater due to a longer tightening screw. The taller German frog requires a viol-like underhand bow grip. The French bow, on the other hand, is shaped and held overhand much like the cello bow. Furthermore, the playing styles of both versions of bows are influenced due to the bow hold and bow shape, because of this variance, bass sections of orchestras around the world may prefer certain holds over the other to fit into the established version of the ensemble.

Tuning Strategies

In Lesson 3 we discussed a scholastic ensemble tuning sequence. In an educational setting in the early stages of study, tuning single strings is the preferred method. As the student becomes more proficient it is possible to start tuning by way of adjacent strings for all instruments, and natural harmonics for the low strings. To describe tuning we must first describe sound waves and the way those waves interact with one other.

When we play an a' (A_4) at 440 Hz, each complete sound wave occurs 440 cycles per second (CPS). This is called wave frequency. If we play A an octave below it, a (A_3), it will have 220 Hz, or cycles per second, at a ratio of 1/2. Each simple sound wave, also known as simple sine wave comprises a peak (crest) and valley (trough). When the two notes are played together, one of the sound waves occurs twice the speed of the other, or coincidentally at perfectly twice the speed and we hear a perfect octave. When we play two perfectly matching A pitches at the same octave as in 440 Hz, both wave frequencies occur simultaneously and we hear a perfect unison. However, if we play one A at 440 Hz and the other at 445 Hz, the five hertz fluctuation between two pitches will cause a wobble, a phenomenon known as a beat (440 vs. 445=5 beats per second). Therefore, the further apart the two pitches the more beats we will hear (440 vs. 450=10 beats per second). By this calculation the closer the two pitches, the fewer the beats, and in tuning it is our goal to eliminate those wobbles completely.

A) **Bowing Principles for Tuning Considerations:** For tuning purposes the same bowing principles apply to all strings: place the bow at the upper 1/3, and continually bow at a piano dynamic level as if floating on the string without any break between bow changes. As excessive bow pressure on strings causes fluctuations in pitch, this is the most assured approach to tuning. Furthermore, piano bowing allows all students to hear themselves and be able to tune promptly without frustration.

B) **Adjacent String Tuning:** All string instruments are tuned to perfect fifths (violin, viola, and cello) and perfect fourths (double bass). To tune to adjacent strings, the student will follow the same order as the scholastic ensemble tuning sequence: A, D, G, C/E. Always tune A first, then tune D to A, and G to D. In the case of viola and cello, tune C to G, and in the case of violin and double bass, tune E to A. As it is in tuning in unison, eliminating the wobbles or beats is the main goal in tuning by way of playing two adjacent strings. To realize that objective the student must be able to play two strings with equal weight and with constant bow speed without any imperfections, so that reliable pitch is heard without any differences caused by bowing faults. Also, the student must become familiar with the way perfect fifth and perfect fourth intervals ring. A perfect unison is 1/1, a perfect octave is 2/1, a perfect fifth interval is 3/2 and a perfect fourth is 4/3 ratio. For instance if a' is 440 Hz, an octave below a is 220 Hz (2/1), a fourth below e' is 330 Hz (3/4), and a fifth below d' is 294 (3/2). Once the student becomes proficient in tuning in unison, the perfect fifth, and in the case of double bass, perfect fourth tuning is rather uncomplicated. Eliminating beats in adjacent string tuning is the exact same procedure as tuning in unison, it is also an effective introduction to double-stop playing.

C) **Natural Harmonic Tuning:** Each open string is considered the fundamental of its harmonic series. Therefore, we can compare each open string to the lowest note on a woodwind or a brass instrument.[1] The complete series of natural harmonics can be heard if a player travels throughout the string lightly touching it. The most commonly played harmonics are the first partial, although through the fourth partials natural harmonics are used. First partial is an octave above the fundamental [a perfect 8th] (a" on a' string), then a fifth above it [a perfect 12th, or a compound fifth], and the second octave [a perfect 15th, or a double octave] (Figure 5.7). Natural harmonics are played by way of lightly touching the string at the placement shown in figure 5.7. The first partial occurs at the midpoint of the playable portion of string and it sounds the same as the stopped note, indicated by a perfect circle above it. However, starting from second partial, all subsequent partials can be played on either below or above the midpoint of the string as depicted in figure 5.7. The "played"

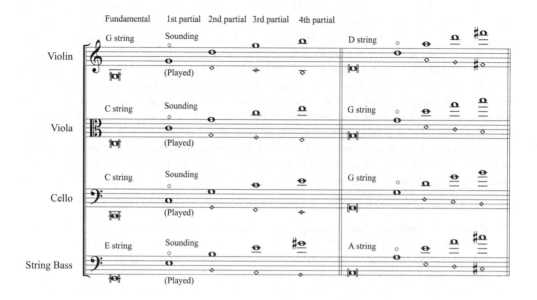

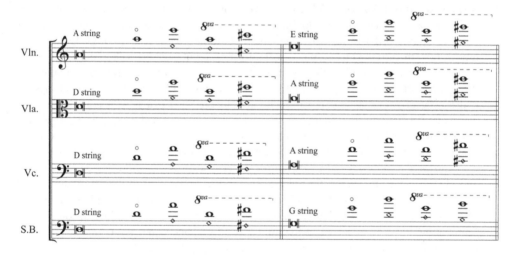

Figure 5.7 Natural harmonics of the violin family

location of those notes are indicated with a diamond notehead, and sounding notes, also playable, are with a regular notehead. Since the first partial sounds the same as the notated pitch, a regular notehead is used to notate it.

D) **Tuning with the First Partial:** There are several ways of tuning with natural harmonics and they are most commonly employed by the low string players. Since lower pitches are more difficult to distinguish, natural harmonics substitute those notes with more suitable ranges for the human ear. Also, in the case of receiving only one a' (A_4) to tune, both cellists and bassists can produce a perfect unison on their instruments. This is the first step for students to discover the natural harmonics on four strings, by locating the midpoint between the bridge and the string nut on the instrument. Both pizzicato and arco will produce the first partial, although arco will produce a better-speaking sustained note. It cannot be overstated how lightly the left-finger touch needs to be. If there is any excessive finger pressure on the string, or any other finger makes contact with it, natural harmonics will not speak. Conversely the bow *should* make good contact and students may play natural harmonics at the forte dynamic range. Once the students locate the midpoint of the playable or resonating portion of the string, they lightly touch it with their third fingers on the cello, and fourth fingers on the bass. Once confident with the third and fourth fingers, respectively, students can replace those fingers with the thumb, as first-partial tuning is a perfect opportunity to get comfortable with the thumb position.

Upper Strings

Find the midpoint on the A string. Lightly touch it at a flatter-than-normal playing angle with the pulpous portion of your fourth finger. The first joint of thumb will wrap around the corner of the neck and no other part of the left hand will make contact with the string or fingerboard (Figure 5.8). Student will play arco at a regular weight of bow as a regular stopped note.

Low Strings

Find the midpoint on the A string. Lightly touch it at a flatter-than-normal playing angle with the pulpous portion of your third or fourth finger. The thumb will hover right above and no

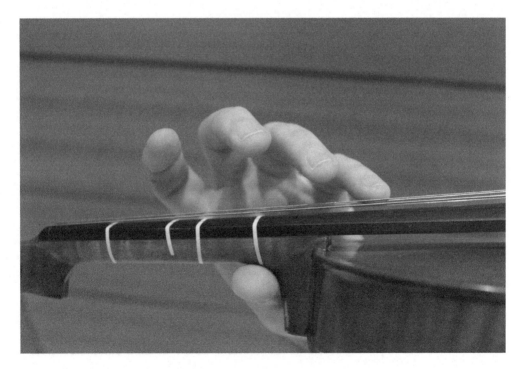

Figure 5.8 Finding midpoint of string for a first-partial harmonic on upper strings

other part of the left hand will make contact with the string or neck (Figure 5.9). Student will play arco at a regular weight of bow as a regular stopped note. Once the A string is tuned, adjacent strings may be tuned by way of tuning the neighboring string to perfect fifth in the case of the cello, and to perfect fourth in the case of the double bass.

Natural-Harmonic Tuning with First through Third Partials

Once comfortable with the first partial, we will move onto the second and third partials that the low strings may be tuned with those matching unison tones. First through third partial tuning is essential for accuracy and efficiency for the low strings. For tuning purposes, most commonly the double bass employs second and third partials and cello first and second partials. Tuning by way of harmonics allows the low strings players to tune their instruments by using a general A (440 Hz). Since general A is in unison with the A strings of the violin and viola, natural-harmonic tuning is not necessary for upper strings, therefore will not be discussed in this section.[2]

Cello

Find the midpoint on the A string with the third finger and lightly touch it. It will be a', or the first partial. Tune the A string to the tone generator's a' (440 Hz). Then, with the first finger, find the second partial on the D string, which is unison a' (this finger placement is the fourth position). Tune the D string to the A string by matching the unison pitch. Once in tune, move onto the first partial on the D string d' with the third finger and its matching unison second

Figure 5.9 Finding midpoint of string for a first-partial harmonic on low strings

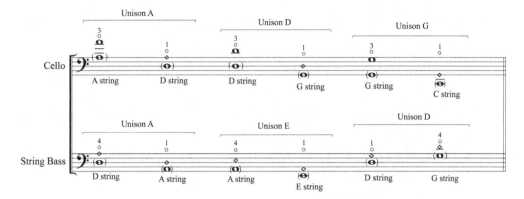

Figure 5.10 Low strings tuning with natural harmonics

partial on the G string. Tune it to the D string by matching this unison. Once in tune, move onto the first partial on the G string, g with third finger and its matching unison on the C string, and tune it to the G string (Figure 5.10). Once in tune, it is a good idea to double-check the overall tuning by placing the third finger across the first partials of adjacent strings and hear ringing of perfect fifths.

Double Bass

On the D string find the A with the fourth finger, which is a perfect fifth above the open string (third position) and lightly touch it. It will sound a (220 Hz) or the second partial. Tune the D string by matching this partial to the tone generator's a' (440 Hz). Then with the first finger, find the third partial A on the A string, which is in unison. Tune the A string to the D string by matching this unison pitch. Once in tune move onto the second partial on the A string, which is E (165 Hz) with fourth finger and its matching unison third partial on the E string. Tune the E string to the A string by matching this unison. Once in tune, move onto third partial on the D string with first finger, or d' (294 Hz) and its matching unison on the G string, and tune it to the D string (refer back to Figure 5.10). Once in tune, it is a good idea to double-check the overall tuning by placing the fourth finger across the first partials of adjacent strings and hear ringing of the perfect fourths.

E) **Tuning with Pegs:** Tuning with pegs is not a highly difficult process, however, in the beginning stages of playing it may first appear daunting. Similarly, for a string teacher charged to teach a class of young beginner students, it is a relatively time-consuming process and it takes up a considerable portion of valuable class time. If students are primarily dependent on fine tuners, it is the teacher's job to help with tuning and loosen the fine tuners that have been wound to their limit. To be able to tune with pegs, students must know the assigned pitch of each peg. The tensile strength of each string has been determined with the assigned pitch of the string. If a student tries to tune a string more than a major second above it, there is a good chance for it to break. The higher above pitch, the higher the likelihood of the string breaking, and for an inexperienced student to break a string may cause injury. To understand the process of tuning with pegs, students must understand how they are constructed and how they function. Pegs are made to fit within a peg hole at a two-degree taper and are held in place only by friction. For a simple friction device as a peg to function properly, it needs to fit into the peg hole perfectly. To accomplish that violin makers use a peg shaper (or peg shaver) to fit the peg into the peg hole, which has been shaped with a peg hole reamer. Due to the two-degree taper, pegs should be pushed into the peg hole as turning to adjust tuning. Both the peg and peg hole need to be well maintained to function properly, allowing the peg to move smoothly and hold the string perfectly in pitch.

The students must learn how to tune their instruments only with the left hand while bowing to achieve efficiency in their tuning. For the left-handed tuning the student must have acquired independent bowing ability and sufficient ear training to know the assigned pitch of each four strings.

Upper Strings

For two pegs on the bass side of the instrument (G and D pegs for violin, C and G pegs for viola), hold the peg between your index finger and thumb, push in from the opposite side of the pegbox with your middle, ring, and pinky fingers (Figure 5.11). For two pegs on the treble side of the instrument (A and E pegs for violin, D and A pegs for viola), hold the peg with your middle finger and thumb, push in from the opposite side of the pegbox with your index finger (Figure 5.12).

Figure 5.11 Upper strings tuning on bass side of pegbox

Figure 5.12 Upper strings tuning on treble side of pegbox

Low Strings

Cello is the largest instrument with wooden pegs in the violin family and it takes more strength to tune than both the violin and viola. For this reason it is critical for pegs to be in perfect working condition and for the cello students to be well prepared for the task. Furthermore, it is not possible to push in pegs with the same ease as upper strings while turning them. Therefore, the instrument must be well secured while tuning and it is necessary to push the peg into the peg hole while turning. To accomplish that, fully grip the peg in your palm and rotate while pushing it into the peg hole (Figure 5.13).

Some Idiosyncrasies of Pegs

As students will discover, pegs may not always move easily due to excessive resistance in the peg hole. Consequently, in order to tune up a string, the pitch needs to be lowered first, essentially breaking the peg's frictional resistance, and then bought back up to the desired pitch. This pitch fluctuation may be on the order of a minor second (or half step). The practice of lowering pitch and bringing it back up may also be necessary to tune without the assistance of a fine tuner. As pegs stick rather imprecisely, as far as the exact pitch is concerned, this process may need to be repeated until the desired pitch is obtained. In the case of double bass, machine heads may have some play between screw threads (or worm) and actual gears, and those metal pegs may also need to be lowered and brought back up to pitch.

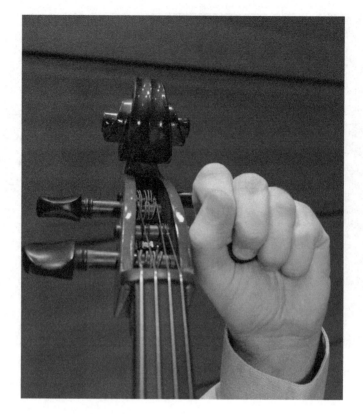

Figure 5.13 Peg grip for cello tuning

Assignment

1) Write a typed, one-page, double-spaced essay that answers the following, to be turned in at next class: how do modern bows differ from their earlier counterparts before 1780s?
2) Practice pizzicato exercises.
3) Practice Preparatory Bow Exercises and the bow hold.
4) Review today's lesson and read Lesson 6.

Notes

1 As tone holes of a woodwind or valves of a brass instrument shorten the column of air, stopped notes on strings shorten the overall length of the playable or vibrating portion of the string (from string nut to bridge). Therefore, whenever a fingered note is played, the fundamental changes and for every fingered note, or string length, there is a series of natural harmonics.
2 Natural harmonics will be discussed more in depth in Lesson 12.

Lesson 6

Contents

This lesson's objectives are:

- Work on arco tuning.
- Practice bow exercises.
- A discussion on necessary accessories.

Applied: Arco Tuning

So far we have discussed the scholastic ensemble tuning sequence, pizzicato tuning, and arco tuning (tuning to adjacent strings, tuning with natural harmonics, and tuning with pegs). With our readily improving ability to play arco, in this class we will start tuning with sustained tones. The class will be tuning to an A produced by a tone generator and once in tune, move through the scholastic ensemble tuning sequence of A, D, G, C, and E. At the instructor's discretion, pegs may be used, although mostly fine tuners will be employed to tune. Remember to tune at a piano dynamic and bow continuously in the upper 1/3, and play *only* the string being tuned.

Guided Practice: Bow Exercises

First, repeat Three-Step Low-String, and Four-Step Upper-String Pencil Bow Hold exercises with drawing of imaginary shapes. Continue onto the Swimming Octopus motion and apply it to the pencil bow hold, and repeat the Opening and Closing the Imaginary File Cabinet exercise.

Next "play" the following exercise with the paper towel roll. Make decisive and quick forearm movements with the bow. Use short and equal-length motions for all note values. After each repetition stop to check the bow grip, making sure that it is not collapsed. If collapsed, correct it and continue with the exercise. Once comfortable, apply the exercise to all strings on respective instruments. Perform the figure on each string, starting from lowest to highest. Make sure to pause in-between each string, check the bow grip and correct it if necessary (Figure 6.1).

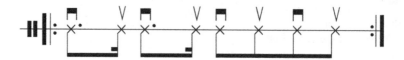

Figure 6.1 Paper towel roll exercise no. 2

Figure 6.2 String-crossing exercise no. 1

After completing the paper towel roll exercise, pick up instruments and pencils and air bow the following exercise. First, stop in-between each measure to adjust arm elevation for the following measure, then play the entire exercise seamlessly (Figure 6.2).

Accessories

In this section we will discuss accessories as they apply to string pedagogy and instrument, bow, and string purchases will be discussed in Lesson 9. As accessories needed to play string instruments evolve over time, it is desirable to remain well-informed of the latest technologies and improvement in products. The decision to include or omit any of the following items is a string educator's prerogative, however, one can make sound choices only if knowledgeable. The selection criteria for accessories comprise practical, acoustical, and philosophical rationale. Density of material, weight, durability, access, and cost are also valid factors that play a significant role in making those decisions.

Shoulder Rest

Among the most contentious matters in upper string instruction, a shoulder rest is an item that carries significant impact on the instrument hold both for violin and viola. Instrument angle, setup solidity, and player's comfort level are greatly affected by the selection of a well-made and well-fitting shoulder rest. As each student's physical attributes to fit a particular instrument are different, there is not one cookie-cutter solution. Although upper string teachers may have preconceived opinions when it comes to shoulder rest selection, it is the author's firm opinion that shoulder rest selection must be done with an open mind that allows for students to try as many makes and models as possible. Much like shoe shopping, there is no substitute for trying a shoulder rest personally. Towards that end if there is a close by violin shop, students and teachers should consider taking a field trip to try as many shoulder rests as possible.

The question is "what makes a good shoulder rest?" Even though preferences are incredibly personal and varied, a well-chosen and well-made shoulder rest works in conjunction with the chinrest, in keeping the instrument supported at a proper angle without any extra effort needed to keep it in place. If the shoulder rest is structured, legs with adjustable height allow for proper angling and heightening of the instrument to conform to the unique physique of the student and shape of the instrument's lower bout. Furthermore, legs should be sturdy and immovable throughout performances and must be made of durable rubber. Too many instruments have been scratched by exposed metal or hard plastic legs of shoulder rests due to worn rubber fittings.

If for some reason the student does not require a shoulder rest, or the private teacher is altogether against the idea of using a shoulder rest, a material such as a chamois leather or beaded non-adhesive shelf liner provides reliable friction to keep instrument in place. If the student needs more structure, half cut pool noodle can be rolled with the shelf liner (Figure 6.3). Most, if not all violin virtuosos of the early- to mid-20th century did not use shoulder rests, therefore, some notable professors still prefer this practice by choice, and argue that there is no need for a shoulder rest if the student can properly hold instrument without it. For beginners on upper string instruments properly fit shoulder rests, along with properly fit chinrests, provide a secure foundation and work extremely well in avoiding injury. The preference of shoulder-rest use, may be a worthy discussion for *much* later in years of practice, well after the instrument setup is solidified for the student.

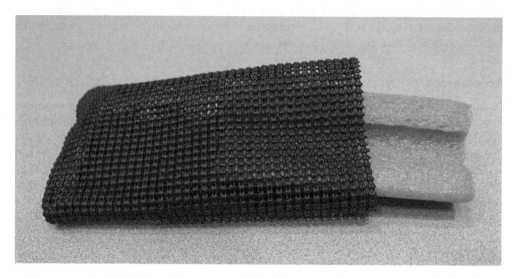

Figure 6.3 A homemade shoulder rest

Foam shoulder pads provide an inexpensive and quick solution for a large class of young students. Smaller and lighter student instruments particularly work well with foam shoulder pads, as those pads are often shaped to fit the collarbone, afford a dependable support, and can easily accommodate any smaller instrument including a 1/32 violin.

In the case of structured shoulder rests (Everest, Kun, et al.), stable body and solid rubber legs that provide reliable grip on ribs are preferred features. The shoulder rest must be light, yet strong enough to deliver the required stability where it does not tilt, flex or move throughout extended performances and nowadays carbon fiber and composite materials offer excellent solutions. If the student's neck height requires further accommodation, many brands offer extended legs for their shoulder rests. In such exceptional cases the instrument might become unwieldy, therefore, part of the lengthening should be done by the chinrest.

Chinrest

Not nearly as contentious as shoulder-rest use, all educators agree on chinrest's necessity—only Baroque instruments do not feature chinrests. Perhaps this categorical acceptance is partially due to the fact that its inventor is none other than Louis Spohr, who depicted a center-mounted chinrest in his 1832 treatise *Violinschule* as "violin-holder" (Figure 6.4).[1]

There are numerous variables with chinrests as its placement (bass-side or center mounted), material (rosewood, boxwood, plastic, or composite), height, tilt and overall shape. Much like the selection of shoulder rests, nowadays there is an abundant variety of relatively inexpensive chinrests capable of accommodating any body type. Established brands as Wittner produce height and tilt adjustable chinrests made of composite materials, in addition to the conventional ebony, rosewood, boxwood, or plastic. Composite chinrests not only provide height and tilt variations, but also eliminate any potential skin irritation due to nickel allergy (contact dermatitis,

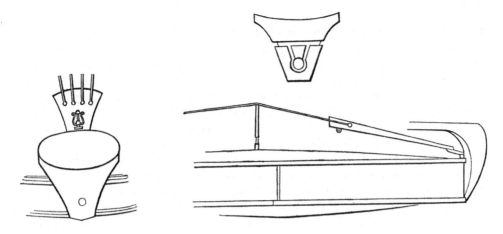

Figure 6.4 Spohr's chinrest, as depicted in *Violinschule*

or contact eczema) caused by metal chinrest clamps. Both with nickel allergy, or if chinrest material itself is causing a skin irritation, a cotton handkerchief may be used to address it.

In summary, a good chinrest must provide secure contact of the jawbone without causing teeth to clench, head to tilt, or instigate any other symptom of tension. Both the groove and bulbous portion of chinrest must fit the student perfectly without any discomfort. While it is impractical to attempt to personalize all school-owned instruments, string teachers must strive to match and assign well-fitted instruments to students and if necessary, update older chin rests with excessively shallow grooves or sharp edges known to cause discomfort and setup deficiencies.

Fine Tuner or String Adjuster

It is likely that most of the classroom instruments have tailpieces with built-in fine tuners or string adjusters—with the exception of double bass, because machine heads do not need fine tuners. There is a chance that some instruments may not be fitted with fine tuners on all strings, a choice many professionals make on their instruments. Indeed, solo instrumentalists may choose to use only one fine tuner on the highest string with exacting aesthetic or acoustical rationales. However, tasked to keep multiple instruments in tune, a string teacher's motivation for fitting fine tuners on *all* strings of violins, violas, and cellos is well justified. Tailpieces with pre-fitted fine tuners may be made of aluminum alloy, composite graphite, plastic, wood, or carbon fiber. If the instrument is not fitted with four fine tuners, separate string adjusters are relatively inexpensive and easy to install.

Tailgut

A Sacconi-style tailpiece adjuster is likely the tailgut fitted on student instruments, and it is a safe, reliable and climate-proof component. If an older instrument is fitted with catgut, it is best to replace it with a nylon tailpiece adjuster. If a double bass is fitted with a coat wire hanger, it would be advisable to replace it with an aircraft-rated stainless steel cable assembly, or seek a similarly healthy solution.

Mute

Historically, mutes evolved as pronged clamps that fit directly on the bridge to dampen the tone for a veiled, translucent quality. In an educational setting it is most sensible to choose a practical slide-on mute, however, the mute should remain on the instrument without any concern of buzzing. Similarly, removable wooden mutes (now mostly-obsolete) take too much time to apply and remove to be practical, not to mention the discoloration they cause on the bridge. Aside from slide-on wire mutes, the simplest and most appealing answer might be rubber mutes. Most ubiquitous orchestra mutes are Tourte-style, which come in two shapes: single hole and two hole. Two-hole mutes are prone to buzzing and so are the single-hole ones if not pushed into the string. For that reason Super-Sensitive brand Spector violin mute is a superior solution to Tourte, as it eliminates all buzzes and rattles. An altogether different alternative to manufactured options, any standard vinyl aquarium airline tube (3/16 inch inner diameter) may be cut to bridge-length, weaved onto strings and used as a slide-on mute. An entire ensemble may be fitted with this homemade mute inexpensively, quickly and effectively.

Practice mutes are much heavier than orchestral mutes and their sole purpose is to dampen as much sound as possible during practice. In an educational setting, five-pronged rubber practice mutes are the preferred option. Metal practice mutes function just as well, although they pose unnecessary hazards especially when they slip or fall onto the top plate of the instrument.

Rosin

Also known as colophony,[2] rosin is distilled by evaporating turpentine, and hardened from pine tree sap, or resin. Although the exact formulas are trade secrets, commercially available rosins include some additives such as beeswax. Its color varies from light amber to dark brown. The selection criteria for a particular rosin formula include personal tonal preferences, climate, bow hair, bow, and instrument response. In a broad sense, the lighter colored rosins produce smoother tone and the darker rosins produce a grittier tone. Although instrument-specific rosins abound, a generic rosin may be used for the violin, viola, and cello. A specific rosin with a stickier formula is preferred for the double bass, since those lower strings require more resistance from the rosin. Most student-grade rectangular rosins are molded in protective frames with open sides, but are not immune from breaking when dropped. Round-shaped cake rosins are protected in fabric or thin foam material and should be handled with extra care. When applying a cake rosin, the student must alternate the direction, or rotate the cake regularly to avoid getting groves from forming. Unlike the rectangular rosins, cake rosins may remain flat throughout their useful lives.

It is possible to repair a broken rosin by melting and remolding it. Additionally, broken rosin pieces may be pulverized for easy application on an unrosined bow, since it is a time-consuming effort to rosin a rehaired or a new bow.[3]

Wolf Tone Suppressors

Wolf tone or wolf note is a tonal irregularity caused by the construction of the instrument, which excessively enhances the resonance of a particular note and causes it to waver or wobble, much like the howling of a wolf. The wolf tone manifests itself most predominantly between a major 6th and an octave on the G string of the cello. Since this is a regularly used part of the string, cello wolf suppression may be necessary. To address it, a brass fitting with a rubber sleeve is installed on the non-playable part of the string between the bridge and tailpiece. Once installed on the string, it may need some adjustment before the wolf tone is suppressed. It must be noted this device not only suppresses the wolf, but also the overall resonance and overtones, therefore, the smallest possible wolf suppressor is the preferred option in addressing this anomaly. There are additional ways to suppress wolf tone by modifying Tourte-style mutes or installing double-sided magnets just below the bass side f-hole of the top plate.

Endpins

A standard feature of a cello or double bass, most full-size student cellos come with a retractable steel endpin rod between 17 inches and 20 inches (an extendable length of 16 inches and 19 inches, respectively). The double bass endpin is likely to feature equidistant notches on the rod and the cello is not likely. Newer cello outfits may feature a 20 inches carbon fiber endpin rod, although steel is the most common material. The conical ebony plug is fitted onto the endpin hole of the cello or bass with a reamer with a taper of 1:17. To reduce cost instrument manufacturers use relatively shorter endpins, especially in the preceding days of carbon fiber, therefore, an alternative solution for taller cellists or bassists may be necessary. To that end carbon fiber endpins, with a composite plug with a cork inner sleeve, are excellent solutions for both cellos and double basses. They are acoustically superior, inexpensive, light, strong, do not bend, buzz, and feature ergonomic and secure tightening screws.

Endpin Anchors and Stops

Much like with shoulder rests and chinrests of the upper strings, the low string instruments need to be securely grounded so that players do not have to worry about stability of their instruments. In addition, endpins of the low strings can cause damage to flooring or carpet, therefore, endpin anchors and stops are needed. Since the cello has a more shallow playing angle than the double bass, there is greater force pushing the endpin away from the student and for that reason an endpin anchor may be a more secure option. Available for both the cello and the double bass, the basic principle of an endpin anchor is an adjustable nylon strap that attaches to a leg of the chair, and a solid plate with a rubber bottom to secure the endpin. Endpin anchors are extremely durable, portable, and work well on most surfaces. Wooden endpin anchors that attach to two front legs of the chair, however, are more secure than single-leg attached anchors.

Although there are numerous variants, most common student-grade endpin stops are made of a brass ring, or a solid top with a rubber disk. In addition, there are rubber tips that attach to the endpin itself to prevent it from slipping and causing damage to the floor. A couple of concerns with endpin stops are that they may not work well on all surfaces, and in time rubber becomes brittle and slippery. It is a good idea for a low string player to carry an endpin anchor and a stop for use on any flooring. Many string teachers and low string players come up with homemade endpin anchors that are most suitable for them.

Bridges

All bridges are pre-fitted onto student instruments as part of the shop setup. Although bridges with self-adjusting feet are available, it is best for a bridge to be fitted by a qualified violin maker as its precise placement is critical to maintain proper measurements of a given instrument and has a significant acoustical impact. For particular double basses that are used both for classical and jazz settings, an adjustable-height bridge with wheels provides a practical solution. Pizzicato playing in the jazz setting does not require the string height necessary for primary arco playing of classical ensembles, therefore, instruments used in a dual setting can be fitted with an adjustable bridge by a qualified violin maker. Therefore, a jazz-fitted double bass complete with a bridge-installed pickup and bow quiver may quickly transition back-and-forth with the classical setting and remain mostly unchanged.

Peg Compound

Also known as peg dope, peg compound is made by a few well-known manufacturers as the W. E. Hill and Pirastro, with specific proprietary formulas. It helps with both friction and lubrication of pegs in the pegbox and ensures smooth functioning of pegs.

Assignment

1) Write a typed, one-page, double-spaced essay that answers the following, to be turned in at next class: describe the setup-related reasons why it is important to fit a student with proper accessories such as chinrest, shoulder rest, endpin anchors and stops.
2) Practice pizzicato exercises.
3) Practice Preparatory Bow Exercises, and the bow hold.
4) Review today's lesson, and read Lesson 6 prior to next class.

Notes

1 Spohr, *Violinschule*, 8.
2 Rosin from the ancient city of Colophon in Asia Minor.
3 Alternately using a sticky bass rosin is a marvelous solution to jumpstart the process of rosining an unrosined bow.

Lesson 7

Contents

This lesson's objectives are:

- Continued work on arco tuning.
- Practice bow exercises.
- Arco playing.
- A brief discussion on string ensemble traditions.

Applied: Arco Tuning

In this class we will continue to tune with sustained tones. The class will be tuning to an A produced by a tone generator and once in tune, and will then move through the scholastic ensemble tuning sequence of A, D, G, C, and E. At the instructor's discretion, in addition to fine tuners, pegs may be employed to tune: bow continuously in the upper 1/3 at a piano dynamic and play *only* on the string being tuned. Throughout tuning no practicing or "doodling" is allowed as it impedes the process and erodes morale.

Bow Exercises

First, repeat Three-Step Low-String, and Four-Step Upper-String Pencil Bow Hold exercises with the drawing of imaginary shapes. Continue onto the Swimming Octopus motion and apply it to the pencil bow hold, and repeat the Opening and Closing the Imaginary File Cabinet exercise.

Next "play" the following three exercises with the paper towel roll. The following bow strokes are slurred staccato (A), hooked bowing (B), and a combination of both bowings (C). To achieve those bow strokes make a decisive and quick forearm movement with a clear stoppage in-between each note. After each section stop to check your bow grip, making sure that it is not collapsed. If collapsed, correct it and continue with the exercise. Once comfortable, apply the exercise to all strings on respective instruments. Perform the figure on each string, starting from the lowest to the highest. Make sure to pause in between each string, check the bow grip and correct it if necessary (Figure 7.1).

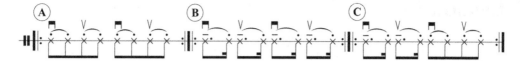

Figure 7.1 Paper towel roll exercise no. 3

Arco Playing

After completing the paper towel roll exercises, pick up instruments and pencils and air bow the following variation of Lesson 6's string crossing exercise. First, stop in between each measure to adjust arm elevation for the following measure, then play the entire exercise seamlessly with the bow (Figure 7.2).

Figure 7.2 String-crossing exercise no. 2

String Ensemble Playing Traditions

The earliest written description of a stand-alone mixed ensemble with strings, playing without any relation to text, singing, dance or other incidental elements, is the performance of five *sinfonias* during a Florentine *intermedi* in 1589 on the occasion of the grand duke of Tuscany Ferdinando de' Medici's marriage to Christine of Lorraine.[1] The term "concerto" initially described an ensemble or orchestra.[2] In England, small ensembles or consorts were created for the purpose of performing instrumental and vocal music. By the middle of the 17th century, both homogeneous and heterogeneous consorts were established.[3] Not until later in the 17th century did the instrumental concerto in the form of concerto grosso become prominent as we understand it.

The origins of the form initiated from the sonata, to be performed by a large ensemble. The accompanimental or secondary voices [ripieno] could be performed by players of lesser ability and primary voices [concertino or concertato] by advanced performers, thus, doubled string parts developed around the late 17th century in Italy. During this time period, sonata, trio sonata, concerto grosso, and solo concerto were chief instrumental forms. The term sonata was used interchangeably with sinfonia (canzone, capriccio, fantasia, et al.) and was used to designate a volume of instrumental pieces by a single composer, as in Arcangelo Corelli's (1653–1713) 12 violin sonatas, Op. 5, published in 1700 in Rome in two volumes: *Parte prima* (sonatas 1–6) and *Parte seconda* (sonatas 7–12), under the title of *Sonate a violin e violone o cimbalo* [sonatas for violin and double bass viol or harpsichord]. Furthermore, sonata could have meant a composition for two or three melody instruments with continuo, trio sonata, or five melody instruments with continuo, *sonata à cinque*. Maurizio Cazzati (1616–1678), Giuseppe Torelli (1658–1709), Arcangelo Corelli (1653–1713), and Tomaso Albinoni (1671–1750/51) were among the influential composers that had a significant involvement with the development of instrumental forms, ensembles, style and technique. Albinoni's Op. 2, twelve sinfonias and concerti for five melody instruments, titled *Sinfonie e Concerti à cinque* and his Op. 5, *XII Concerti à cinque* feature two violin and two viola lines dedicated to alto viola and tenor viola, as it was commonplace to find in instrumental ensemble works to offer a wide variety of organization for the string ensemble.

Antonio Vivaldi (1678–1741) made a vast contribution to instrumental technique, style, solo concerto form, program music, and orchestration as the most prolific concerto composer. For example, Vivaldi implemented the ritornello form in instrumental writing, where he transferred it from the church aria to the outer fast movements of concertos. This practice is exemplified in *L'estro armonico* Op. 3 (1711), a collection of double concertos for strings and harpsichord. Ritornello form (a diminutive of *ritorno* or return in Italian), in an instrumental sense, is a refrain of a short melody alternated with solo instrumental episodes that afford soloists an expansion of tonality and diverse technical difficulties.

Johann Sebastian Bach (1685–1750), who studied and arranged several of his concertos, actually adapted Vivaldi's string writing style into his own. In the case of his six so-called Brandenburg Concertos (1721), Bach not only expanded the concerto grosso idiom notably, but also placed significant demand of the virtuoso playing on all involved solo instruments. When it comes to large-scale orchestral compositions, not involved with singing or dance as in operas, oratorios, and other liturgical compositions, Bach's four orchestral suites (BWV 1066–69), one overture (BWV 1070, although spurious), and sinfonia (BWV 1046a formerly BWV 1071), are noteworthy multi-movement works. In 1730, Bach's municipal orchestra in Leipzig included the following string forces: three first violins, three second violins, two violas, two cellos, and one *violone* (double bass viol). Both leaders of the first and second violins were professionals, and the section players were students. His orchestra for instrumental music were as many as 20 players altogether with the winds, percussion and keyboard instruments, although his ensemble dedicated to church music comprised seven professionals and one apprentice.[4] He employed not only the members of the standard violin family, but also now-defunct instruments such as the violino piccolo, violetta, viola d'amore, violoncello piccolo, in addition to the viola da gamba and violone in his works as the cantatas.[5] Bach personally owned numerous string instruments, among which was a violin made by Jacob Stainer.[6]

George Frideric Handel's (1685–1759) strings totaled fourteen violins, five violas, four cellos, and two double basses in a mixed ensemble of 50.[7] Among Handel's largest string sections included 22 violins, four violas, six cellos, and five double basses. The pay-lists for the two *Messiah* charity performances at Foundling Hospital (1754/58 respectively) list the following string sections: 14 first violins, 12 second violins, six/three violas, three cellos, one/three double basses.[8]

The orchestra of Mannheim's electoral court (1740–78) was among the most influential forces on the development of orchestral styles and forms, particularly of the symphony. Among Mannheim school's prominent representatives was Johann Stamitz (1717–1757). Adopting the orchestral idiom characterized in Italian opera overture in the works of Alessandro Scarlatti (1660–1725), Leonardo Leo (1694–1744), Baldassare Galuppi (1706–1785), Niccolò Jommelli (1714–1774), and Leonardo Vinci's (1696?–1730), Stamitz greatly expanded the orchestral idiom. He wrote both for strings and continuo, and for full orchestra in the following multi-movement forms: orchestra quartets, sinfonias, sinfonia concertantes, symphonies, and concertos. Another composer associated with the Mannheim court, Franz Xaver Richter (1709–1789) wrote six string quartets, Op. 5 (publ. in London in 1768).

The string quartet and symphony become some of the most substantial expressions for string writing for the three representatives of the Viennese Classicism: Haydn, Mozart, and Beethoven. The string quartet at the heart of a symphonic orchestra exemplified the relations between sections of the strings and in the symphonic idiom this relationship was expanded with the use of non-string instruments. Joseph Haydn (1732–1809) wrote 68 string quartets (No. 68, Op. 103 is unfinished), and 106 symphonies. He is known as the "father of" string quartet and symphony due to the immense number, sublime excellence and lasting influence of his output in both areas. Haydn's symphonies could have as few as three first violins, three second violins, one viola, one cello, and one double.

Wolfgang Amadeus Mozart (1756–1791), while paying homage to Haydn further developed the expression of both symphonic writing and string quartet. His 23 string quartets (written between 1770 and 1790), including the last three known as the "Prussian" (K. 575, K. 589, and K. 590) are among the exemplary representations for this setting. In his 41 symphonies Mozart did not simply follow the symphonic traditions established in Vienna, Salzburg, and Mannheim but actually broke the established norms. His Salzburg symphonies (written in 1770s), and late symphonies, especially Nos. 35–41 "Haffner" through "Jupiter" contain both superlative and stylistically challenging writing for strings. When it comes to string section size, a Mozart symphony performance in Vienna in 1781 featured 68 strings altogether. A much more likely string section in the same timeline would have been a total of twenty-three: six first violins, six second violins, four violas, four cellos, and three double basses. In 1781, in Vienna, a symphonic orchestra featured 21 violins, 22 violins, ten violas, eight cellos, and ten string basses.[9]

Third representative of the Viennese Classical tradition Ludwig van Beethoven (1770–1827) has expanded the technical and individual responsibilities of the violin family both in the symphonic and chamber setting. His string quartets are studied under three distinct periods:

early Nos. 1–6 (1798–1800), middle Nos. 7–11 (1806–11), and late Nos. 12–16 and Op. 133 *Grosse Fuge* (1824–26). The string quartets, particularly the late quartets present technical and stylistic challenges to chamber musicians and influence composers for the next two centuries. His symphonic output and particularly the nine symphonies (1799–1824) are the cornerstone of orchestral repertoire. In Beethoven's symphonic writing, overall demand of range for expression placed on all sections of strings, enhanced the individuality of cellos from double basses, and the increase in responsibility is paramount. Due to the expanded number and sustained use of winds and percussion, which greatly increased the dynamic and tessitura demands placed on string instruments, as in extensive passages in higher positions, those string sections had to be increased in number. In a letter to Archduke Rudolph dated 1811, Beethoven requested a diminutive string section for the period: four firsts, four seconds, four violas, two cellos, and two double basses for his middle symphonies and two overtures. Only a few years later his string section that performed the Seventh and Eighth Symphonies in 1814 in Vienna featured 18 firsts, 18 seconds, 14 violas, 12 cellos, and seven string basses.

In less than a century the dependence of amateur musicians to bolster string sections, a practice that served late Baroque composers as Bach fairly well, had become unsustainable. Therefore, by the mid-19th century, Europe conservatories of music started to focus on the production of orchestral musicians capable of performing highly technical writing found in the symphonic repertoire of Beethoven, Franz Schubert (1797–1828), Robert Schumann (1810–1856), and Johannes Brahms (1833–1897).

Following Beethoven's exceptional treatment of orchestra, Romanticism further expand the size and involvement of each section of the violin family for the rest of the 19th century and with Richard Wagner's (1813–1883), Gustav Mahler's (1860–1911), and Anton Bruckner's (1824–1896) significant influences has reached its height. Vienna Philharmonic's string section in the 19th century was 12/12/8/8/8, in comparison to Wagner's Bayreuth Festspielhaus's (opened in 1876) robust string section of 16/16/12/12/8, and around the same time New York Philharmonic featured a string section of 37 violins, 14 violas, 14 cellos and 14 double basses.

Assignment

1) Study String Ensemble Playing Traditions for a quiz on this material in the next class and write a one-paragraph summary of the same section to be turned in next class.
2) Review instrument hold and bow hold.
3) Practice pizzicato exercises, preparatory bow exercises, and arco exercises for your first playing test.
4) Review today's lesson, read Introduction of Lesson 8 and the String Playing Test Rubric.

Notes

1 Coelho and Polk, *Instrumentalists and Renaissance Culture, 1420–1600*, 184.
2 "Concertato" was used as a descriptor for a list of instruments at the marriage celebration of grand duke of Tuscany Ferdinando de' Medici to Christine of Lorraine (1565).
3 Adler, *The Study of Orchestration*, 4.
4 Terry, *Bach's Orchestra*, 9.
5 Ibid., 238.
6 Wollny, "Bach and the Violin," 96.
7 Hogwood, *Handel: Water Music and Music for the Royal Fireworks*, 13.
8 Stahura, "Handel and the Orchestra," 243.
9 Zaslaw, "Toward the Revival of the Classical Orchestra," 177.

Lesson 8

Contents

In this lesson students will demonstrate the following:

*   Proper posture.
*   Proper setup.
*   Good tone production.

Videotaping of First Playing Test

This lesson is dedicated to performing the first playing test. The instructor will be videotaping the playing test and evaluating it on the spot. Each student will play the selections which have been decided by the instructor. Each student will watch the videotape and complete the following Self-Evaluation Form I, using the posture, setup, and tone production guidelines established in class.

Videotaping Number 1

Name:_____**Instrument:**_____**Date:**_____**Grades**____/_____

STRING PLAYING TEST RUBRIC I

First watch your video and read your instructor's evaluation of your playing. Afterwards, watch your video again and fill out the below rubric. Leave correct items blank, mark any exceptional element by a plus sign and any element in need of improvement by a minus sign. You will receive a grade for full and accurate completion, and timely submission of this form. The form is due at the beginning of next class.

POSTURE—INSTRUMENT HOLD, LEFT HAND, PIZZICATO POSITIONING AND BOW HOLD

VIOLIN AND VIOLA

POSTURE, INSTRUMENT HOLD AND LEFT HAND

_____ torso is square
_____ shoulders are relaxed
_____ feet are positioned correctly
_____ head is not tilted and is free of tension
_____ instrument is supported on the collarbone without tension
_____ instrument is placed parallel relative to the floor and kept with the "nose-scroll-elbow-toe" alignment at all times
_____ wrist is straight from all angles
_____ hand is free of tension
_____ four fingers are curved and tips of fingers are hovering right above strings
_____ thumb is at a proper height and is free of tension

PIZZICATO POSITIONING

_____ hand and arm are at a proper angle to play pizzicato
_____ tip of thumb is placed at the corner of fingerboard for secure pizzicato anchoring
_____ pizzicato is played with the index finger at a proper distance from the bridge

BOW HOLD

_____ shoulder is relaxed at all times
_____ elbow is relaxed and functioning smoothly
_____ wrist is slightly higher than knuckles
_____ all fingers are properly curved and spaced
_____ thumb's first joint is curved and tip of thumb is wedged against end of frog
_____ pinky finger is on top of stick

_____ forearm and wrist are slightly pronated and index finger is leaning toward the stick
_____ bow is always parallel to the bridge
_____ bow is at proper distance from bridge with a constant contact point
_____ arm weight and index finger produce a sustained and even tone
_____ bow direction changes are executed smoothly and without stoppage
_____ string crossings are executed smoothly and without disruption

CELLO

POSTURE, INSTRUMENT HOLD AND LEFT HAND

_____ seated on front four inches of seat with feet positioned correctly and flat on the floor in a position that can allow the student to stand up at any given time
_____ endpin is at a proper length with cello at a proper angle
_____ C peg is behind left ear, neck is one fist width above left shoulder and cello is tilted slightly to the left
_____ cello is not pinched and knees are relaxed with instrument balanced without assistance of arms
_____ wrist is straight from all angles and draws a straight line from elbow to knuckles
_____ elbow height can allow the student to slide up and down on the fingerboard
_____ thumb is behind the second finger and the tip of the thumb is lightly touching the middle of neck
_____ first joint of thumb is slightly rounded but not straightened
_____ first finger is slightly tilted toward the fingerboard and fourth finger is parallel to the first finger
_____ first to second and second to fourth fingers are equidistant from each other

PIZZICATO POSITIONING

_____ hand and arm are at a proper angle to play pizzicato
_____ tip of thumb is placed at side of fingerboard, last three- to four-inches of fingerboard for secure pizzicato anchoring
_____ pizzicato is played with the index finger at a proper distance from the bridge

BOW HOLD
_____ shoulder is relaxed at all times
_____ elbow is relaxed and functioning smoothly
_____ wrist is slightly higher than knuckles
_____ all fingers are properly curved and spaced
_____ thumb's first joint is curved and tip of thumb is wedged against end of frog
_____ forearm and wrist are slightly pronated and index finger is leaning toward the stick
_____ bow is always parallel to the bridge
_____ bow is at a proper distance from the bridge with a constant contact point
_____ arm weight and index finger produce a sustained and even tone
_____ bow direction changes are executed smoothly and without stoppage
_____ string crossings are executed smoothly and without disruption

DOUBLE BASS

SITTING POSITION

_____   seated tall with left knee behind bass right foot planted firmly on the floor
_____   endpin is at a proper length with bass at a proper angle
_____   instrument is slightly leaning back with the right corner of instrument in front of
          sternum with f-holes facing the conductor

STANDING POSITION

_____   standing tall, shoulders back with a straight spine
_____   endpin is at a proper length with bass at a proper angle with right corner of
          instrument in front of sternum
_____   the instrument is positioned diagonally in-front of the player with f-holes facing the
          conductor

INSTRUMENT HOLD AND LEFT HAND

_____   first finger is at eye level when placed on the first tape
_____   wrist is straight from all angles and draws a straight line from elbow to knuckles
_____   elbow height can allow the student to slide up and down on the fingerboard
_____   thumb is behind the second finger and the tip of the thumb is lightly touching the
          middle of the fingerboard
_____   first joint of thumb is slightly rounded but not straightened
_____   first finger is tilted toward the fingerboard and the fourth finger is reaching the
          fourth finger tape with a K-shaped hand
_____   first to second and second to fourth fingers are equidistant from each other

PIZZICATO POSITIONING

_____   hand and arm are at a proper angle to play pizzicato
_____   tip of thumb is placed at side of fingerboard, last three- to four-inches of fingerboard
          for secure pizzicato anchoring
_____   pizzicato is played with the first joint of the index finger at a proper angle

GERMAN BOW HOLD

_____   shoulder is relaxed at all times
_____   elbow is relaxed and functioning smoothly
_____   thumb, index and middle fingers are joined at the tips
_____   all fingers are properly curved and spaced
_____   thumb's first joint is curved and tip of thumb is behind stick, but not on top
_____   forearm and wrist are supinated at a proper angle
_____   bow is always parallel to the bridge
_____   bow is at a proper distance from bridge with a constant contact point
_____   arm weight and index finger produce a sustained and even tone

_____   bow direction changes are executed smoothly and without stoppage
_____   string crossings are executed smoothly and without disruption

FRENCH BOW HOLD

_____   shoulder is relaxed at all times
_____   elbow is relaxed and functioning smoothly
_____   wrist is slightly higher than knuckles
_____   all fingers are properly curved and spaced
_____   thumb's first joint is curved and tip of thumb is wedged against end of frog
_____   forearm and wrist are slightly pronated and index finger is leaning toward the stick
_____   bow is always parallel to the bridge
_____   bow is at a proper distance from the bridge with a constant contact point
_____   arm weight and index finger produce a sustained and even tone
_____   bow direction changes are executed smoothly and without stoppage
_____   string crossings are executed smoothly and without disruption

Scale: intonation, accuracy, and fingering

Piece: intonation, accuracy, and fingering

Evaluation Summary: provide a summary of your playing test by writing one paragraph on the positive elements of your playing and one paragraph on those elements in need of improvement

1)   A summary of positive elements.

2)   A summary of elements in need of improvement.

Assignment

1)   Complete String Playing Test Rubric I, to be turned in next class.
2)   Practice pizzicato exercises.
3)   Practice Preparatory Bow Exercises, and the bow hold.
4)   Read Lesson 9.

Lesson 9

Contents

This lesson's objectives are:

- A bow placement exercise.
- A discussion on bow management and string crossings.
- A brief discussion on selection and maintenance of string instruments, bows and strings.

Guided Practice: A Bow Placement Exercise

Mental imagery is central to playing a string instrument. The following exercise by Dr Rodney Schmidt, featured in an article, titled "Contours, Images, and the Bow" in *Journal of the Violin Society of America*, helps visualize the motions associated with bowing. To accomplish that, students pick up their bows and drop their right arms on their side loosely. Close their eyes, imagine the body and following a circular motion, upper string players bring the right thumb to their nose, and low string players to their belly button. Make sure to imagine the body as vividly as possible and make any adjustments necessary to the mental picture while the arm is moving. Once an accurate picture of the movement is memorized, upper string players touch the nose with the middle and tip of the bow, and low string players, touch the belly button with the middle and tip of the bow.

Now pick up your instrument and hold in the playing position. Close your eyes and imagine the playing area of the D string between the bridge and fingerboard. Divide the area into five bow hair widths or tracks. With the right arm holding the bow and hanging loosely at the side, visualize the circular movement necessary to bring the arm and bow to the string with the frog touching the bridge. Perform the movement—out, up, and around—then visually check for accuracy. Repeat the movement sequence until it is completely accurate. Then place the middle and the tip of the bow at the bridge using the same procedure. Once the bridge can be found using a variety of bow areas, begin experimenting with different tracks or hair-width areas on the D string until they can be found with complete accuracy with any part of the bow on any track, visualizing the entire procedure with the eyes closed, only opening them to check accuracy.[1]

Bow Management and String Crossings

A substantial part of bow technique on all string instruments is bow management, or the ability to distribute the bow within any given musical context. Often music necessitates the use of unequal lengths on down and up bows and string players have to negotiate the difference. The uneven down and up bows could be due to unequal note values, or an inconsistent number of notes in a slur. The ability to distribute the bow to overcome any unevenness presented in the music is a skill gained through intense practice and years of experience.

In the beginning stages only the middle 1/3 of the bow and similar note values are presented. This approach allows the student to focus on constant bow weight and speed without having to compensate the disproportionate note values or uneven slurs. Similarly, in graded repertoire, editors work meticulously to avoid uneven slurring and when necessary provide hooked bowing to even out dotted rhythms. It is a significant part of a string teacher's responsibilities to provide level-appropriate exercises in introducing students to the challenges of bow management as they develop this essential skill. As the student gains more experience and comfort with varied bow strokes, more and more uneven bow distribution and alternating bow strokes are introduced in playing.

String crossings pose yet another challenge to bow distribution that it takes away from finite bow length to cross strings. To minimize the loss of bow length, pedagogues advocate string crossing exercises to acquire proficiency in this area. Often, both challenges are combined in uneven slurring and string crossings, and the added issue of varied dynamics and musical phrasing make matters only more complicated.

Selection and Maintenance of String Instruments, Bows, and Strings

Regarding instrument selection string teachers must be well-acquainted and judicious with their options, as acquiring a high-quality instrument with proper shop setup is critical. Shop setup comprises the fitting of pegs, ensuring proper string width and height (proper string nut and bridge height and profile), and a sound post adjustment. The instrument must be made with suitable materials such as high quality and properly dried wood, and must be made within proper measurements. All of the required knowledge makes it absolutely necessary to purchase instruments only from a reputable shop, whether it is a local brick-and-mortar violin shop, or an online store. A limited budget is almost always a determining factor when making an instrument purchase, however, it is never a good idea to compromise quality. The advice must be shared with students and parents looking into purchasing an instrument or a bow. An online auction or classified advertisement site is never a good place to make such purchases by a layperson.

When making a purchase the teacher must perform due diligence in researching and understanding all components and fittings featured on an instrument. Reputable shops list all of those features in detail, a very good sign of a quality instrument. In quality instruments the principal components are made of spruce, maple, and ebony. Sometimes ebony is replaced by high-quality composite materials. Most often major manufacturers and large online stores offer named series for different grade instruments as AV5-SC by Yamaha, SR41 by Scherl & Roth®, Franz Hoffmann® by Shar, and Klaus Mueller by Southwest Strings.

Customer service is also a significant part of this decision. If the string teacher is close to a local dedicated violin shop, customer service and maintenance are often bundled into the purchase. If the string teacher is far from a brick-and-mortar violin shop, reputable online shops offer comparable assurances.

String instruments require regular maintenance. Open seams are among the most common issues and can be glued by a reputable violin repair person. When gluing seams, appropriate water-soluble hide glue is used, but not permanent glues. Depending on the severity, repair of cracks may range from a rather simple fix to a more involved restoration. To find open seams and cracks, instruments should be inspected visually. In the case of buzzes and rattles of an unknown cause, an open seam or a crack may be the culprit. In any case, the open seam or crack must be addressed in a timely fashion to avoid further damage to the instrument. Certain cracks in vulnerable areas, such as near the bass bar or sound post may reduce the value of an instrument.

Major instrument repairs may involve opening the instrument, removing or resetting the neck and neck grafting. The decision to proceed with such a major repair depends on the value of an instrument versus the cost of repair. Only a reputable and established shop and repair person should be trusted with instrument maintenance and repair consultations. For string teachers to educate themselves in overall maintenance, *Emergency String Repair Manual for School Orchestra Directors* (1972) by Lowell G. and Douglas Bearden is an invaluable resource that covers an extensive competency level from checking for correct measurements of string instruments to changing strings, to sound post adjustment, to resetting a neck. Two additional diminutive pocket references are *An A to Z of Instrument Care for Players of the Violin Family, 2nd ed.* (1996) by Jane Dorner and *String Reference Guide* (1996) by Knilling.

Bow Rehairing Frequency

One of the most common questions from parents is "How often do we need to rehair our student's bow?" Depending on care and playing frequency, a bow may be rehaired from six months to a year, if not longer. Realistically, many student bows do not get rehaired nearly as frequently as they should and when this lapse of maintenance occurs, the bow will not hold rosin and fails to produce a healthy tone.

As a rule of thumb the bow hair should not be touched by bare hands. The natural oils and dirt of the player's hands will cause gunk to build, particularly in the frog area where the right thumb may make contact with the hair. Darkening of the white bow hair is a sign of grime building. It is possible to clean gunked up bow hair by wiping it with an alcohol swab, however, after the cleaning, hair will need to be rosined, as cleaning will take away all rosin along with oils and built up grime. It is imperative not to touch the stick with alcohol swab, as it will remove polish.

Rosining and Maintenance of Bow Hair

Much like bow rehairing frequency, how much and how frequently to rosin a bow is determined by a player's needs. Under rosining a bow will cause uneven tone production and skidding of bow and in contrast, over rosining a bow will cause crunching and extraneous sounds. Rosining from once a day to several times a week works for many players, although the amount of playing dictates how much rosin the bow hair requires.

Breaking a bow hair during a performance is not an uncommon occurrence and it does not affect the playability, since a violin bow has 140 to 200 strands of hair.[2] Under proper conditions of storage and playing, breaking bow hairs should not be an issue. In other words, bow hair should be changed long before excessive breaking of hair becomes an issue.

String Maintenance and Replacement Frequency

The most basic string maintenance is to wipe off rosin every time the instrument is put away. To that end, it is advisable to keep two separate dust towels: one dedicated to wiping off rosin by the bridge and the belly of the instrument, and one dedicated to wiping off the fingerboard and strings away from the bridge. This practice of keeping dirt and rosin from getting caked on the string ensures the free resonance of strings.

Strings have a limited life expectancy and need to be replaced at least once a year. Student-grade strings are most commonly made of steel or synthetic core and winding. With regular use, strings go false and winding gets frayed. Arguably, somewhat more difficult to detect on a student's instrument than a frayed one, a false string will sound somewhat dull and flat. When an open string is played and it does not resonate for a reasonable length of time and sounds flatter than the initial attack, the string is false. To determine if a string is false, turn on a tuner and bow the open string. If the tuner indicates initially in tune, and shortly after the bow is released a flat pitch, the string is false.

The first parts of the string to unravel are the most played areas, such as the first position and contact points of the playable portion of the string: string nut and the bridge. This unravelling is a sign of normal wear of strings. However, an improperly grooved string nut channel or a poorly-notched groove of a bridge will cause chafing and result in unravelling in those areas. As part of regular maintenance, it is a good practice to treat those contact points with graphite at every string change by marking the channel with a pencil at the string nut and groove on the bridge.

String Replacement

It is ideal to replace all four strings as a set to ensure even wear, reliable intonation and optimum sound production. In doing so, removing all four strings at once may cause the sound post to fall, therefore, it is good practice to remove one string at a time and replace it. First remove the old string and inspect it to see if there is any unusual wear caused by string nut or the bridge. Remove the peg and wipe off any excessive peg compound from the peg and the peg hole. Reapply a judicious amount of peg compound if the peg appears shiny at the peg hole contact points. Reinsert the peg, insert the string through the string hole with the help of tweezers pulling it out by 5 to 10 mm. Start winding the peg away from you: clockwise on the treble side, and anticlockwise on the bass side. Capture the end of the string under the winding on the peg, making sure no bunching or overlapping of winding occurs. Tune up to pitch before moving onto the next string. Make sure to inspect neat and consistent winding of string because problems with pegs may be caused by incorrect winding. Too close a winding to the inner wall of the pegbox or bunching may cause pegs to stick, and too far winding from the inner wall of the pegbox may cause pegs to be pulled outward and slip (Figure 9.1).

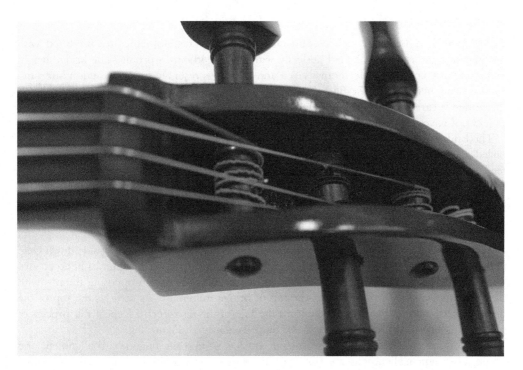

Figure 9.1 Correct winding of strings in the pegbox

Peg Maintenance

To keep string instruments in perfect playing condition pegs need to be well maintained. Changing seasons and weather conditions may cause issues with pegs and tuning. Since it is part of the string teacher's responsibilities for all instruments to be tuned prior to any playing, it is in the interest of optimal instruction time to keep pegs in perfect condition. As pegs are wedged and held in place only by friction, the conical taper of pegs and corresponding peg holes need to be matched perfectly. Outside any emergency, pegs should be inspected and maintained regularly at the time of string replacement. Wiping pegs of excessive peg compound or graphite peg soap and reapplying a judicious amount to shiny parts of a slipping peg is adequate maintenance on the part of the teacher. If the pegs are beyond their useful life, that is, they are inserted too far into the peg holes, a new set needs to be installed by a qualified repair person. It is also possible for a new set of string holes to be drilled if they are moved further than their intended placement on old pegs.

Chinrest Tightening

The chinrest is secured by two brackets and turnbuckle barrels possibly conjoined at the bottom. In normal use those turnbuckle barrels may loosen and cause buzzing. If the chinrest is moving or making contact with the tailpiece, it must be realigned and tightened with a chinrest tightener. The bottom of the chinrest and bracket's contact point with the instrument feature padding of a 1–2 mm thin sheet of cork and overtightening should be avoided. Also, the tightening holes on the turnbuckle barrels go through and the chinrest tightener can scratch the rib if not done carefully.

Bridge Care

As mentioned in Lesson 6, all instruments with a proper shop setup are pre-fitted with a bridge and the crown is aligned perfectly with the fingerboard's profile. The bridge height and string distances are perfectly measured and let strings resonate freely without a buzz and feature string height from the fingerboard that allows player to perform without difficulty. If the bridge is cared for and the instrument is stored within acceptable conditions, the bridge should not have any issues.

The bridge should stand at a 90° angle from the tailpiece side. During tuning the bridge is pulled away from the tailpiece with the tightening of the pegs. The friction of the string will tend to pull the bridge every time the instrument is tuned and over time it will cause the bridge to lean, and if unchecked, warp. To keep the bridge straight, using graphite to lubricate the string grooves (as mentioned in String Replacement Frequency discussion) and straightening it when necessary, are considered regular maintenance. It is a good idea for the teacher to inspect each student's instrument visually during tuning to ensure perfect playable condition.

To straighten the bridge of a violin or a viola hold the instrument in an upside-down cello playing position, securing the upper bout between the knees, place the thumbs between two upper and two lower strings along the edge of the bridge crown, and opposing thumbs with the index and middle fingers pulling the top of bridge minimally. As soon as the top of the bridge moves, stop and check visually from the side of the instrument. Repeat this process of moving and checking until the desired 90° angle is achieved (Figure 9.2).

If the bridge's feet are not in their intended place, so that the fingerboard alignment and f-hole inner notch alignment are not true, the bridge itself must be realigned with those

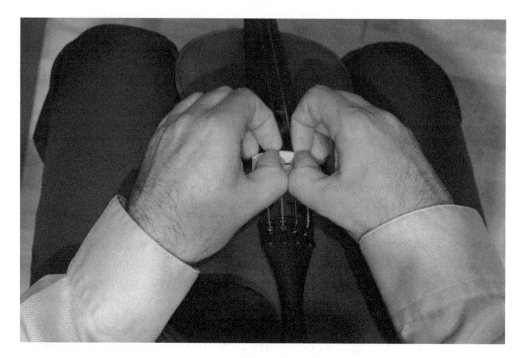

Figure 9.2 Straightening the bridge of a violin

reference points. To accomplish that task strings may need to be loosened to move the bridge. Also, due to the greater pressure of strings on the bridge, it is best to loosen the strings to adjust the bridge of a cello or a bass. To work on a low strings instrument, place it flat on its back on top of a soft case. Care must be exercised not to loosen the strings completely, which may cause the sound post to fall. If you are uncomfortable with performing these tasks, the string teacher may elect to call for the help of a qualified string repair shop.

Bow Selection and Care

Much like the selection of a high-quality string instrument, bow selection requires the string teacher to understand the qualities of a well-made and reliable bow. A bow made of high-quality materials by an expert bowmaker is sought after by professional players. In an educational setting the use of high-quality student-grade bows is necessary to achieve a good tonal result, therefore, help students to have a positive experience. It is likely to encounter fiberglass bows in an educational setting. Some inexpensive student bows feature synthetic hair, considered by many to be inferior to real horse hair, and should be avoided. Although acceptable at the beginner level, a serious student will soon require a better quality bow.

Student bows made of wood most likely feature brazilwood, a generic term used to denote any lighter density wood used in place of the rare pernambuco. Another viable option for student-grade bows is carbon fiber. A higher quality product than fiberglass, carbon fiber bows are durable and suitable alternatives to inexpensive brazilwood student-grade bows.

After daily use, wiping off rosin from the stick and loosening the bow is the proper way of storing it. Loosening the hair relieves pressure and allows the stick to get back to its natural shape and wiping rosin off the stick will keep it from caking on the varnish. If the bow is stored without loosening the hair, it may warp the stick and lessen the camber in time. Even if well cared for, all bows need regular maintenance to remain in perfect playing shape. Rehairing the bow regularly by a reputable shop is an essential practice and is the best way to uphold the perfect playing condition of a bow. Getting a bow rehaired by an unqualified person may create much damage to the bow. For example, if the bow hair is installed unevenly it may cause the stick to warp. If there is too much hair or if the spreader wedge is poorly fit then the ferrule could deform. If the plugs are not perfectly fit to the inside of the head or frog mortise, if they are fit too tightly, or if too much pressure is used while inserting the plugs then the head of the bow could crack or the frog could break.

Regular bow maintenance includes replacing the worn leather grip, securing undone silver winding, cleaning and polishing the stick, adjusting or replacing a worn eyelet and lubricating the tightening screw. Inexpensive fiberglass bows feature a plastic grip and if unglued, an unsecured grip will cause discomfort and may negatively influence the bow grip of the student, therefore, it must be glued at the proper distance from the frog. Much like in the repair-cost-versus-instrument-value equation, in some cases it is more expensive to rehair a student-grade bow than purchase a new bow.

Humidifiers

Internal humidifiers that are inserted through the f-hole are known to cause internal water damage to instruments, therefore should be avoided. It is best practice not to expose string instruments to sudden changes of humidity and temperature, and to store them in a controlled environment absent from direct sunlight.

Endpin Rods

If the low-string instrument is furnished with a steel endpin rod, it may be bent due to mishandling. If possible, it is best to avoid double bass endpin rods with a thin diameter. Also, the endpin rods for double basses (and some cellos) may feature notches and those offer limited adjusting possibilities and tend to slide, particularly if the tightening screw is worn.

Planing a Fingerboard

As part of regular maintenance planing or dressing the fingerboard may be necessary. The violin repair person will plane the fingerboard to shop specifications if any unevenness or grooves are formed by regular use. An uneven fingerboard may impede ease of playing and strings from resonating freely. For financial reasons makers of inexpensive instruments may use black paint to give the appearance of ebony on certain parts of the instrument, like the fingerboard, which cannot be planed since it will take away the black paint.

Sound Post Adjustment

To keep a string instrument in top playing condition the sound post may need to be adjusted and it is part of a shop setup. A well-adjusted sound post will yield the optimal sound production from the instrument, therefore it is a critical component. From time to time a new sound post may need to be cut and fit into the instrument.

Assignment

1) Write a one paragraph summary on bow management and one paragraph on bow selection criteria, to be turned in next class.
2) Practice pizzicato and arco exercises.
3) Practice Preparatory Bow Exercises, and the bow hold.
4) Review today's lesson, and read Lesson 10 prior to next class.

Notes

1 Schmidt, "Contours, Images, and the Bow," 107–9.
2 Guettler, "Some Physical Properties of the Modern Violin Bow," 8.

Lesson 10

Contents

This lesson's objectives are:

- A discussion on error detection and string rehearsal techniques.
- A discussion on Teaching Cycle.

Conducting Strings: Error Detection and Rehearsal Techniques

Within the scope of this text we will focus on the pedagogy aspect of conducting strings rather than the conducting craft itself. However, skills gained in conducting, as in the ability to conduct while listening critically and determining the source of a given problem, would be considered wholly relevant. In error detection there are both physically observable problems and physically unobservable problems. When compared with voice or wind instruments, most technical issues of string instruments are external and easily recognizable, which means all string teachers must be keenly observant. To accomplish that when instructing, the string teacher must remain outside the score and heed the conducting adage of "score in head, not head in score." Taking quick mental snapshots of the full score to remain out of it is a good habit for any string teacher and conductor. That is the only way to ensure how students are performing at any given time. General posture, instrument setup, direction of bow, amount of bow, contact point, and bow alignment, are some critical elements only observed when out of score.

In addition, it is a good practice to remain mobile, walk around and not be pinned to a conducting podium. It will give the teacher a better perspective and catch all setup issues which can only be spotted from different angles: as a straightened left thumb, left wrist, and a misaligned left elbow. Some teachers rotate each section of the ensemble to keep a close eye on less advanced students and bring them to the front seats regularly.

In score preparation the string teacher should map out the entire class or rehearsal to be prepared for the predictable issues. Finger pattern problems for upper strings, as in high 2 versus low 2, forward and backward extensions for low strings, shifting and awkward string crossings for all strings are areas that will take extra rehearsal and sectional time. In intonation, as in bow planning and uniform bow placement, some students in each section may be flawless, whereas some students may not. In error detection it is incumbent upon the teacher to identify which students are inaccurate and fix those individual issues within the section.

Sectional work is an efficient way to address problems and transform each section to solid ground. However, it is not always possible to break down classes into separate sections. If that is the case, the entire ensemble can participate in soli sections. To accomplish that, the teacher must plan ahead and produce warm-up sheets for the entire ensemble to familiarize students with articulations, specific runs, and phrasing directions well ahead of programming the particular work. One example is Brandenburg Concerto, Number 5 by Bach (first movement—abridged, arranged by Merle J. Isaac, published by Highland/Etling, Alfred, graded 3 by publisher). The opening ritornello figure in this educational strings-only edition is assigned to the first violin section. In the original work (BWV 1050) all violins play it in unison (Figure 10.1). In the Isaac graded string orchestra edition, only the first violins play the original ritornello figure in a simplified eighth-note value. It is an effective pedagogical approach to integrate this particular figure into a D major and A major scales and use it during the class warm-up regimen (Figure 10.2). The original ritornello figure can also be transcribed for the entire ensemble, which will give the bass section an opportunity to work on this bow stroke, since in the Isaac transcription the bass section never plays this eighth-note bow stroke. Having the entire ensemble play a selection meant for a particular section is an effective way to include all students in the introduction process of an idea, keep all the class involved and avoid any class management issues.

Furthermore, passages that feature obvious technical and rhythmic challenges must be taken into account when planning for class or rehearsal time. In lesson planning the above-mentioned issues will dictate the time management in a way that is predictable and repeatable. Setting goals to accomplish certain metronome markings, intonation, even note values, and any other benchmark clearly set forth by the teacher helps to keep the class motivated, informed, and enthusiastic. Some teachers use a drawing of a target with identified goals to inform the class of its real-time progress and inspire students to keep on task. Effective string teaching and modeling are inseparable. Successful teachers are known to model regularly and demand consistent results from their students.

Figure 10.1 Manuscript detail of Bach Brandenburg Concerto in D Major, No. 5, BWV 1050, movement 1, Allegro

Figure 10.2 A string ensemble warm-up exercise based on Bach Brandenburg Concerto in D Major, No. 5, BWV 1050, movement 1, Allegro

Incorporating Good Teaching Habits in Strings: the Teaching Cycle

The teaching cycle is an approach to assess student progress continuously within each class period or teaching unit. The continuous teaching cycle can be described as: pre-assess, plan, implement instruction, evaluate learning outcomes, analyze and reflect, and repeat the sequence. Designed to determine student needs and assess outcomes, the continuous teaching cycle can be summarized with the following model:

Pre-Assess

1) Plan
2) Implement Instruction
3) Evaluate Learning Outcomes
4) Analyze and Reflect
5) Repeat

Pre-Assess

At this stage of collecting information, the teacher evaluates the overall goal of the following unit (class period, rehearsal, etc.). Both desired musical outcomes and standards-based pedagogical objectives as dictated by the state, district, and school must be considered within the lesson plan.

1) Plan: this is the step where the teacher determines what the students should know and are able to perform at the end of the class or unit. The teacher writes a lesson plan, including all concepts and terminology to be covered, along with a scaffolding plan to reach out to every student at different learning and playing abilities.

2) Implement Instruction: in this step the teacher executes the activity, or the learning unit. During class or rehearsal, the teacher must be mindful of the ability of class participation and success in achieving the planned outcome for each student. Accordingly, adjust speed, repeat certain concepts if necessary, and change teaching methods to accommodate those learning inconsistencies.

3) Evaluate Learning Outcomes: a formative end-of-lesson assessment is an independent practice session. This is a way to assess student learning at the end of the lesson that follows the teacher-guided instruction.

4) Analyze and Reflect: in this section of the cycle, the teacher analyzes student work and scrutinizes the student errors. This can be done with or without the use of rubrics. Identifying the underlying causes of mistakes, re-evaluating the initial supposition or pre-assessment, and moving onto the next lesson or unit.

Musical Rehearsal Planning Parallels with the Teaching Cycle

A common rehearsal technique used in professional settings is the "macro–micro–macro" outline. This is an effective way to rehearse an ensemble and it is equally well suited both in the professional and pedagogical settings. It can be summarized as tackling a large chunk of musical material such as a movement or a section of a movement with the following plan: run through (macro), rehearse in detail (micro), and run through again (macro). The first run through provides the empty canvas on which learning activity will take place, and it is comparable to the Pre-assessing and Planning portions of the Teaching Cycle. Rehearsing in detail is akin to the Implementing Instruction portion of the Teaching Cycle. Arguably the most critical segment, the post run through is comparable to Evaluating Learning Outcomes, and as a result this section completes the cycle. In a musical setting, it is critical for the string teacher to leave enough time to run through the same section without rehearsing, in order for students to put to practice what they have learned during the rehearsal portion of class. This post-instruction run-through functions as a formative end of lesson assessment.

Another perfect parallel with the Teaching Cycle, and an exemplary trait of a professional conductor, is the flexibility of or acknowledgement of unplanned-for issues and choosing to address or ignore them in the interest of following the pre-determined goal. An example for this is to continue to run through a movement, even though there are ongoing ensemble or individual execution concerns. A conductor's capability of adjusting the overall pace or implementation of goals during a rehearsal is analogous to a teacher's ability of adjusting speed of instruction, re-teaching previously discussed concepts, varying teaching strategies, and offering further scaffolding during Implementing Instruction phase of Teaching Cycle.

Assignment

1) Review Error Detection section and be prepared for in-class error detection exercises.
2) Write a one paragraph summary of incorporating Teaching Cycle in string teaching to be turned in next class.
3) Practice pizzicato and arco exercises.
4) Bring a table tennis ball or a similarly sized rubber ball for the collé exercise.
5) Review today's lesson and read Lesson 11 prior to next class.

Lesson 11

Contents

This lesson's objectives are:

- A collé bowing exercise for right hand and finger flexibility.
- A discussion on classroom and string orchestra setup.

Collé Bowing Exercise

Before we discuss this exercise we must be mindful that collé, as a part of the bow arm and its technique, is a relatively small motion. In *Problems of Tone Production in Violin Playing*, Carl Flesch unmistakably indicates: "If assigning the change of bow to the fingers as their exclusive privilege, one will achieve exactly the opposite of an inaudible change."[1] Indeed, all of the movements discussed in this article must be approached with great care so that the desired motions associated with the collé action must remain barely noticeable, but by no means insignificant as collé action is among the principal elements of the bow technique.

In the literature, the term collé is often identified in the sense of a stroke like an off-string martelé, or a combination of spiccato and martelé (those bow strokes will be discussed in detail in Lesson 13). Flesch, on the other hand, labels the use of fingers in a connected, on the string bow stroke as "the fingerstroke." This is, however, the same motion described in the collé stroke with the following differences: it is a smooth motion that occurs on the string.

The smooth and inaudible bow direction change requires the involvement of the wrist and the fingers, and the greatest challenge of achieving an imperceptible bow change emerges at the frog. Evidently, the bow weight and insufficient counterbalance of the pinky finger cause this difficulty. To add to this problem, an incorrect version of the Russian bow hold—as in an exaggerated wrist and forearm angle and the overall height, which cause the right-hand fingers to straighten and stiffen—keeps the player from achieving a smooth and inaudible bow change at the frog.

Before applying it on the instrument, it would be advisable to break down the collé action into its divisible building blocks (i.e. fingers and the wrist), and practice them separately. Then, put those actions together, and practice the combined motion in different sections of the bow.

Let's first take the finger motion:

- With your right arm raised to the chest level in front of you, rotate your forearm counter clockwise to a 45° angle (Figure 11.1).
- To isolate the finger motion, with your left hand, hold the top of your right hand, and restrict its movement (Figure 11.2).
- Extend (open) and flex (close) the fingers, including the thumb (Figures 11.3 and 11.4).
- Do not allow the fingers to stiffen in a completely straight and locked position.

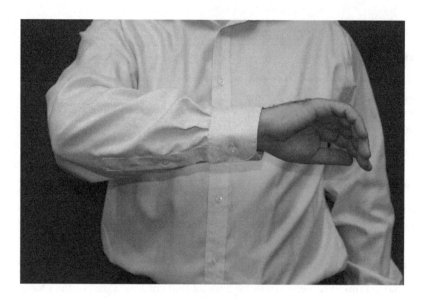

Figure 11.1 Forearm rotated counterclockwise to a 45° angle

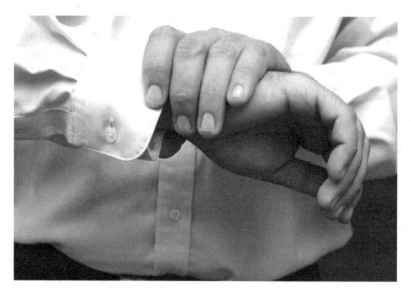

Figure 11.2 Right hand with a restricted movement

Once the student is comfortable with the fingers, let's move to the wrist motion:

- With your right arm raised to the chest level in front of you, rotate your forearm counter clockwise to a 45° angle.
- To isolate the wrist motion, hold an object as a rubber ball in your right hand (Figure 11.5).
- Extend (open) and flex (close) the wrist (Figures 11.6 and 11.7).

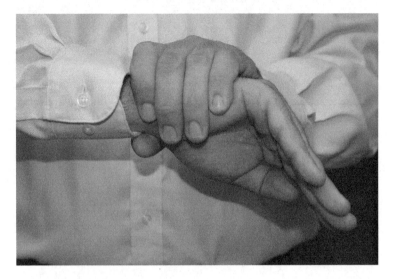

Figure 11.3 Right hand extension of fingers (opened)

Figure 11.4 Right hand flexion of fingers (closed)

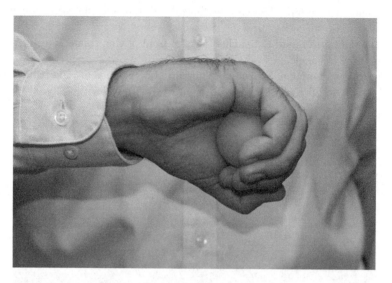

Figure 11.5 Isolated wrist with a rubber ball

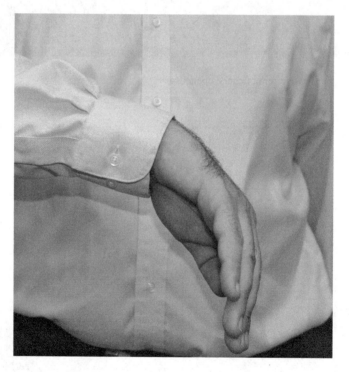

Figure 11.6 Extension of the wrist (opened)

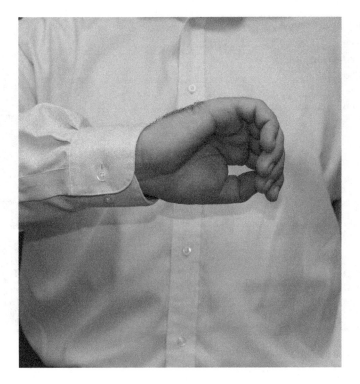

Figure 11.7 Flexion of the wrist (closed)

Once the student is comfortable with the above exercises, repeat with a light object as a pencil or a straw held like a bow (Figures 11.8 and 11.9).

Adjustment of Collé for the Low Strings

The collé exercises apply to low strings only with minimal adjustments. The cello bow hold and French hold for the bass are nearly the same. When applying collé on those bow holds, pronation of the forearm is simply reduced. When it comes to German bass bow hold, first create the "chop-stick" hold (refer back to figure 2.33) and apply the collé action extension of the wrist and flexion of fingers and flexion of the wrist and extension of fingers.

Exercises on the Instrument

Apply this first exercise at the balance point, only with the use of fingers and the wrist (no forearm motion is allowed). Tone production is not the main concern, but the correct collé action is (Figure 11.10). To isolate the finger and wrist motion, the student may restrict the forearm movement with the left hand.

Next, we move onto the smooth collé motion and apply it to a simple one-octave scale as D Major (Figure 11.11). Making sure that the student remains at the absolute frog and the absolute tip, but does not drift into a "middle-ish" bow placement.

Figure 11.8 The collé action extension of wrist and flexion of fingers

Figure 11.9 The collé action flexion of wrist and extension of fingers

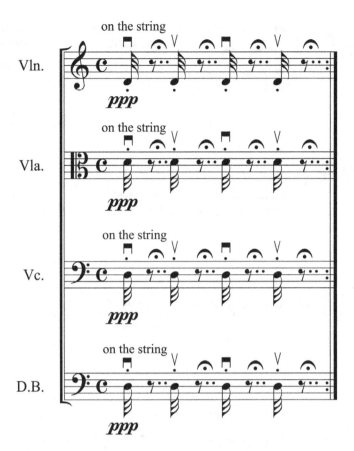

Figure 11.10 First collé action exercise

Classroom and String Orchestra Setup

The instructor of any beginning string class must establish an instrumental setup for each student to allow the production of a beautiful, resonant, and enjoyable sound. It must also provide an ease of playing and decrease the likelihood of pain or injury in the student. This task is often complicated due to the large numbers of students in class, as well as the nature and possible inadequacies of the classroom. Eminent string pedagogues have pondered this issue and offered solutions consistent with their teaching philosophies.

Teachers in secondary school systems across the US, prominently follow a standard score-order seating: first violin, second violin, viola, cello, and double bass. An alternative educational string setting is the row seating for beginning string classes. An influential string pedagogue and champion of heterogeneous string teaching, Jacquelyn Dillon-Krass (b 1936) stresses the correct playing position by way of the row seating, where the teacher can walk around each student and physically make adjustments. This early educational seating comes with a warning from her, that "row seating is not a performance seating when students are to be conducted." Another alternative type of seating is used for rote learning, a circle formation around the teacher that allows the teacher close visual contact with each student. The circle

Figure 11.11 Collé action one-octave D major scale exercise

formation arrangement may be used for heterogeneous teaching as well as homogeneous setting—this arrangement has been employed at Indiana Jacobs School of Music String Academy.

Influential string pedagogue Paul Rolland (1911–1978), advocates violin students to stand and prefers the use of a room spacious enough for the teacher to move around students, and for rhythm activities. Also, he the use of rote technique in "eliminating the paraphernalia and distraction of music stands." Having the upper string players stand not only makes efficient use of precious space, but also cultivates better posture in the beginning stages. In this class we will follow this model and have all upper string players stand. When it comes to the cello, from chair height to front-side seating position, the student's weight is distributed on the feet, more than on the chair. To promote this seating position, Dillon and Kriechbaum suggest "Up" and "Bingo" games to allow students to "be able to get up quickly without shifting their weight forward." Hamann and Gillespie suggest similar game as "Jack-in-the-Box" to encourage the same seating balance. Lastly, regarding standing vs. stool use preference for the double bass, Professor of Bass at Wichita State University, and Principal Bassist of Wichita Symphony, Dr Mark Foley recommends sitting at stool for bassists in the pedagogical settings, as in secondary school classrooms and orchestras.

There are multiple options for string ensemble seating, the standard US string quintet setup (Figure 11.12), and its alternative—also known as Furtwängler variation (Figure 11.13); furthermore, antiphonal seatings are possible—also known as European (or German) (Figure 11.14), and its variation (Figure 11.15). Currently, both the American and European (or German) orchestra traditions continue. Having started due to recording equipment deficiencies in the 1920s and advanced with Leopold Stokowski's efforts, the American seating has become popular around the world by the mid-20th century.[2] The orchestral seating as late as the 19th century was wildly varied, and the conductor did not face the audience, but stood half-way toward the orchestra and was sometimes surrounded by the musicians. As a matter of fact, throughout the 18th and into the 19th centuries, often times, the musicians were not even seated except for the cello section. Austrian music critic and historian Eduard Hanslick accredited the "Viennese custom" as to the origins of playing while seated.[3]

In an educational setting, shared spaces are a reality and unfortunately our room setup may be far from optimum for string classrooms, as we share our rehearsal halls and orchestra rooms with other disciplines. Often times, permanently-installed crescent-shaped risers, otherwise stepped rooms, weight-bearing columns, and all other immovables stand in our way of providing a healthy, accommodating string classroom.

Truly, all seating, both in the classroom and performance hall, should allow players to perform without any physical strain to maintain a good setup, or to see the conductor. Whether students are sharing a music stand or not, they should have both enough room to move around and always be situated to face the teacher. These critically important orchestral requirements are not readily apparent to students, or some students might have motivation to

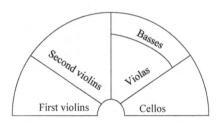

Figure 11.12 American Seating

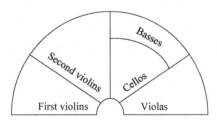

Figure 11.13 An Alternate American Seating

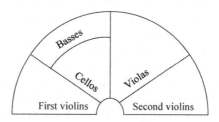

Figure 11.14 European (or German) Seating

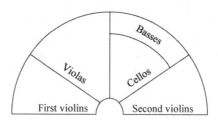

Figure 11.15 An Alternate European (or German) Seating

hide from the teacher, it is the teacher's responsibility to implement seating. Some students might be aware of a problem or discomfort but do not wish to seem disruptive or confrontational and therefore will not speak up. Again, the responsibility falls to the teacher to condition the students to react when setup issues arise.

Experimenting with various seating plans will provide a new sort of rotation, the rotation of sections, and will afford students a different perspective on stage: both visually and aurally. Splitting sections would not be advised in an educational setting, however, moving the basses to the middle of the stage may be a good compromise so that their centralized position would make them more prevalent on both wings, and equally audible to all sections. The European seating plan of antiphonally splitting the first and second violins is a good start to break away from the current American standard of score-order left-to-right string section. As antiphonal seating variants do not necessarily lend themselves as easily to all repertoire, by nature, they prepare the conductor and players to accept seating changes as part of the orchestra experience.

If the classroom is set up with load-bearing beams or columns, steps and permanent risers, the exercise and flexibility of alternate seating will be most helpful in finding an optimum solution. If the orchestra teacher is sharing a room with the band (as many of us do), they are likely to find a room composed of multiple crescent rows. The first order of business is to break the crescent rows, as they are rather inflexible, do not leave enough room to play a string instrument, do not allow single chair rotations, and do not allow teachers access to the students. For example, to alleviate the above space problem, it is a good idea to split the first and second violin sections antiphonally as two facing rows and take the violas, cellos, and double basses on the top platform. This seating will allow all sections more room to move, and allow them to rotate as needed. However, it must be stressed that the antiphonal seating requires both violin sections to be independently strong. In the words of Arturo Toscanini, who likens both violin sections to shoulders: "Like shoulders, they must be equally strong and equivalent."[4]

As string teachers, the more knowledge and awareness we possess, the more options we will have and seating is no exception. Student health, both aural and neuromusculoskeletal, as acknowledged by the National Association of Schools of Music (NASM) and Performing Arts Medicine Association (PAMA), is paramount in all activities we participate. All rehearsals and performances must comply with good judgment on the teacher's part, as students may not possess the knowledge or experience needed to maintain their own health. We as teachers must act on the account of our students and assure to provide a healthy learning environment at all times.

Assignment

1) Repeat collé action and practice collé exercises on your instrument.
2) Write a one paragraph summary of orchestral string ensemble seating options, to be turned in next class.
3) Practice pizzicato and arco exercises.
4) Review today's lesson and read Lesson 12 prior to next class.

Notes

1 Flesch, *Problems of Tone Production in Violin Playing*, 14.
2 Alois Melichar, *Der vollkommene Dirigent: Entwicklung und Verfall einer Kunst.* (München: Langen–Müller, 1981), quoted in Jürgen Meyer, *Acoustics and the Performance of Music: Manual for Acousticians, Audio Engineers, Musicians, Architects and Musical Instrument Makers*, 267.
3 Koury, *Orchestral Performance Practices in the 19th Century: Size, Proportions, and Seating*, 175.
4 Meyer, *Acoustics and the Performance of Music*, 264.

Lesson 12

Contents

This lesson's objectives are:

- A discussion on left-hand techniques.
- A brief discussion on orchestral performance practices.

Left-Hand Techniques

Among the most important fundamental objectives in the first stages of string instruction is to establish a reliable and tension-free left arm and hand position that allows for an unrestricted facility. In the beginning stages establishing finger patterns for the upper strings, C-shape and forward and backward extensions for the cello, and K-shape and half and first positions on the bass are among the first goals for a string teacher. Once the initial left-hand facility within the diatonic scale framework is established, improving upon existing techniques and adding new ones at a manageable pace is a sound pedagogical approach. The below discussion covers most essential left-hand techniques that are common in the beginning and intermediate stages of instruction.

Positions: in heterogeneous string teaching everything that relates to the left hand is optimized for the general classroom, with consideration of specific instrument needs. Beginning method books acknowledge the need and aim to offer globally applicable material that benefits all instruments at the same time. With regard to range, all strings are at an advantage over the double bass, in that their range in the first position exceeds two octaves, conversely bass is only an octave and a perfect fifth. This inequitable problem is solved with the early introduction of a shift on the bass. As far as keys are concerned, D major and G major are considered string-friendly and allow beginning students to perform simple melodic material with minimal left-hand challenges. The overall goal of string instruction in the beginning stages is to cover as much musical material without overwhelming students in the pursuit of establishing a solid instrument setup, and foundational left-hand and bow-arm techniques.

Shifting: shifting is a central element both in technical and expressive areas of string playing in that it helps define schools of playing and the very individuality of specific players, therefore, it may be scrutinized both as a technical and expressive device. As a technical element it expands the instrument's range and is used in minimizing awkward string crossings by way of using different positions for certain portions of a passage, and as an expressive element it allows the player to execute a slide within a great range from a slight lilt to a portamento, to a full glissando. It also allows the player to individualize the shift by choosing with which finger to execute the slide portion.

Simply put, every shift can be defined as travelling between two different positions on a string instrument. The travel starts with a departure finger, also known as the guide finger, and ends on an arrival finger. In a simple shift, both departure and arrival fingers are one and the same, where in a compound shift, both are different fingers (Figure 12.1). In introducing the concept, a simple shift on the same string, between adjacent or close positions is used.

Lack of frets on fingerboards of orchestral string instruments allow for a smooth and unobstructed slide between any two pitches. A shift may occur within a single string, or between two different strings. Either way the player will depart from a given position and arrive in another. Also, a shift may occur from a lower position to a higher position, or vice versa. Technically, the direction of a shift will not make a difference, however, expressively it will matter whether to expose the slide of the departure finger or to disguise it (Figure 12.2).

From a technical point of view, a shift can occur between adjacent or distant positions on the same string or on different strings. Regardless of the distance, shifting may occur with the same finger or two different fingers. If it is a single finger, for example departing and arriving with the first finger between two positions, it is a straight forward slide as a portamento. The slide in a shift may be disguised by executing it quickly and subtly, or may be revealed by executing it slowly and deliberately for expressive purposes. In orchestral performances, practice members of a section do not possess such expressive allowance, and may not take extra time or make such individual expressive decisions unless a portamento or a glissando is indicated by the composer. Furthermore, as Flesch warns against excessive use of portamento,[1] it should not be used as a crutch for shifting deficiencies.

Figure 12.1 Simple and compound shifts

Figure 12.2 An exposed shift

The timing of the bow change will also help disguise or expose a shift. If a shift occurs within a bow, only the timing will impact the outcome. A bow direction change within a shift will help disguise or expose it.

Teaching Shifting: in teaching the sequence students should be comfortable playing in a given position before shifting to and from it. In other words, shifting should be introduced once students are comfortable playing in different finger patterns, as in playing in different keys in the half and first positions. Additionally, before shifting is introduced, all left-hand technical issues must be addressed. If there are pre-existing left hand technical problems, as in a collapsed wrist and overall tension in the left hand, introducing shifting will only compound those existing issues.

Shifting may be broken down to its basic components and taught first as a slide between two notes, that is departing from one position and arriving in another. Using the first finger, a smooth and deliberate slide between two positions takes place. The finger weight into the string and fingerboard must be minimal and the thumb should not be clamped into the neck. The first joint angle of the guide finger *must* remain constant and cannot roll forward or backward. The left-hand shape and finger distances *must* remain intact during the shift. In other words, the wrist or a finger cannot lead and the entire arm should move as a single unit. Because of this, shifting between close positions, particularly between the half and first positions, the line may be blurred and the student may be confused. The remedy for this possible confusion is the reminder that the entire hand must be situated as a whole in any given position, and the thumb moves along with the entire arm during a shift while keeping the finger distances intact. Another common issue with shifts is undershooting or clamping down with both the guide finger and the thumb. One exercise to solve this issue is tapping and rolling the thumb against the neck. Additionally, the thumb may be removed altogether to demonstrate the possibility of maintaining guide finger's own minimal weight into the string, but not pushing against it with the thumb. The goal is to remove any unnecessary friction caused by the tip of the guide finger and first joint pad of thumb during the shift, much like the untimely application of brakes would cause while trying to pedal a bicycle. Just enough weight to keep the string down during a shift is necessary, any more weight or pressure will only hinder a smooth shift. This exercise and similar exercises will help relieve excessive weight and unnecessary pressure in achieving unobstructed and smooth shifts.

Portamento: described as "*portamento della voce*" or "carriage of voice," vocal portamento finds its roots in the 17th century's established legato singing traditions and has been adopted in string playing as an expressive gesture. In the instrumental tradition, Flesch's indication of "emotional connection between two notes" helps explain the instrumental meaning of portamento as exposing a chosen portion of a slide. Either an upward or downward gesture, portamento makes use of shifting as an expressive device. Although sometimes a composer provides a diagonal line to indicate a portamento, it is not always the case. For string players we may label four approaches to a portamento:

1) **A simple portamento** is a simple slide starting and ending on the same finger and on the same string.
2) **A compound portamento** is a slide starting with the departure or guide finger, and ending with the arrival finger. Any portion of the portamento to any extent can be exposed (departure finger, arrival finger, or both).

On an upward portamento an early placement of the arrival finger will provide the latter portion of the slide (Figure 12.3), conversely on the downward gesture, the departure finger will provide the earlier portion of it (Figure 12.4). How much of the portamento will be audible may be determined by placement timing of the departure and arrival fingers, and as a matter of taste, the guide finger's slide within a shift itself may be used as portamento (Figure 12.5).

Glissando: an Italianized French term, originates from the French verb *glisser*, "to slide." Sometimes a composer may indicate a glissando on a string instrument as a simple slide like a portamento. In performance practice such an indication is executed as a dedicated slide where all of the slide between the departure and arrival pitches is heard. A chromatic glissando, defining all minor seconds (semitones) in between the two pitches is a much more advanced technique than portamento. One virtuoso technique of executing a glissando is the imitation of a chromatic scale with a vibrato-like motion during the slide. Unless the composer indicated a chromatic glissando by defining all minor seconds (semitones) in between those two pitches, in an orchestral setting all glissandos are done as a slide, much like a portamento. One significant difference is exposing the entire slide between the departure and arrival pitches in the glissando, where only a chosen portion of the slide may be exposed in a portamento.

Vibrato: originating in Italian, *vibrare* means to shake and vibrato is the past participle form of the verb. On orchestral string instruments vibrato is the continuous wavering of pitch

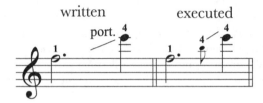

Figure 12.3 Upward portamento

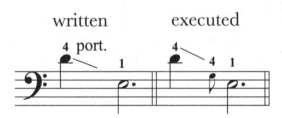

Figure 12.4 Downward portamento

Figure 12.5 Guide-finger portamento (from first to fifth position), Spohr, *Violinschule*

on long or expressive notes. An early definition of vibrato is close shake, even though before the 19th century, vibrato was generally considered an ornament savored for long and expressive notes, in his cornerstone treatise on violin playing, titled *The Art of Playing on the Violin*, Francesco Geminiani (1687–1762) advocates the use of vibrato not only on long notes, but also on short notes, and "be made use of as often as possible."[2] Not until the first quarter of the 20th century did continuous vibrato on all notes become fashionable. Continuous vibrato ultimately became a part of a player's tone production, particularly with Fritz Kreisler's (1875–1962) influence. Today, the use of continuous vibrato is expected of any orchestral player, and by definition it is consistently provided throughout each note. From one string instrument to another, and from lower to higher registers, both the speed and width of vibrato differ greatly. In the lower instruments and registers, vibrato is slower and wider. In higher registers vibrato gets faster and more narrow, a necessary adjustment to keep the pitch unaffected by the width of the vibrato. Although with artistic choice, alterations to vibrato's intensity, starting a note senza vibrato and slowly introducing an increasing use of vibrato, or intensifying the middle of a note as in a vocal expressive technique of *messa di voce* (placing of the voice), are variations used in solo playing.

Sulla Corda: the expression indicates to play on a particular string. The particular string may be indicated with a Roman numeral: the highest string of a given instrument is I, second II, third III and the lowest is IV. Also, solmization technique as well as a letter system may be used to indicate the given string. To indicate a section to be performed on only the G string, *sul G*, *sul sol*, *sulla IV corda* or *sul IV* could be used for the violin. In the orchestral setting, string sections should play on the same string for consistency of tone color. When a composer indicates *sulla corda*, the given string section will remain on the indicated string for the duration of the dashed lines, if no dashed lines are present for the duration of the passage (Figure 12.6).

Trills: a simple definition of a trill is a quick alternation of a main note and the note above it. The exact interval may or may not be indicated in music. If not indicated otherwise, the key signature dictates the quality of the second: minor, major or an augmented second. How many turns to execute in a trill is dictated by the note value and tempo. The most essential part of executing a trill is the evenness of it.

Finger Tremolos: a natural extension of a trill, finger tremolos refer to the rapid alternation of intervals greater than a second. Generally, finger tremolos are executed on the same string and the rapid alternation of strings, or rapid string crossings should *not* be necessary. Therefore, whenever possible, all tremolos are fingered in a way to keep them on the same string, that is, constant shifting may be necessary. If a tremolo between intervals

Figure 12.6 Rimsky–Korsakov, *Sheherazade*, movement 3, mm 1–5, first and second violin *sulla corda*

greater than a fourth is necessary, then string crossings are necessary (see Lesson 13: Ondeggiando). Finger tremolos may be measured or non-measured.

Natural Harmonics: although this topic was covered earlier in Lesson 5 as it applies to tuning, natural harmonics, sometimes referred to as *flageolet*, are used often and offer a significant color option in string playing. Most commonly the first partial, located an octave above an open string, offers an extension in any given position and a solid intonation reference point. Indicated with a round zero, or a zero above a finger number, the first partial produces a consonant and clear tone. When it comes to second through to fourth partials, notation choices of a composer can be confusing, and sometimes a composer may notate the sounding note or the actual placement on the string notated as a diamond head (see figure 5.3). It is exceedingly rare to encounter second through the fourth partials in graded editions, though not as rare in the standard orchestral repertoire (Figure 12.7).

Double Stops: among the most challenging aspects of the left-hand technique, double stops allow a player to sustain two adjacent strings at the same time. In string pedagogy the student's earliest introduction to double stops occurs with tuning by way of adjacent strings. This standard tuning approach requires a player to keep an even weight on both strings and a constant bow speed, therefore, it helps create a solid foundation for double stops. Once bow independency and control is achieved, double stops are introduced by playing two open strings, then adding a fingered strings to open strings, and finally playing two fingered strings at a time. Use of natural harmonics, particularly the first partial, is another good way to introduce double stops and sustain without having to put much weight to produce sound and sustain (Figure 12.8).

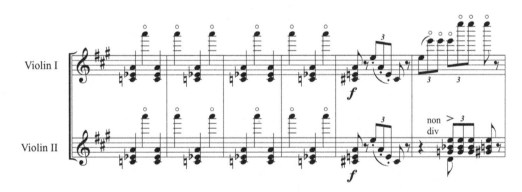

Figure 12.7 Rimsky-Korsakov *Capriccio Espagnol*, movement 5, *Fandango asturiano*, rehearsal V, first- and second-partial natural harmonics

Figure 12.8 Ševčík, *Preparatory Exercises in Double-Stopping*, Op. 9 (1901), p 3

Chords: due to the curvature of the bridge, no orchestral string instrument can sustain more than two notes at a time. Therefore, in solo playing most commonly triple- and quadruple-stop chords are executed as broken chords. Broken quadruple-stop chords are executed as the lower two notes at a time, as grace notes, to be quickly followed by sustained upper two notes. For the upper portion of chord to be on time, the lower two notes are placed right before the beat (Figure 12.9). Triple-stop chords can be executed as three notes at a time, although this approach can cause crunching if excessive weight is applied on the string and the chord cannot be sustained. Therefore, most commonly triple-stop chords are executed as lower two notes placed right before the beat as grace notes, break the chord to sustain the upper two notes (Figure 12.10). In a softer dynamic triple- and quadruple-stop chords can be rolled as one note at a time, although this is a rare occurrence (Figures 12.11 and 12.12).

Figure 12.9 Executing a broken quadruple-stop chord

Figure 12.10 Executing a broken triple-stop chord

Figure 12.11 Executing a rolled quadruple-stop chord

Figure 12.12 Executing a rolled triple-stop chord

Performance Practices Specific to Orchestra

Divisi: in a string section, whenever multiple notes are written players execute only one note at a time, unless indicated non-divisi. When sharing a stand, the <u>outside</u> person, seated closer to the audience, plays the higher note and the <u>inside</u> person plays the lower note. If more than two notes are present at a time, sometimes "by the player" and sometimes "by the stand" approach may be taken. If by person, the composer indicates *div. a 3*, *div. a 4*, etc. The end of divisi is indicated by tutti or unison, or abbreviated as *unis*. It must be noted that composers or editors do not always indicate divisi. It is then up to the conductor to decide when to divide the section and when not to do so.

Chords: in solo playing breaking or rolling a chord is not a cause for concern as the player executes the bottom of the chord on the beat. In contrast, the large ensemble setting poses a timing challenge that needs to be addressed, as exact timing of breaking or rolling of a chord must be synchronized among all players. Furthermore, students tend to press or crunch when playing chords. By executing chords as divisi, the inside person plays the lower notes, and the outside person plays the higher notes, both timing and pressed tone quality issues are addressed (Figure 12.13). There are certain exceptions, as the opening of Beethoven's First Symphony, where the first violin chord in the fourth measure cannot be played as divisi, and the first violins must sustain the highest note and continue without an interruption as part of the melody, and therefore, it must be broken (Figure 12.14).

Use of Open Strings in the Large Ensemble Setting: in the interest of uniformity and to be able to vibrate, the use of open strings is avoided in large ensembles and is part of orchestral performance practice. The only exceptions are when open strings happen on quick, passing notes, on a weak beat, and on non-divisi chords. Especially the open E string of the violin is avoided because it stands out of texture.

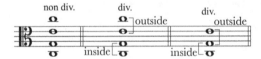

Figure 12.13 Chord divisions for quadruple- and triple-stop chords

Figure 12.14 Beethoven Symphony No. 1, opening measures

Arco and Pizzicato Transitions: sometimes there is no time between arco and pizzicato passages. If the pizzicato passage is short enough, and that there is no time between arco and pizzicato notes, the player may keep the bow grip in order to switch smoothly and without missing any notes. If the bow grip is kept intact while playing those pizzicato notes, the index finger is used to pluck the string on all string instruments.

Extended Pizzicato Sections or Pizzicato Movements: when a long section of a pizzicato passage or a pizzicato movement is played, the teacher may designate exact spots where the bows should be put down and picked back up.

Pizzicato chords: much like regular chords, pizzicato chords can be executed both as non-divisi and divisi. When executing a pizzicato chord, the direction is from bottom up, or from lowest string to the highest string, although there are some exceptions to this rule (Figure 12.15).

Orchestral Notation Shortcuts: in orchestral writing, often times, engravers use short-hand notation and the most common ones are on repeated notes. Shorthand notation on repeated notes may be unclear and non-measured tremolo and measured repeated note values can be mixed up. Non-string players may not be as familiar with this practice, although all shorthand notation is likely to cause confusion on all players (Figure 12.16).

Figure 12.15 Rimsky-Korsakov *Capriccio Espagnol*, movement 5, *Fandango asturiano*, mm 38–43, guitar-like pizzicato chords

Figure 12.16 Orchestral notation shorthand samples

Assignment

1) Write one paragraph explaining reasons for shifting and the relationship between shifting and portamento, to be turned in next class.
2) List all left hand techniques and their brief explanations discussed in this lesson, to be turned in next class.
3) Practice pizzicato and arco exercises.
4) Practice rolled and broken chords on your assigned instrument.
5) Read Lesson 13 prior to next class.

Notes

1 Flesch, *The Art of Violin Playing: Book One*,15–16.
2 Geminiani, *The Art of Playing on the Violin*, 8.

Lesson 13

Contents

This lesson's objectives are:

* A discussion on principal schools of bow hold.
* Common bow strokes and expressions.

Principal Schools of Bow: German, Franco-Belgian, and Russian; French Vs. German Bass Bow Holds

The three standard schools of upper-strings bow hold may be categorized as German, Franco-Belgian, and Russian. In the interest of practicality both violin and viola bow holds can be discussed under the same heading. Similarly, both cello and French bass bow holds are similar and can be combined despite their minimal differences, and lastly the German bass bow hold is the only other grip to discuss separately.

Above all, the introduction and maintenance of a technically solid bow hold is imperative, and an overfocus on school-of-bow choice may be considered superfluous. Furthermore, every student's physical attributes are different and bow hold must make sense for that particular student's physical individuality. In other words, both upper and low strings choice of bow, and school of bow, may have been made by a previous teacher and if there are no technical deficiencies, should remain the same.

1) **Upper Strings:** when categorizing schools of bow, index finger placement in relation to the stick is taken as a reference point. This placement has a direct effect on the initial pronation and supination of the fingers, wrist, forearm, and the overall arm height. The thumb pivoting is the other vital variable that remains flexible and continually adjusts the pronation and supination while playing. Although national affiliations offer little service other than streamlining different approaches, influential pedagogues ultimately endorse their own synthesis when it comes to bow hold. The three main schools of bow hold are:

- German school: index finger makes contact with stick at the first joint.
- Franco-Belgian school: index finger makes contact with stick at the second joint.
- Russian school: index finger makes contact with stick at the third joint.

Today, the German school is mostly outdated, so much so that contemporary violinists and violists gravitate towards Franco-Belgian and Russian, or an amalgamation of the two schools. In this text the Franco-Belgian school is the preferred approach to cover as many bow grips as possible.

2) **Cello:** although it closely resembles the Franco-Belgian grip of the upper strings, in that the right index finger makes contact with the stick at the second joint, the cello bow hold is slightly less pronated and the pinky finger is placed in front of the frog, not on the stick.

3) **Bass:** the French bass bow hold, or overhand hold, is almost identical to the cello with the following exceptions that pronation is less than the cello grip, the finger separation is possibly greater, because of that, either the middle two fingers or the ring finger may be aligned with the thumb, and the ring finger may be resting on the ferrule. Owing to its ancestry in the viol family, German traditions continued with the viol lineage of bows, hence the underhand bow hold. Both German and French bow holds have such a profound influence on the bow technique and bowing preferences, that some orchestras tend to hire musicians with a particular bow hold as established within their traditions. Unlike the upper strings so-called national bow schools, among European orchestras, Franco-Belgian and Germanic affiliations with bass bows are quite nationalistic.

Bow Strokes and Expressions

Bow strokes prior to the 1780s included slurred notes, staccato, tremolo, ondeggiando, arpeggiando, among others, however, Baroque and earlier shorter bows without a convex curve and a weighed tip limited the length of sustained notes and extended groupings of slurred notes. When performing pre-Tourte era early music, it is prudent to be informed of period bows, instruments and gut strings available to those musicians. From the mid-16th century to the late-18th century the French practice of *notes inégales* (Fr. "unequal notes") refers to a performance practice of dotting notes that are written as equal note values. Although this is a limited practice it stresses the preference of heavier down bow strokes and lighter up bow strokes.

The French bow maker François Xavier Tourte's pioneering work and revolutionary bows that were refined in the mid-1780s, with prominent German violin pedagogue Louis Spohr's endorsement, helped create the basis of modern bows and bow strokes. A heavier frog and heavier hatchet head (tip), as opposed to the Baroque pike tip which helped improve legato playing, longer slurs, expressive portato articulation and elasticity of the stick made a variety of off-string bow strokes become part of regular string lexicon. Until the mid- to late-19th century bowing articulations, both in vocabulary and notation, were wildly inconsistent, as an interchangeable use of the terms of staccato, spiccato, and sautillé, even to date some discrepancy on terminology and disagreement on interpretation exist. Below are some bow strokes and expressions that represent bow technique. Most of the below strokes and expressions will be found in graded repertoire, although some strokes are listed to give historical perspective, and some to give a broader knowledge on this vast subject.

Détaché

A ubiquitous bow stroke, the term denotes separated notes without a slur or articulation. Despite the common misconception, détaché notes are neither detached nor legato.

Legato Slur

Slurred notes are played in a single bow direction, connected without any articulation. In a legato slur, there are no articulation shapes between the note head and slur.

Legato

The term simply means to play connected. Legato may apply to separate notes in addition to slurred notes.

Portato or Louré

A re-articulation of the same pitch or different pitch under the same slur. Most commonly it is indicated as tenuto lines under a slur, however, some editions may place dots or tenuto lines under dots to indicate portato. To execute a portato the bow may be paused in between notes slightly, or the right index finger may pulsate without stopping the bow.

Staccato

Detached notes on the string. It is denoted by a dot above or below the note head and articulated by stopping the bow in between notes. How much to shorten the note depends on the note value, tempo, style, and other factors.

Slurred Staccato

Detached notes under a slur on the string. It is denoted by dots under the slur and articulated by momentarily stopping the bow in between notes.

Martelé

(Fr. from *marteler* "to hammer") an incisive, hammered bow stroke. It may be described as an accented staccato. It is executed most commonly on the upper half or upper 1/3 of the bow by the use of the forearm and the bow is stopped in between each note. Due to its distinct quality, only the forearm motion is engaged to execute the stroke with inflexible wrist and fingers. It may be denoted by a wedge (an arrow-head stroke) or an accent by the note head.

Spiccato

In present-day string playing the spiccato term indicates to play short and off-the-string notes.[1] To execute those bouncing notes, spiccato is played at or around the balance point and its exact location depends on the speed in which it is played: the slower the spiccato, the closer to the frog, the faster, the further towards the middle of bow. It is denoted by a dot by the note head. When more-brisk than regular spiccato is called for, molto spiccato indication may be provided by the composer or editor.

Brush Stroke

Although a made-up term, it indicates the exact opposite of molto spiccato where a lengthier contact than regular spiccato is made with the string.

Slow or Artificial Spiccato

To execute a heavier and controlled spiccato at slower speeds, the bow is carried, bounced, and controlled by hand. An artificial spiccato is the speed where the bow cannot spring on its own accord and if slow spiccato is played at or above the balance point, bow control cannot be maintained. It is denoted by a dot by the note head.

Sautillé

(Fr.; It. saltando) is a fast spiccato where the bow cannot fully bounce due to the quick pace. The sautillé is played in the middle of the bow, slightly further than the balance-point placement of spiccato. It is denoted by a wedge (an arrow-head stroke) or a dot by the note head.

Staccato Volante

Or "flying staccato" is a fast slurred staccato where numerous notes are played in one bow in a rapid succession. This is a soloistic bow stroke that will not occur in orchestral writing (Figure 13.1).

Ricochet

(Fr. "rebound" or *jeté* from *jeter* "to throw") a thrown bow stroke that bounces on the same bow direction to execute anywhere from two to several notes. It is denoted by dots by the note heads under a slur. It is different from flying staccato in that the bow is thrown onto string and made to bounce, or dribble on the string on its own volition. Naturally the bow will run out of energy at some point, which limits the number of notes to be played within rhythmic accuracy within a given tempo (Figure 13.2).

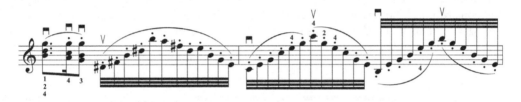

Figure 13.1 Paganini Caprice Op. 1, No. 7, mm 50–51, up and down bow flying staccatos

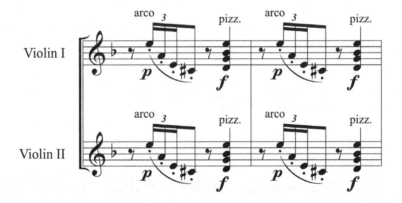

Figure 13.2 Rimsky-Korsakov *Capriccio Espagnol*, movement 4, *Scena e canto gitano*, rehearsal L, first and second violins, ricochet bowing

Collé

(Fr. from *coller* "to stick" or "to glue") although not a truly classified bow stroke, collé is executed with the fingers on the string, with a light and defined pinching attack and a slight lift at the end of stroke, much like a diminutive martelé stroke.

Ondeggiando

(It.; Fr. *ondulé*) an undulated bow stroke where continuous alteration between two strings takes place, commonly within a slur or multiple slurs. Ondeggiando may or may not involve open strings (Figure 13.3).

Bariolage

An undulated bow stroke where continuous alternation between stopped and open notes with the involvement of an open string. Often times, executed within a slur or multiple slurs, the particular illusion of bariolage is the color change caused by the alternation between the stopped note and the open string (Figure 13.4).

Arpeggiando

In Baroque performance practice, rolled chords may be written as block chords and executed in an arpeggiated manner, or in contemporary writing arpeggiated notes are written out. Often times, executed within a slur or multiple slurs, it may involve three or four strings. Additionally, it may be mixed with a ricochet bow stroke as in Paganini's Caprice Op. 1, No. 1 or Mendelssohn Violin Concerto in E Minor, Op. 64 (Figure 13.5).

Figure 13.3 Mozart Symphony in E-flat Major, No. 39, movement 4, Allegro, second violin section's opening measures, an ondeggiando passage

Figure 13.4 Bach Violin Concerto in A Minor, BWV 1041, movement 3, Allegro assai, mm 105–108, first four measures of the bariolage passage

Figure 13.5 Paganini Caprice, Op. 1, No. 1, opening, ricochet arpeggiando bow stroke

Multiple Stops

Although in orchestral performance practices, often times, multiple stops are divided, in some cases non-divisi chords are indicated by the composer (Figure 13.6).

Hooked Bowing

Is executing a dotted rhythm stopped within the same bow direction with a defined or portato articulation. Sometimes it is used to remove an unintentional accent caused by the shorter note value's bow recovery (Figure 13.7). It may be indicated with a dot under the slur by the longer and shorter note values, sometimes only by the shorter note value. Sometimes, however, indicated with only bow directions with no articulation attached. If the bow is stopped between two notes as a distinct articulation, for instance, if the hooked bowing is for the repetition of the same pitch, the first or the longer note value is somewhat shortened, however, the second or the shorter note value is always on time (Figure 13.7).

Tremolo

Rapid non-measured restatement of the same note with quick down and up bow repetitions, played at the tip or in the upper 1/3 portion of the bow. It may be indicated by the term tremolo, or abbreviated as trem., but more often it may not be denoted (Figure 13.8). With the common orchestration shorthand of repeated sixteenth notes or thirty-second notes, distinction between measured and tremolo notes is sometimes veiled.

String Crossings

Occur anywhere in the bow from the frog to the tip, from separate notes to notes within a slur, from a single crossing to multiple crossings (as in ondeggiando). Therefore, a comprehensive bow technique is capable of executing any string crossing without any interruption or wasteful use of bow. The only way to execute string crossings in an optimized manner is to get as close to the adjacent string as possible without making it sound. This approach necessitates a smooth and organic elevation change, but not an angular motion.[2]

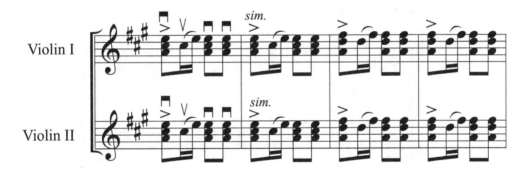

Figure 13.6 Rimsky-Korsakov *Capriccio Espagnol*, movement 1, Alborada, mm 33–36, first and second violins, down-bow retakes

Figure 13.7 Hooked bowing

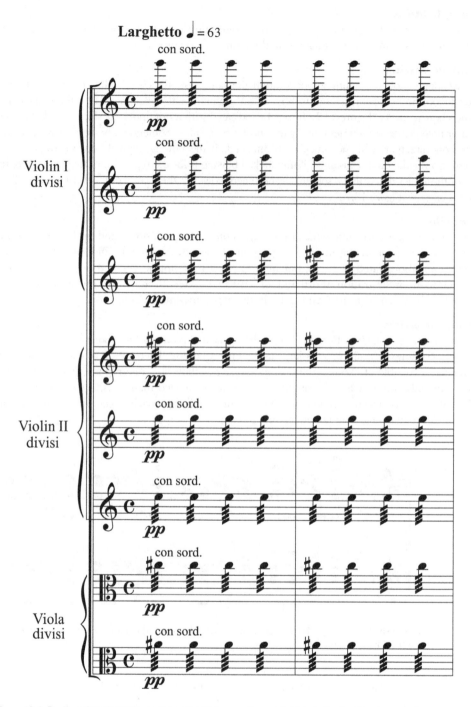

Figure 13.8 Berlioz *Symphonie Fantastique*, Op. 14, movement 5, A witches' sabbath, opening measures, upper strings, tremolo

Retakes

Generally, composers do not indicate bow directions unless a particularly accented or unaccented section calls for it. In accented figures a composer may indicate multiple down bows, which will require multiple retakes (Figure 13.9). In contrast, for unaccented but separate notes players may be called to execute with multiple up bows (Figure 13.10).

Figure 13.9 Rimsky-Korsakov *Capriccio Espagnol*, movement 2, *Variazioni*, mm 73–75, first and second violins, down-bow retakes

Figure 13.10 Prokofiev Third Piano Concerto in C Major, Op. 26, II. *Tema con variazioni*: Andantino, first two measures, violins, violas and cellos, up-bow retakes

© Copyright 1923 Hawkes and Son (London) Ltd. A Boosey & Hawkes Company. Copyright Renewed. International Copyright Secured. All Rights Reserved. Reprinted by Permission.

Effects Acquired with Contact Point

The following two items are not bow strokes, but effects acquired by an intentional contact point placement.

Sul Tasto

(It. also *sulla tastiera*; Fr. *sur la touche*; Ger. *am Griffbrett*), an Italian term indicating to bow on the fingerboard. The same effect is also known as flautando (It.) and it produces a softer, breathy, more veiled flute-like tone quality. Contact point having been moved onto the fingerboard requires additional bow length.

Sul Ponticello

Indicates to play at the bridge (It.; Fr. *au chevalet*; Ger. *am Steg*) and it produces overtones resulting in a glassy or a metallic tone quality. Often times, sul ponticello is coupled with tremolo.

Assignment

1) Write a one paragraph summary of bow schools discussed in this lesson, to be turned in next class.
2) List all bow-related terms and their brief explanations discussed in this lesson, to be turned in next class.
3) Practice pizzicato and arco exercises.
4) Read Lesson 14 prior to next class.

Notes

1 Boyden and Walls, "Spiccato."
2 For a comprehensive list of bow motions expressed in graphs, see Hodgson, *Motion Study and Violin Bowing*, 35–63.

Lesson 14

Contents

This lesson's focus is:

- A discussion on common technical issues and their remedies.

Common Technical Problems and Their Remedies

All aspects of string playing, from instrument setup to bow hold to tone production, present various challenges. Although technical challenges manifest themselves in various forms, there are commonalities found with each of those issues. The remedies for the following common problems are abundant in method and delivery, and all experienced string teachers establish their individual solutions through years of teaching, this lesson will examine common challenges and provide proven strategies to remedy them in the beginning and intermediate stages of string playing.

Posture and Instrument Setup Issues cause faulty tone-production, because a misaligned instrument is just as problematic as a misaligned bow arm, and a contributing factor to tension and other technical deficiencies. The center of each school of teaching, stable posture and instrument hold create the foundation for all techniques to develop. Even though at first look both posture and instrument hold appear to be static, they are wholly dynamic aspects of string technique that allow players to move while performing without any restriction. Static instrument hold and unnatural posture are a recipe for tension, and are the exact opposite of a healthy motion in string playing.

Posture and setup concerns of upper strings:
Problems while standing:

- Student is leaning toward the instrument.
- Student is leaning back.
- Student is leaning forward.

Problems while sitting:

- Student is slouching.
- Student is leaning back.

Solution: have the student stand with one heel off the floor as described in Lesson 2, and sway sideways. Place the instrument in the playing position, have the student repeat the sway motion. The natural posture must remain throughout this exercise and no lean should ever occur. Have the student lie on the floor in the supine position with knees flexed and feet tucked by the torso and hold the instrument in the playing position.

Problems:

- Instrument is placed on the chest.
- Instrument is placed too far on the shoulder.
- Instrument angle is too steep.
- Instrument angle is too flat.

Solution: make sure that the chinrest and shoulder rest fit the student perfectly. The left shoulder should never be elevated while playing the instrument, conversely the shoulder rest and chinrest should not cause the jaw to be raised and head tilted away from the instrument. Making sure that the instrument size is correct for the given student and finding well-fitting and well-functioning accessories, as the chinrest and shoulder rest are critical. For a drooping instrument hold, Rolland's Balancing a Ball exercise, or Holding Game, is an effective way to keep the instrument from drooping (Lesson 2).

Left hand and arm problems with upper strings:

Problem:

- Left wrist is extended (known as collapsed wrist).
- Left wrist is flexed.
- Left wrist is bent sideways (ulnar or radial deviation).
- Left thumb is straightened.
- Left thumb and index finger are clamped on the neck.
- Left hand carries the instrument.

Solution: while playing the upper strings, the left wrist should be in the natural position. Some students may be supporting the violin that causes the wrist to collapse (extension). If that is the case the instrument hold must be re-examined and any issues with the chin rest and shoulder rest must be addressed, then the wrist must return to its natural position. The opposite of a collapsed wrist is a flexed wrist and it also causes tension in the hand and restricts free movement of fingers. Since there is no causal relation with instrument hold, left arm position must be re-evaluated and the wrist should be returned to its natural position.[1] Sideway motion of the wrist, or ulnar and radial deviations, is caused by the entire arm not engaging in a pendulum motion when moving from one string position to the other and for the wrist to move sideways to accommodate string changes. "Pendulum" exercise (Lesson 3) helps resolve this issue efficiently. In the case of a straightened left thumb or lack of a squirrel hole with the left hand that carries the weight of the instrument, "A-OK" position and squirrel hole must be created (much like the C-position of the cello). A thumb exercise of tapping and drawing circles with the pad of thumb on the side of the neck will relieve tension and help release the neck from the hand's clutch, allowing fingers to function freely.

Problem: left arm extended to the left while playing on the highest string and fingers are placed too low in relation to the fingerboard.

Solution: in the first stages of playing it is a relatively common issue for a student to extend and abduct the left arm out to the left of the instrument while playing on the highest string and lower left fingers in relation to the fingerboard. This creates tension in the shoulder (glenohumeral) joint, an unnecessary playing angle for the left arm. The simplest way to make the student aware of this undesirable motion is to place the four fingers in the playing position on the second string (A string and D string, on the violin and viola respectively) and move all four fingers onto the first string (E string and A string, on the violin and viola respectively). This will assure that the highest string can be played with the first finger placed high enough to be squared like a hook and the elbow position is perfectly vertical (Figures 14.1 and 14.2).

Problem: left-hand's mold of rounded fingers is not kept intact and fingers move away from the fingerboard, furthermore, the fourth finger may be curled under.

Solution: in the initial stages of string playing it is common for fingers to lift higher than necessary and move away from the fingerboard and that can cause issues in intonation, accuracy, and withhold the student from achieving agility. If corrective work is necessary, work with the student on their left-hand position (Lesson 2). A simple exercise of holding a crumpled piece of paper and placing the hand on the neck assures a perfectly rounded shape of the left hand. Subsequently, reminding the student to imagine a crumpled piece of paper in the left hand helps ensures the perfect left-hand mold. If the student is curling the fourth finger, tapping the first joints of the third and fourth fingers will confirm that the fourth finger is not curling under.

Problem: avoiding the use of the fourth finger causes awkward string crossings, random color changes, and interruption of vibrato on arbitrary open-string notes.

Solution: avoiding the fourth finger is an exceedingly common issue where it is dismissed as an "age-related laziness" or "carelessness" on the account of younger students all the way to

Figure 14.1 Correct first finger height on upper strings

Figure 14.2 Incorrect first finger height on upper strings

high school and even some college students. The avoidance of the fourth finger may be a deeper problem, that some method books and some teachers delay introduction of it for an extended period of time in the earliest stages of instruction. First, this practice gives the student a false impression that the fourth finger is *not* part of the basic left-hand technique and should be used *only* when an open string is not an option. Whether that message is given verbally or not, the student identifies it as such and the avoidance of the fourth finger becomes an accepted manner of playing. The only way to avoid this from becoming an issue, the fourth finger *must* be introduced right along with finger numbers one, two, and three.

Problem: avoiding the use of second position causes awkward string crossings, and redundant shifting.

Solution: with the exception of half position, an upper-string student's first encounter with a new position is third position. The reason second position is initially bypassed is that the finger patterns between first, third, and fifth positions are more similar than that of the second and fourth positions. Therefore, it is quite common for students to avoid the second position. The only solution to this problem is to practice two-octave scales in second and fourth positions as in *Scale-Studies* by Jan Hřímalý, and work on studies in those positions. *Introducing the Positions for Violin: Volume II—Second, Fourth, Sixth and Seventh Positions* by Harvey S. Whistler, and *New Violin Study School*, Op. 182, *Book 4* (2nd position) and *Book 7* (4th position) by Arthur Seybold, and *Introducing the Positions for Viola: Volume 2—Second, Fourth and Fifth Positions* by Harvey S. Whistler, *Practical Viola School* by Hans Sitt, and viola transcription of his *Études for the Violin: Book II*, Op. 32 are invaluable resources.

Setup concerns of low strings:

- The cello is held at too steep an angle.
- The cello is held at too shallow an angle.
- The cello is tilted too far to left.
- The cello is tilted right.
- The cello is tilted left in the vertical plane.
- The student is leaning too far into the bass.
- The bass is leaning too far into student.
- The student is positioned behind the bass.
- The student is positioned on side of bass.

Solution: making sure that proper seat height, stool height for seated bass, and endpin length are maintained for low strings. Following the Cello Sitting Position and Double Bass Standing Position steps and "hugging" the instrument provides a good reference for appropriate instrument angle (Lesson 2). When it comes to bowing for double bass, both with the French and German bows, instrument positioning should allow for free bowing on the lowest and highest strings.

Left hand and arm problems with low strings:

- Left elbow resting on the ribs (both on the cello and the bass).
- Left thumb is straightened behind the neck.
- Left thumb is pointing up.
- Instrument's neck is clutched by the left hand.

Solution: all of the listed issues with the left hand and arm cause tension and all issues of tension must be corrected quickly. Re-evaluate the left arm slope, as it must be maintained at all times (Lesson 2). Imagining a beach ball resting under the left elbow is an efficient way to create a correct slope. Tapping the tip of left thumb and drawing circles with the tip of the thumb behind the neck are effective exercises to fix thumb directional issues (C-shape and K-shape) and tension problems. If the left hand issues are caused by an incorrect bass hold in standing position, getting comfortable with balancing the instrument is necessary and will help relieve tension of the left hand (Lesson 2).

Tone Production: is among the most intimidating challenges in early string instruction. It may take years to acquire an advanced proficiency in bow technique, but that does not mean the student cannot enjoy the process in the interim and make steady improvement in achieving a good tone. The most essential tenet in early string education is to keep students from getting overwhelmed and letting bad habits take over while challenging them at an appropriate pace to assure their improvement. Below are the most common causes for faulty tone production:

Problem: a bow-arm misalignment creates an uneven contact point that causes an uneven tone production, or the contact point is on the fingerboard which results in an unintentional and persistent *sul tasto*. Directly related to this issue, a faulty instrument hold, a drooping instrument onto the chest for upper strings and misalignment on the vertical plane for low strings may also be contributing factors in this problem.

Solution: videotape students to show bow misalignment and contact point irregularities from the teacher's point of view and work with students on the paper towel roll exercises in front of a mirror (figures 4.4, 6.2, and 7.2). If the misalignment is caused by faulty posture and instrument hold, work with the student on posture and instrument hold to remedy the problem (Lesson 2).

Problem: the student hesitates in between bow changes.
Solution: commonly encountered in the early stages of string playing, the ability to keep weight into the string during bow changes is the true solution for hesitant bow changes. Work with the student to relax the wrist and fingers with the pencil exercise (Lesson 2) and legato rubber-band exercise (Lesson 19).

Problem: the student avoids the frog area due to a stiff wrist and fingers, resulting in a longer articulation when short, crisp notes are needed (e.g. spiccato), and because of avoiding the frog, retakes of the bow are inadequate.
Solution: work with students on preparatory bow exercises (Lesson 2) to remove tension in the wrist and fingers.

Problem: the right shoulder is elevated and tense, causing labored bowing and preventing an optimal tone production.
Solution: most often, string crossings from high to low strings allow shoulder elevation to sneak into the motion. In fact, the shoulder is not a moving component of the bow arm and it should not elevate when crossing strings. The lifting may occur to a varying degree and in certain passages. Therefore, it is imperative for students to realize when this unintentional lift of the shoulder is occurring to fix the problem. To accomplish that, have the student place the left hand on the right shoulder to realize the extent of the shoulder lift on a scale from one to ten. To remedy the issue work with the student on the bow placement exercise (Lesson 9).

Problem: right elbow is locked and preventing the student from legato playing.
Solution: work with students on the paper towel roll exercises in front of a mirror (figures 4.4, 6.2, and 7.2).

Problem: the student produces a wispy, surface tone that does not carry.
Solution: first have the student weigh the right arm by holding it with the left hand at the elbow and help realize the natural weight of the right arm. There are two possible issues in play that cause a wispy tone quality: not enough weight applied into the string, or too much bow length is used for a given note. If not enough weight is applied into the string, the bow-arm weight must be utilized and index-finger transfer of that weight into the string is not taking place. On the lowest strings of the cello and particularly of the double bass, due to gauge thickness of the string, a slower, more deliberate bowing is required than that of the high strings. Refer to Gearhart's "recipe" for speed and weight ratio (Lesson 3). Furthermore, work with students on supplemental preparatory bow exercises (Lesson 2).

Problem: the student does not sustain the tone: after an initial attack tone withers.
Solution: the continuous use of the right index finger to transfer arm weight into the string is the solution to this problem. On a down bow the weight of the index finger must increase, and on an up bow it must decrease to keep the same amplitude of tone or dynamic level. Without the increased weight of the index finger, tone will wane on all down bows. Work with the student on Gearhart's "recipe" for speed and weight ratio (Lesson 3) and legato rubber-band exercise (Lesson 19).

Common Bow Hold Issues
In the pursuit of bow technique, maintaining a reliable bow grip, moving the entire arm in a coordinated manner, smooth bow changes, smooth string crossings, and flexibility of fingers

are not overnight achievements. In the earliest stages of string instruction on the teacher's part, an empathetic yet determined approach is necessary to accomplish all of the above in a timely.

Problem: an overly pronated bow hold.
Solution: overpronation of bow hold causes a raised forearm and hinders smooth bowing. To address this issue work with the student in gaining a reliable and flexible bow grip with corrective pencil exercises (Lesson 2) and reevaluate the right arm slope.

Common Faults with Intonation

Problem: minor seconds are not close enough with upper strings.
Solution: work with the student on remedial finger pattern exercises and scales as Otakar Ševčík's *Violin School for Beginners*, Op. 6, Part 1, and Castleman and Koob II's *The Tonal Application of Finger Patterns to Violin Scale Technique* and *The Tonal Application of Finger Patterns to Viola Scale Technique*. Furthermore, the use of open strings as a drone in placing minor seconds is a proven formula in solving this issue.

Problem: first finger is too sharp and fourth finger is too flat with low strings.
Solution: this problem may be due to lack of a proper C-shaped cello left hand and K-shaped bass left hand. Work with the cello student on remedial left-hand positioning (Lesson 2), finger pattern exercises and scales as Kummer's *Violoncello Method*, Op. 60, Lee's *First Steps in Violoncello Playing*, Op. 101 and Fischer's *Method for the Violoncello*, and for the bass student Nanny's *Complete Method for Double Bass*, and Simandl's *New Method for the String Bass*.

Common Faults Associated with Vibrato

When vibrato is introduced, both intonation and a tension-free left-hand technique must be established so that adding vibrato may aggravate those deficiencies. In its initial stages, vibrato sounds out of place, because it is slow and applied only to longer notes. However, once established, vibrato should fit into any passage without being noticed, unless an indication such as non-vibrato or molto vibrato is given by the composer. The below are some common issues encountered in early to intermediate stages of string studies.

Problem: vibrato is infrequent, suddenly starts and stops on a given note, and is affected by fingering.
Solution: although during the initial stage vibrato is only applied to longer notes, once it is fully implemented, students should be able to vibrate on all notes regardless of fingering and note value. The main principle of vibrato practice is to gain the ability to vibrate on all four fingers throughout one's playing. Any deficiency of vibrato on a given finger, or changes in its speed and continuity, are signs of a partially-developed vibrato. Establishing the complete ability to vibrate takes time and practice. Vibrato must be nurtured throughout its infancy, and it will sound out-of-place for a considerably long period of time. As this newly-acquired skill will consume substantial amounts of concentration for the student, technically challenging pieces of music are not appropriate repertoire choices for vibrato application. For that reason, the string teacher must be clear in defining expectations when the students should apply vibrato, and when not to apply it.

Problem: finger initiates the vibrato, and sideways finger motion is used to achieve vibrato.
Solution: separate from appropriate finger vibrato, finger-initiated sideway vibrato causes intonation problems and vibrato limitations. A common issue with upper strings, this faulty

vibrato is cause for concern on the accounts of intonation and tension. All vibrato motion *must* be initiated by arm and transferred to fingertip, but not the other way around. Such faulty vibrato should be addressed with proper pre-vibrato and vibrato exercises (Lesson 21).

Problem: wrist flexes or collapses during vibrato.
Solution: if vibrato causes the wrist to flex or collapse, it is a sign of improper motion to achieve vibrato. Remedial work may be required to re-evaluate left-hand position, remove tension (Lesson 2), and supplement with pre-vibrato and vibrato exercises (Lesson 21).

Problem: vibrato causes pitch to sharpen.
Solution: if vibrato affects pitch, it may be too wide to maintain pitch. Depending on the register, vibrato must remain within acceptable parameters: the lower, the wider and slower, the higher, the faster and narrower. If it exceeds those benchmarks, vibrato may cause pitch to become unreliable and sharp. Therefore, vibrato should be controlled in its amount of width and speed (Lesson 21).

Problem: vibrato is too wide and slow or too narrow and fast for the given piece of music.
Solution: as long as there is no causal relation with tension, both vibrato width and speed are refined through practice and experience (Lesson 21).

Common Faults Associated with Shifting

When introducing shifting, both a reliable intonation and left-hand technique must have been established, all deficiencies such as tension issues must be addressed, so that shifting is not going to compound those problems. For example, if there is any existing tension in the left hand, smooth and reliable shifting can never be achieved. Therefore, much like with the vibrato, preventive medicine in shifting is starting with a solidified left-hand foundation.

Problem: a clamped-down guide finger and thumb cause a jerky and undershot shift.
Solution: work with the student to remove all tension in the hand by remedial work (Lesson 2), by pre-shifting exercises (Lesson 21), and by removing thumb from neck to accomplish the shifting motion without it.

Problems:

- The thumb and first finger separate during shift.
- The wrist anticipates shift.
- The distance between fingers is collapsed during shift.

Solution: the shifting motion must be accomplished without any apparent change to the left hand's shape and functionality. The string teacher must be vigilant in observing any of the abovementioned tendencies and must address them in the pre-shifting phase, so that when shifting is introduced they are not an issue. However, if any of these problems are encountered, the teacher must work with the student on pre-shifting exercises (Lesson 21).

Common Faults Associated with Trills

Although an in-depth discussion of trill is not within the scope of this text, the ability to play trills in an unimpeded manner is an imperative component of the left-hand technique, therefore, common problems related to trill will be discussed below. Much like with the vibrato and shifting, trill exercises are necessary to acquire this skill and maintain proficiency (Lesson 21).

Problem: trill is uneven in its speed, intermittent, and is affected by fingering.
Solution: whether on weaker third and fourth fingers, or stronger first and second fingers, trills may be undermined by inadequate control. The only way to address this problem is

through trill exercises and evenly strengthening all fingers. Otakar Ševčík's *Studies Preparatory to the Shake*, Op. 7 is an invaluable resource for the violin, however, all string instruments should transform vibrato exercises to trills and practice them with the metronome to improve and maintain trills. In acquiring control, fewer turns of trill should be applied first and sped up in time. As good taste dictates, trills with open strings should be avoided by way of shifting up to keep an even tone color.

Problem: vibrato is mixed with trill.
Solution: it is a common issue for a student to mix vibrato with a trill. The problem of a trill mixed with vibrato causes the trill to become muddy. The teacher must work with the student on trill exercises (Lesson 21).

Problem: tension with left hand causes the wrist to flex or collapse (extend) during trill, therefore the upper auxiliary, or upper neighbor note of trill sounds flat.
Solution: an indiscernibly slight flexion of the wrist is acceptable as it allows for a quicker trill, however, if an excessive flexion or any extension (collapse) caused by tension is present, the left wrist must be relaxed and straightened during trills. The upper auxiliary note sounding flat is most likely related to extension (or collapse) of the wrist, however, at times may occur independently of this issue. If that is the case, practicing trills with drone tones or drone open strings will address the intonation issue.

Problem: trill shortens or lengthens the note value.
Solution: it is imperative to treat trills in multiple layers of challenge and introduce them in succession only after gaining complete control of each layer. First, the student should remove all ornaments including the trill and turns, play the note unembellished with a metronome. Once comfortable with the length of the note, the student should add the trill, then add turns before and after it in sequence. In this building practice *only* a limited number of turns must be executed for all ornamentation, including turns before or after trill, to be accommodated within the allotted time.

Assignment

1) List common faults on your assigned instrument, to be turned in next class.
2) Practice pizzicato and arco exercises in preparation for second playing test.
3) Review today's lesson and midterm test preparation prior to next class.

Note

1 The only exception to flexing left wrist is in higher positions where some flexion movement is required, although this occurs at negligibly shallow angles.

Lesson 15

Contents

In this lesson students will demonstrate the following:

- Proper posture.
- Proper setup.
- Good tone production.

Videotaping of Second Playing Test

This lesson is dedicated to performing the second playing test. The instructor will be videotaping the playing test and evaluating it on the spot. Each student will play the selections which have been decided by the instructor. Each student will watch the videotape and complete the following Self-Evaluation Form II, using the posture, setup, and tone production guidelines established in class.

Videotaping Number 2

Name:_____**Instrument:**_____**Date:**_____**Grades**____/____

STRING PLAYING TEST RUBRIC II

First watch your video and read your instructor's evaluation of your playing. Afterwards watch your video again and fill out the below rubric. Leave correct items blank, mark any exceptional element by a plus sign and any element in need of improvement by a minus sign. You will receive a grade for full and accurate completion, and timely submission of this form. The form is due at the beginning of next class.

POSTURE—INSTRUMENT HOLD, LEFT HAND, PIZZICATO POSITIONING AND BOW HOLD

VIOLIN AND VIOLA

POSTURE, INSTRUMENT HOLD AND LEFT HAND

_____ torso is square
_____ shoulders are relaxed
_____ feet are positioned correctly
_____ head is not tilted and is free of tension
_____ instrument is supported on the collarbone without tension
_____ instrument is placed parallel relative to the floor and kept with the "nose-scroll-elbow-toe" alignment at all times
_____ wrist is straight from all angles
_____ hand is free of tension
_____ four fingers are curved and tips of fingers are hovering right above strings
_____ thumb is at a proper height and is free of tension

PIZZICATO POSITIONING

_____ hand and arm are at a proper angle to play pizzicato
_____ tip of thumb is placed at the corner of the fingerboard for secure pizzicato anchoring
_____ pizzicato is played with the index finger at a proper distance from the bridge

BOW HOLD

_____ shoulder is relaxed at all times
_____ elbow is relaxed and functioning smoothly
_____ wrist is slightly higher than knuckles
_____ all fingers are properly curved and spaced
_____ thumb's first joint is curved and tip of thumb is wedged against end of frog
_____ pinky finger is on top of stick
_____ forearm and wrist are slightly pronated and index finger is leaning toward the stick

_____   bow is always parallel to the bridge
_____   bow is at a proper distance from the bridge with a constant contact point
_____   arm weight and index finger produce a sustained and even tone
_____   bow direction changes are executed smoothly and without stoppage
_____   string crossings are executed smoothly and without disruption

CELLO

POSTURE, INSTRUMENT HOLD AND LEFT HAND

_____   seated on front four inches of seat with feet positioned correctly and flat on the floor in a position that can allow the student to stand up at any given time
_____   endpin is at a proper length with cello at a proper angle
_____   C peg is behind left ear, neck is one fist width above left shoulder and cello is tilted slightly to the left
_____   cello is not pinched and knees are relaxed with instrument balanced without assistance of arms
_____   wrist is straight from all angles and draws a straight line from elbow to knuckles
_____   elbow height can allow the student to slide up and down on the fingerboard
_____   thumb is behind the second finger and the tip of the thumb is lightly touching the middle of the neck
_____   first joint of the thumb is slightly rounded but not straightened
_____   first finger is slightly tilted toward the fingerboard and fourth finger is parallel to the first finger
_____   first to second and second to fourth fingers are equidistant from each other

PIZZICATO POSITIONING

_____   hand and arm are at a proper angle to play pizzicato
_____   tip of thumb is placed at side of fingerboard, last three- to four-inches of fingerboard for secure pizzicato anchoring
_____   pizzicato is played with the index finger at a proper distance from the bridge

BOW HOLD

_____   shoulder is relaxed at all times
_____   elbow is relaxed and functioning smoothly
_____   wrist is slightly higher than knuckles
_____   all fingers are properly curved and spaced
_____   thumb's first joint is curved and tip of thumb is wedged against end of frog
_____   forearm and wrist are slightly pronated and index finger is leaning toward the stick
_____   bow is always parallel to the bridge
_____   bow is at proper distance from bridge with a constant contact point
_____   arm weight and index finger produce a sustained and even tone
_____   bow direction changes are executed smoothly and without stoppage
_____   string crossings are executed smoothly and without disruption

DOUBLE BASS

SITTING POSITION

_____   seated tall with left knee behind bass right foot planted firmly on the floor
_____   endpin is at a proper length with bass at a proper angle
_____   instrument is slightly leaning back with the right corner of the instrument in front of the sternum with f-holes facing the conductor

STANDING POSITION

_____   standing tall, shoulders back with a straight spine
_____   endpin is at a proper length with bass at a proper angle with right corner of instrument in front of sternum
_____   the instrument is positioned diagonally in-front of the player with f-holes facing the conductor

INSTRUMENT HOLD AND LEFT HAND

_____   first finger is at eye level when placed on the first tape
_____   wrist is straight from all angles and draws a straight line from elbow to knuckles
_____   elbow height can allow the student to slide up and down on the fingerboard
_____   thumb is behind the second finger and the tip of the thumb is lightly touching the middle of the fingerboard
_____   first joint of thumb is slightly rounded but not straightened
_____   first finger is tilted toward the fingerboard and fourth finger is reaching the fourth finger tape with a K-shaped hand
_____   first to second and second to fourth fingers are equidistant from each other

PIZZICATO POSITIONING

_____   hand and arm are at a proper angle to play pizzicato
_____   tip of thumb is placed at side of fingerboard, last three- to four-inches of fingerboard for secure pizzicato anchoring
_____   pizzicato is played with the first joint of the index finger at a proper angle

GERMAN BOW HOLD

_____   shoulder is relaxed at all times
_____   elbow is relaxed and functioning smoothly
_____   thumb, index and middle fingers are joined at the tips
_____   all fingers are properly curved and spaced
_____   thumb's first joint is curved and tip of thumb is behind stick, but not on top
_____   forearm and wrist are supinated at a proper angle
_____   bow is always parallel to the bridge
_____   bow is at a proper distance from the bridge with a constant contact point
_____   arm weight and index finger produce a sustained and even tone
_____   bow direction changes are executed smoothly and without stoppage
_____   string crossings are executed smoothly and without disruption

FRENCH BOW HOLD

_____   shoulder is relaxed at all times
_____   elbow is relaxed and functioning smoothly
_____   wrist is slightly higher than knuckles
_____   all fingers are properly curved and spaced
_____   thumb's first joint is curved and tip of thumb is wedged against end of frog
_____   forearm and wrist are slightly pronated and index finger is leaning toward the stick
_____   bow is always parallel to the bridge
_____   bow is at a proper distance from the bridge with a constant contact point
_____   arm weight and index finger produce a sustained and even tone
_____   bow direction changes are executed smoothly and without stoppage
_____   string crossings are executed smoothly and without disruption

Scale: intonation, accuracy, and fingering

Piece: intonation, accuracy, and fingering

Evaluation Summary: provide a summary of your playing test by writing one paragraph on the positive elements of your playing and one paragraph on those elements in need of improvement.

1)   A summary of positive elements.

2)   A summary of elements in need of improvement.

Assignment

1)   Complete Playing Test Rubric II, to be turned in next class.
2)   Practice pizzicato exercises.
3)   Read Lesson 16 prior to next class.

Lesson 16

Contents

This lesson's objectives are:

- A discussion of studio teaching of string instruments.
- Studio teaching of violin.
- Studio teaching of viola.
- Studio teaching of cello.
- Studio teaching of bass.

Studio Teaching

This lesson will be dedicated to specifics of teaching orchestral string instruments in one-on-one instructional setting. In the studio setting the teacher has the vital responsibility of selection, correct sizing, and fitting of the instrument. An improperly sized and fitted violin and viola can cause permanent injury. A great number of string students do not have access to private teaching: they either never received one-on-one instruction, or received it intermittently for one reason or another. It is common to encounter a student playing an instrument for years without any access to private instruction. In a large classroom, string teachers have limited time and resources to devote to an individual student, even though they can be significantly helpful by taking necessary steps to promote and uphold good techniques and resolve pre-existing technical issues. Therefore, the essential role of studio teachers is to devote their attention to guide their students with knowledge, experience, and sound pedagogical philosophy in a systematic development timetable.

Instrument Quality

The concern of instrument quality has been examined in the Instrument Selection discussion (Lesson 9). In continued instruction it may become necessary for a serious student to upgrade to a better student model due to acoustic limitations, or growing out of the current instrument. The teacher must exercise due diligence when it comes to finding a local reputable shop or a reputable online vendor and help the student select a perfect instrument.

Instrument Sizing

When compared with the violin, viola sizing issues are much more prevalent because unlike a fairly standard 4/4 violin size of a 14 inch body length, a "full" viola size may vary anywhere from 15 inches to 17 inches, and bout and neck widths vary. Although young students are much more pliable than adult students, significant harm can be done by assigning a student too-large an instrument with the promise of "growing into" it. The student should be able to maintain left-hand position without an excessive stretch. When the violin is in the proper playing position on the collarbone and the student can reach around the scroll with the left hand comfortably with a relaxed elbow, the instrument size is proper as far as the arm is concerned. If the student can place first, second, third, and fourth fingers on the first position tapes without an excessive stretch, the neck size is correct as well.

How is the body length of an instrument determined? The measurement is taken on the back of the instrument from the side of the button to the bottom of the instrument (Figure 16.1). The string length is measured from string nut to the bridge and under

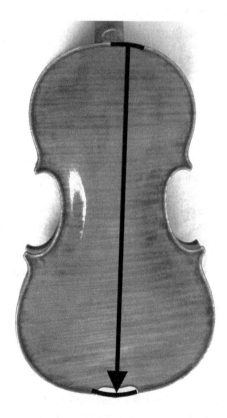

Figure 16.1 Back of violin for a body length measurement

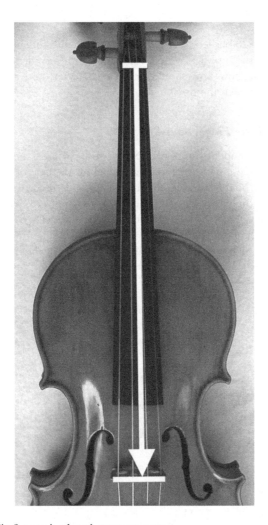

Figure 16.2 Front of violin for a string length measurement

normal circumstances a properly fitted bridge should line up with inside notches of F-holes (Figure 16.2). In the US, standard measurement of instruments is the body length expressed in inches. As an industry standard both makers and shops use fractional sizes for string instruments (from 1/32 to 4/4 for violin, 1/10 to 4/4 for cello, and 1/10 to 3/4 for bass) with the exception of viola. Viola sizes are expressed in inches and can be found from 12 inches to 16 ½ inches for student-grade instruments, and 15 inches to 17 inches among artist-grade violas. 17 inch plus instruments are rare but not unheard of. The current standard bass body size is 3/4 due to playability concerns. The same is the case for the viola, since accommodations must be made with regard to neck width and string length to make larger instruments playable. In addition to standard fractional instruments, petite sized or non-standard 7/8 size violins and cellos are possible to acquire.

Bow Length

Once instrument size is established, there is a chance that the student cannot stretch the bow arm all the way to the exact tip. It is perfectly acceptable for a student not to be able to reach the tip of the bow. The bow arm should *never* be contorted and shoulder should *never* be extended in an effort to reach the tip.

Strip Preparation of the Fingerboard

To prepare a violin for a student you may affix four strips of 1/16 inch white striping tape on the fingerboard and a hole punch reinforcement label on the side of the neck for the thumb alignment. For the fingerboard marking, the most commonly used two tape arrangements are the three-tape pattern: whole, whole, 1/2; or the four-tape pattern: whole, whole, 1/2, whole for upper strings (Figure 16.3), whole, whole, 1/2 for the cello (Figure 16.4), and whole, whole, whole, 1/2 for the bass (Figure 16.5). For the thumb alignment with the first finger, you may place a hole punch reinforcement label on the side of the neck, although this is not as common as the fingerboard tape patterns.

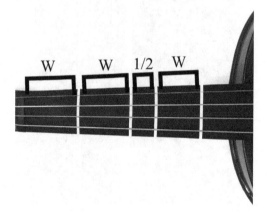

Figure 16.3 Upper strings fingerboard tape placement

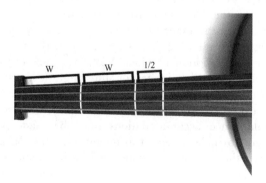

Figure 16.4 Cello fingerboard tape placement

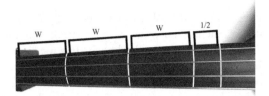

Figure 16.5 Bass fingerboard tape placement

The old fingerboard tapes need to be replaced if they are dirty, worn, and are out of tune. You may remove them and clean the fingerboard with the help of an alcohol swab, making sure no alcohol touches the neck or the instrument as it will dissolve varnish. When placing new tapes, use a pencil to mark the side of the fingerboard as tuning the correct placement of tapes. Once the correct tape placement is determined, cut and slide the tape under the strings using pencil markings as a guide and visually inspect that the tape is affixed straight across the fingerboard to ensure perfect intonation.

Preparation of the Bow

Although there are proprietary bow-grip aids available on the market, through the years string teachers have been preparing bows to help their students develop a correct bow hold by placing a rubber band, affixing corn cushions and hole punch reinforcement labels. The basic idea behind any physical item used as bow-grip assistance is to aid the student by referencing certain contact points and confining fingers into a correct bow hold. Corrective proprietary aids work by securing student's bow hold position into one or two pieces of a molded rubber material. The rubber band is wrapped around the frog and is used to capture the ring finger so it does not migrate up the bow and perch on top of the stick. Affixing corn cushions, or less conspicuous clear hole punch reinforcement labels, can work by marking the proper placements of the thumb, index and pinky fingers (Figure 16.6). The bow-grip aids are extremely helpful in correcting collapsed and slipping thumbs, straightening pinky fingers, perching the middle two fingers, and securing a migrating bow grip.

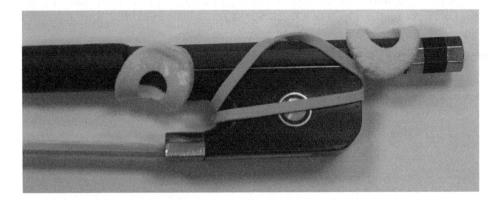

Figure 16.6 Rubber band and corn cushion placements on the bow

Use of Classroom Method Books in the Studio

When it comes to selecting a method book written specifically for private study and not for classroom use, violin studio teachers have diverse and strong opinions. One question that must be asked is: what is the purpose of a method book? It is meant to impart knowledge, for the student to gain technical ability on the instrument and learn a particular way of playing. None of these goals are achieved on the account of a method book without the work and direction of a studio teacher. In essence, a method book is merely a means for an end and it is most effective when used as part of the vision of an enlightened instructor. Therefore, it might be just as effective for an instructor to gather materials outside a single source and use various method books to implement multiple objectives in the studio.

It is a fairly common practice to use method books meant for classroom instruction in the studio. While it is not a completely objectionable practice, in light of the abovementioned method books and scores of unmentioned options, taking a cookie-cutter approach of assigning classroom method books in the studio may not be the preferred choice. Studio teachers are expected to be observant and commit all their focus on one student and modify their teaching *and* teaching materials to accommodate the needs of that particular student. Nonetheless, for the purposes of this class, students may use the classroom method book for the sample lesson teaching (Lesson 27).

Teaching the Violin

Clef

All violin music is written in treble clef (Figure 16.7). Any occasion of alto-clef writing in scordatura passages, is exceedingly rare.[1]

Scales and Double Stops

Two standard violin scale books with worldwide acceptance are *Scale System* by Carl Flesch that features scales, arpeggios, double stops, and artificial harmonics, and *Contemporary Violin Technique* in two volumes by Ivan Galamian and Frederick Neumann that features scales and arpeggios along with rhythmic and bowing variations. Two scale books that can be used in preparation to the above is the first part of *Scale-Studies* by Jan Hřímalý and *Complete Scale Studies* by Henry Schradieck. Preparatory double stops are Harvey S. Whistler's *Developing Double Stops*, and *Melodious Double-Stops* in two volumes by Josephine Trott. Also, *Preparatory Exercises in Double-Stopping*, Op. 9 by Otakar Ševčík.

Methods and Study Books

Among numerous selections, a couple of established methods are Ševčík's *Violin School for Beginners*, Op. 6, Wohlfahrt's *Foundation Studies for the Violin*, and another book worthy of

Figure 16.7 Violin's treble clef and open strings

attention is Erich and Elma Doflein's *The Doflein Method*. When it comes to early violin studies, étude books or compilations, Bériot, Campagnoli, Kayser, Mazas, Schradieck, Seybold (Op. 182), Sitt, Spohr, Wichtl, and Wohlfahrt are among the most influential pedagogues.

First and Half Positions

The explanation of first position on the violin is the ability to play all available consecutive notes of a tetrachord in a diatonic scale above an open string without having to shift: B-natural, C-sharp, D-natural and E-natural on the A string. A passing stretch of the fourth finger does not change that rule. Conversely, half position requires a backward shift of the left hand, meaning the move of the hand as a single unit with the thumb and forearm. Half position reduces the span of four fingers on a string allowing a sharpened version of the same letter of an open string through only a tetrachord: A-sharp, B-sharp, C-sharp and D-sharp on the A string (Figure 16.8). This span can be compressed further to accommodate a chromatic scale as A-sharp, B-natural, C-natural, and D-natural.

Stretches: stretches are a form of an extension and are a means to perform passing notes that are just above or below the regular position of the fingers. In other words, stretching the first finger backward or fourth finger forward allows that individual note to be played without having to cross strings or to shift into another position. The main rule of a stretch is that it is momentary and is done without having to move the thumb. By definition moving the thumb constitutes a position change and passing extensions are simply a stretch of that particular finger (Figure 16.9).

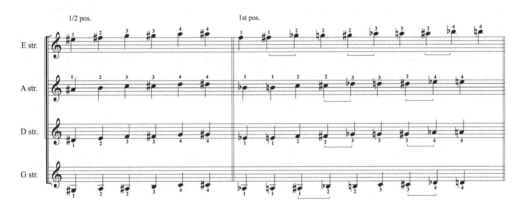

Figure 16.8 Violin fingering chart for half and first positions

Figure 16.9 Violin stretches

Higher Positions

In ensemble playing, higher positions are required primarily of the first violin in higher passages (Figure 16.10). This means that in orchestral playing, with the exception of sulla corda passages, E string is the only region of the instrument a student would have to perform in higher positions. This trend starts with the introduction of third position in enabling the student to play a two-octave D major scale. Aside from range-dictated higher positions, sulla corda playing in the interest of drawing different colors, shifting into positions that eliminate awkward string crossings, all require the student to be conversant in *all* strings in higher positions, not just the highest string. This facility must be acquired by practicing degree scales, or two-octave scales that start and end in a single position, and studies in higher positions. *Introducing the Positions for Violin* in two volumes (*Volume I*: 3rd and 5th; *Volume II*: 2nd, 4th, 6th, and 7th positions) by Harvey S. Whistler and *Above the First Position* by Markwood Holmes and Russell Webber are two wonderful resources when it comes to getting comfortable with higher positions. Arthur Seybold's *New Violin Study School*, Op. 182, a selection of studies including the higher positions (*Book 9: Studies on the Higher Positions*) is an invaluable source for developing proficiency in higher positions on all strings.

Repertoire

An invaluable source of graded solo violin repertoire, in addition to technical works as methods and studies is *String Syllabus Volume One*, edited by David Littrell. In the early stages of violin instruction, it is imperative to encourage the student with as much ability to play technically constructive and musically satisfying pieces. Collection of short pieces as *Violinists' First Solo Album: Volume One Elementary* by G. Perlman, *First Solo Album* by Whistler and Hummel, *World's Favorite Easy Violin Pieces*, published by Ashley, and *Miniature Masterpieces* by W. F. Ambrosio are some outstanding examples of accessible pieces with a rewarding and encouraging piano accompaniment.

Easy student concertos in first position, such as as Küchler Concertino in G Major, Op. 11, Rieding Concerto in G Major, No. 1, Op. 34, and Portnoff Concertino in E Minor, Op. 13 are marvelous examples. These and similar works allow students to build technique and perform melodious works written in the concerto form remarkably early in their violin education. Simple

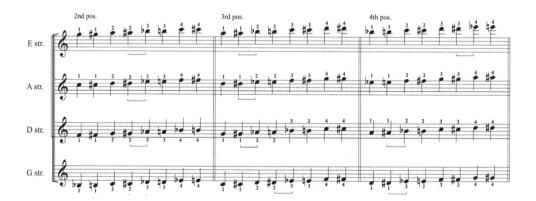

Figure 16.10 Violin fingering chart from second through fourth positions

duos played by two students, or by a student and teacher are also effective formats in the early violin education. Bruni *Six Easy Duets*, Op. 34, Gearhart and Green's *Fiddle Sessions for Two, Three and Four Violins*, Hindemith *14 Easy Pieces for Two Violins*, Kalliwoda *Three Easy Duos*, Op. 178, Mazas *12 Little Duets*, Op. 38 are several excellent examples of this setting.

Teaching the Viola

Instrument Size

An area of intense debate and concern is viola size. As with any string instrument, the overall size of the sound box or body of instrument is the determining factor of sound color of the instrument. Viola, due to its responsibility dictated by location between violin and cello, must be able to take violin-like and cello-like personalities as a particular register and character of a piece calls for it. In simple terms, the larger the body the more cello-like, the daintier the body the more violin-like sound quality the viola produces. Regardless of tone quality differences, the primary concern for a teacher when assigning instruments is proper sizing for the particular student. The greatest danger in assigning students too-large an instrument is twofold: first intonation is problematic when the student is unable to reach the longer span between notes, second continuous stretching over time can cause health problems. Therefore, much like the violin, both arm and finger parameters must be met when assigning a viola as dictated by the left arm slope when holding the instrument and finger span as determined by fingerboard strips.

Left Hand Specifics

When violin instructors teach viola students, some tend to treat the instrument like a "rather large violin," even though overall technique of the instrument is different. Left hand specifics of the viola resemble low strings for the fact that the second finger is used to pivot the hand that due to the large span between first through to the fourth fingers, therefore, viola players do not keep fingers down to the same extent as the violin players. Also, vibrato width and speed are not as narrow and fast as the violin. Aside from those differences most left-hand exercises and technical studies can be used interchangeably for the violin and viola.

Clefs

Majority of viola music is written in alto, or third-line C clef (Figure 16.11). In higher registers treble clef is used to avoid ledger lines and all'ottava or 8va writing (Figure 16.12).

Scales and Double Stops

The viola transcription of two standard violin scale books are *Scale System* by Carl Flesch, edited by Charlotte Karman, and *The Galamian Scale System Adapted for Viola* by Ivan Galamian and Frederick Neumann, edited by Karen Olson. Two scale books that can be used in preparation to the above is the first part of *Scales for Viola* by Enrico Polo, and *Scale Studies for Viola: Based on the Hrimaly Scale Studies for the Violin* by Leonard Mogill. Two preparatory double-stop books are Jane Daniel's transcription of *Melodious Double-Stops: Book 1* by Josephine Trott, and Alan Arnold's transcription of *Preparatory Studies in Double-Stopping*, Op. 9 by Otakar Ševčík.

Figure 16.11 Viola's alto clef and open strings

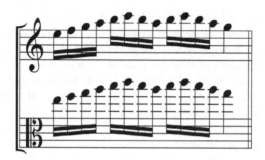

Figure 16.12 Viola's alto and treble clef comparison

Methods and Study Books

Among many, a few noteworthy methods are Hans Sitt's *Practical Viola School*, Antonio Bartolomeo Bruni's *School for Viola: Followed by 25 Studies* (text in Italian, French, and English), Berta Volmer's *Viola Method* (text in German and French), and Etienne Ginot's *New Method of Initiation to the Viola* (text in French, English and German). Influential pedagogues Bruni, Campagnoli, Kayser, Kreuzer, Mazas, Schradieck, Ševčík, Seybold (Op. 182), Sitt, Volmer, and Wohlfahrt are noteworthy authors of early viola studies, étude books or compilations.

First and Half Positions

The explanation of first position on the viola is the ability to play all available consecutive notes of a tetrachord in a diatonic scale above an open string without having to shift: B-natural, C-sharp, D-natural and E-natural on the A string, and a passing stretch of the fourth finger does not change that rule (refer back to Figure 16.9). Conversely, half position requires a backward shift of the left hand, meaning the move of hand as a single unit with the thumb and forearm. Half position reduces the span of four fingers on a string allowing a sharpened version of the same letter of an open string through only a tetrachord: A-sharp, B-sharp, C-sharp and D-sharp on the A string (Figure 16.13). This span can be compressed further to accommodate a chromatic scale as A-sharp, B-natural, C-natural, and D-natural.

Higher Positions

Much like with the violin, with the exception of *sulla corda*, the orchestral setting requires the student to get familiar with playing in the higher positions, albeit mostly on the A string (Figure 16.14). The facility of playing in the higher positions on all strings must be acquired

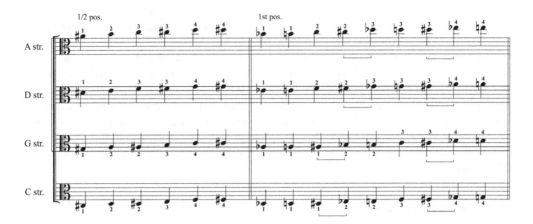

Figure 16.13 Viola fingering chart for half and first positions

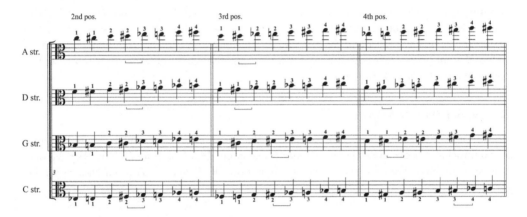

Figure 16.14 Viola fingering chart from second through fourth positions

by practicing degree scales, or two-octave scales that start and end in a single position, and studies in higher positions. *Introducing the Positions for Viola* in two volumes (Volume I: 3rd and 1/2; Volume II: 2nd, 4th, and 5th positions) by Harvey S. Whistler; and the viola transcription of Arthur Seybold's *New Violin Study School Books 6 and 8* (Book 6: 1st–3rd; Book 8: 1st–5th positions) Op. 182 are invaluable sources for developing proficiency in the first five positions on all strings.

Repertoire

A marvelous source of graded solo viola repertoire, as well as technical works as methods and studies is *String Syllabus Volume One*, edited by David Littrell. In the early phases of viola instruction, the student must be inspired by playing both technically beneficial and melodious pieces. Such collections in the first position as *Schott Viola Album: Eleven Transcriptions in the First*

Position by Raymond Dodd, or *First Solo Album* by Whistler and Hummel, are outstanding examples of accessible pieces with a rewarding and encouraging piano accompaniment.

Easy student concertos in the first position as viola transcriptions of Küchler Concertino in G Major, Op. 11, Portnoff Concertino in E Minor, Op. 13, Rieding Concerto in B Minor, No. 1, Op. 34, arranged by Philip Lehmann, Concerto in B Minor, Op. 35, and Concerto in D, Op. 36, and Concertino in G Major by Henri Classens are several good examples. Simple duos for two students or for a student and teacher are a wonderful way to introduce beginners into chamber music early in viola instruction. Samuel Applebaum's *Chamber Music for Two String Instruments: Book 1*, Kalliwoda *Three Easy Duos*, Op. 178, and *Fifteen Viola Duets from Keyboard Works of the Baroque Era*, edited by Lynne Latham are a few excellent examples of this setting.

Teaching the Cello

Clefs

Most cello music is written in bass clef (Figure 16.15). In higher registers tenor and treble clefs are used to avoid ledger lines and *all'ottava* or 8va writing (Figure 16.16). One potentially confusing irregularity for treble-clef writing is, composers like Dvořák and some of his 19th century Romantic contemporaries such as Schumann notated treble clef passages one octave higher than the sounding pitch (Figure 16.17). This octave-higher-than-sounding notation of treble clef still exists in orchestral scores and parts, though some have been corrected by contemporary tenor clef standards.

Scales and Double Stops

At the preparatory level *Elementary Scales and Bowings* by Harvey S. Whistler and Herman A. Hummel and *Scales: Book One* by Samuel Applebaum, *Double Stops for Cello* by Rick Mooney can be mentioned. *Daily Exercises for Violoncello* by Louis R. Feuillard, *Technical Studies* by Julius

Figure 16.15 Cello's bass clef and open strings

Figure 16.16 Cello's common bass, tenor, and treble clef registers

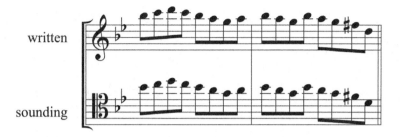

written

sounding

Figure 16.17 Dvořák *Carnival* Overture, Op. 92, mm 270–71, cello treble clef as written and sounding pitch in tenor clef

Klengel, *Violoncello Technique* by Mark Yampolsky, and *The Ivan Galamian Scale System for Violoncello* arranged and edited by Hans Jørgen Jensen are all-encompassing technical proficiency works for cello.

Methods and Study Books

Among others, a few method choices are *Method for the Violoncello* by Carl Fischer, *Practical Method for Violoncello* by Joseph Werner, Studies of the Young Cellist (text in English, French, and German) by Louis R. Feuillard, Method for Cello by Carlo Alfredo Piatti, and *The Art of Cello Playing* by Louis Potter, Jr., *Tune a Day* series by C. Paul Herfurth is a good example of a bifold string method book suitable for both classroom use and individual lessons. *Playing the String Game: Strategies for Teaching Cello and Strings* by Phyllis Young is an invaluable resource to introduce foundational concepts to younger students in the form of games that can be adapted to all string instruments. Early cello studies or compilations by prominent cello pedagogues as Dotzauer, Feuillard, Kummer (Op. 60), Lee (Op. 101), Popper, and Schroeder make up the majority of cello technical repertory.

First and Half Positions, Backward and Forward Extensions

The explanation of first position on the cello is the ability to play all available consecutive notes of a tetrachord in a diatonic scale, including an open string without having to shift: open A string, B-natural, C-sharp, and D-natural (Figure 16.18). Extensions are a significant element of the cello left-hand technique and critical part of early cello education. They are classified as backward, or first finger, and forward, or fourth finger extensions (Figure 16.19). In either case, the distance between second through to the fourth fingers remains the same, and the first finger is the only one stretched from a minor second to a major second by way of pivoting, much like the K-shape of the double bass left hand. Normally the left hand on the cello covers the distance of a minor third: that is E-natural to G-natural on the D string in the first position, also known as the closed position. The extension allows players to expand the span between the first and fourth finger and produce a major third within the position: that is E-natural to G-sharp on the D string in the first position, or E-flat to G-natural, also known as the extended position. An important quality of an extension is that it is momentary, and that the student should not keep the first finger extended to avoid a prolonged static tension. Unlike the thumb rule of the upper strings stretches—that its move signifies a shift—in the cello extensions, the thumb moves with the second finger to allow the second through to the fourth finger distances to remain the same without causing undue tension to the hand.

Figure 16.18 Cello fingering chart for half and first positions, backward and forward extensions

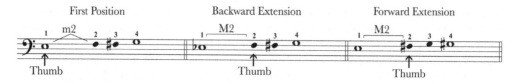

Figure 16.19 Cello extensions

Higher Positions and Thumb Position

A positive initiation into positions can be accomplished with *Introducing the Positions for Cello* in two volumes (*Volume I*: 4th; *Volume II*: 2nd, 2 1/2th, 3rd, and 3 1/2th positions) by Harvey S. Whistler, Otakar Ševčík's *Changing the Positions Opus 8* arranged by Orlando Cole, and *Position Pieces for Cello* by Rick Mooney. Much like upper strings, it is most likely for a cellist to encounter higher positions on the highest A string (Figure 16.20). Therefore, it is necessary for a cellist to gain proficiency in higher positions on all strings. This must be acquired by practicing scales, as in one-octave scales on one string, studies in higher positions, and pieces as *Position Pieces for Cello*, book two (5th through 7th positions) by Rick Mooney.

Cello thumb position can be introduced as a fingering option on the first-partial harmonics during tuning, as explained in Tuning with the First Partial section (Lesson 5). Thumb position is not necessary to reach the highest positions of the fingerboard, however, it is necessary for the fact that it enables the player to move between adjacent strings with agility and execute double stops in higher positions (Figure 16.21). Placing thumb position on the first-partial harmonic serves two purposes: fourth position at the end of the neck provides physical alignment for the thumb with the first finger, then a shift to the thumb position on A harmonic gives further confidence that transitioning the thumb from back of neck onto the string is not as intimidating. In addition to cello method books, particular thumb exercises such as *Thumb Position for Cello*, in two volumes, by Rick Mooney would help students build self-assurance in thumb position.

Figure 16.20 Cello fingering chart from second through fourth positions

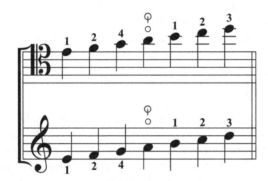

Figure 16.21 Cello thumb position on A string in treble and tenor clefs

Although it is extensively used in higher positions, thumb position can be called upon in lower sections of the fingerboard. For instance, thumb position is used to execute octaves and ondeggiando passages, as low as the first through to fourth position regions on all strings. In the cello repertoire, Boccherini's and Haydn's cello concertos make extensive use of thumb positions: virtuoso passages with continuous string crossings, mixed double-stops, including octaves both in broken and block forms.

Repertoire

An excellent reference of graded solo cello repertoire, in addition to technical works as methods and studies is *String Syllabus Volume One*, edited by David Littrell. Applebaum's *Building Technic Through Beautiful Music* is a collection meant for classroom or individual instruction, containing elementary-level tuneful melodies linked with various bow strokes. Erich Doflein's *Collection of Small Pieces, Playful Book for Violoncello* (duets and solos in first position), and *Bach for the Cello*: *Ten Pieces in the First Position*, transcribed by Charles Krane, and Three Easy Pieces (first position) by Paul Hindemith are good examples of accessible collections for the cello. Jean-Baptiste Bréval's Sonata in C and Fourth Concertino in C (in first position), edited by Ruyssen are attractive yet accessible works that introduce cello students to multi-movement forms of sonata and concerto early in their education.

Teaching the Bass

Clefs and Register

Much double bass music is written in bass clef (Figure 16.22),[2] and sounds an octave lower than notated. In higher registers tenor and treble clefs are used to avoid ledger lines and *all'ottava* or 8va writing in advanced levels (Figure 16.23).

Scales

At the preparatory level, *Elementary Scales and Bowings* by Harvey S. Whistler and Herman A. Hummel and *Scales: Book One* by Samuel Applebaum are classroom materials that can be used for individual instruction. *Scales, Triads, and Exercises for String Bass Beginners* by Dmitri Shmuklovsky, edited by Lucas Drew, can be used in preparation to the below method books that feature comprehensive scales, arpeggios and broken intervals as thirds, fourths, fifths, sixths, sevenths, and octaves.

Methods and Study Books

Representative method book of the French school of playing is Edouard Nanny's *Complete Method for String Bass*. Czech bassist Franz Simandl represents the Prague or colloquially known as German school of playing in his *Complete Method for Double Bass*, a method book with an orchestral emphasis, which is still used in music schools worldwide.[3] Incidentally, classroom studies and method books as *Essential Elements*, *String Explorer*, et al. are based on the Simandl

Figure 16.22 Double bass's bass clef and open strings

Figure 16.23 Double bass's common bass, tenor, and treble clef registers

position organization. *A New Technique of the Double Bass* in three volumes (2012) (text in French, English, German, and Spanish) by François Rabbath (*b* 1931 in Aleppo, Syria), is a unique bass method that uses the thumb pivoting in order to reach a larger span than Simandl or Nanny, reducing the bass fingerboard into six positions. George Vance and Annette Costanzi's book, titled *Progressive Repertoire for the Double Bass: Volume 1* (2000) functions as preparation to the Rabbath method. In preparation to Sturm's *110 Studies: Vol I*, Op. 20, and Simandl's *30 Etudes for the String Bass*; Thomas B. Gale's *Practical Studies for Double Bass, Melodic Foundation Studies*, and *Technical Foundation Studies*, are valuable building blocks.

Simandl versus Nanny System

Simandl and Nanny methods start with half position and advance through positions (or degrees) in sequential order. Simandl breaks down positions into halves: half position, first position, second position, second and a half position, third position, third and a half position and so on (Figure 16.24). Nanny on the other hand labels the same left-hand span by degrees. He labels positions in whole numbers, although he assigns two degrees per lower position: first degree, first position, second degree, first position, third degree, second position, fourth degree, second position and so on (Figure 16.25).

For example, second and a half position in Simandl corresponds with the second position fourth degree in the Nanny system. There is, however, further complications in the Nanny system, where he labels second position fourth degree and its enharmonic equivalency of third position fourth degree as two separate entities. Nanny's explanation of this discrepancy is as follows (Figure 16.26):

> The 3^d position (4th degree) differs from the 2nd (4th degree) in the name of the notes. The place of the fingers of the left hand is about the same: one comma from one another:[4]

Alternatively the more recent Rabbath system reduces half positions into whole positions by way of pivoting the thumb, also known as crab fingering. Preferred by some pedagogues, Rabbath employs left-hand flexibility to eliminate frequent shifting required by both Simandl and Nanny

Figure 16.24 Franz Simandl's Bass fingering chart from half through fourth positions

Figure 16.25 Edouard Nanny's Bass fingering chart from half through fourth positions

Figure 16.26 Nanny's C-sharp to D-flat one comma difference

systems. George Vance breaks down the Rabbath system further and makes it more accessible for beginning students in his *Progressive Repertoire for the Double Bass.*

Higher Positions and Thumb Position

Predominantly, instead of the fourth finger, the third finger is used in the sixth position and above, and thumb position is used for seventh position and above. Therefore, higher-position and thumb-position exercises and scales as Simandl's second part of *New Method for String Bass*, as well as specific studies as *Thumb Position Exercises for the Double Bass*, in addition to the latter two volumes of *Enjoy the Double Bass* method (*Vol 3: 5 1/2–7th positions* and *Vol 4: Thumb Position*) by Gerd Reinke are beneficial in becoming proficient.

Figure 16.27 Bass shift from fifth to thumb position on G string

The thumb position can be introduced for the bass as a fingering option on the first-partial harmonics during tuning, as explained in Tuning with the First Partial section (Lesson 5). Thumb position is not necessary to reach the highest positions of the fingerboard, however, it is necessary for the fact that it enables the player to move between adjacent strings with agility, execute double stops in higher positions, and frees the fourth finger. One example to transition to thumb position on the C string is to shift from fifth position directly to thumb position, for which the thumb can use G harmonic for intonation security in the early stages (Figure 16.27).

Repertoire

An exceptional source of graded solo bass repertoire, in addition to technical works as methods and studies is *String Syllabus Volume One*, edited by David Littrell. Applebaum's *Building Technic Through Beautiful Music* and *Solo Time for Strings*, books 1 and 2, by Forest Etling are two collections designed for either classroom use or studio teaching that feature accessible pieces. Also, *Leichte Spielstücke: für Kontrabass und Klavier: Teil I*, edited by Klaus Trumpf, *String Festival Solos: Volume 1*, by Samuel Applebaum, and *Festival Performance Solos* published by Carl Fischer are ideal examples of easy albums. The earliest student bass concertos require higher technical ability than other string instruments such as the violin. For example, Antonio Capuzzi's F Major Concerto (originally in D major), edited by Francis Baines, Benedetto Marcello's Six Sonatas and Vivaldi's Six Sonatas, both edited by Lucas Drew, are considered grade 4, or early-intermediate. Therefore, short pieces and accessible works like William Presser's Sonatina can be used earlier in bass education.

Assignment

1) Measure your assigned instrument's body length and string length.
2) Write one paragraph on the benefits of fingerboard tape use in string teaching, to be turned in next class.
3) Provide a list of beginner scale books, studies, and grade one repertoire for your assigned instrument, to be turned in next class.
4) Practice pizzicato and arco exercises.
5) Review today's lesson and read Lesson 17 prior to next class.

Notes

1 Alfred Schnittke wrote the scordatura section of second violin part in *Moz-Art* (after sketches by Mozart, K. 416d, for two violins, 1976) in alto clef.
2 This particular figure illustrates standard orchestral tuning, "solo tuning" will be discussed in Scordatura discussion in Lesson 21.
3 Originally published as *Neueste Methode des Contrabass-Spiels* in Vienna: Markus Krämer, 1874.
4 Edouard Nanny, *Méthode complète pour la contrebasse à quatre et cinq cordes*, 36.

Lesson 17

Contents

This lesson's objectives are:

- A brief discussion on influential pedagogical approaches in string teaching.
- Moving students between string instruments.
- A discussion on how to prepare for the secondary-school string program observation assignment.

Pedagogical Understanding of String Teaching

In order to understand string teaching from a holistic perspective, universal pedagogical approaches must be contemplated both philosophically and in practice. Teaching the technical side of strings may be examined separately, however, the philosophical foundation and all other aspects of teaching music should be integrated within the string discipline. In other words, doctrines of various prominent music pedagogues can be incorporated into a cohesive string teaching approach, as movement, singing, and experimentation are all as beneficial to string playing as rote techniques.

Émile Jaques-Dalcroze (1865–1950): Swiss educationist and composer Jaques-Dalcroze embraced his interest in polyrhythms and irregular rhythms in a eurhythmics method he created. The Dalcroze eurhythmics involve rhythmic steps and clapping by students as they react to teacher's improvised piano playing. Dalcroze's approach aims to connect mechanics of music with an internalized sense of musicality.

An article on how to integrate Dalcroze in string classroom:

Barbara Flooding and Kathy Thomsen. (2009). "Practical Dalcroze for String Teachers." *American String Teacher*, 59 (3), 28–32. doi:10.1177/000313130905900306.

Zoltán Kodály (1882–1967): Hungarian educationist, composer and ethnomusicologist, Kodály believed that any student capable of linguistic literacy is capable of musical literacy, a student is most receptive to musical instruction between ages six and sixteen, and it is the school's responsibility to provide it. Kodály's concept includes relative solmization, or moveable do, hand signs (attributed to John Curwen), rhythmic syllables (after Jacques Chevé), and a musical shorthand notation featuring stems without note heads, known as stick notation. In the string classroom there are numerous avenues of incorporating Kodály's approach. One way is for students to sing their parts before attempting on their instruments. As Kodály's method concentrates on developing aural skills, it is particularly advantageous for improving sight reading skills.

An article on how to integrate Kodály in string classroom:

Priscilla M. Howard. (1996). "Kodaly strategies for instrumental teachers." *Music Educators Journal*, 82 (5), 27. doi:10.2307/3398929.

Carl Orff (1895–1982): German educationist and composer, Orff's ground breaking work alongside Gunild Keetman *Orff-Schulwerk: Music for Children* has revolutionized early music education worldwide with the Observe, Imitate, Explore/Experiment, and Improvise/Create model of learning. Although the Orff system does not readily correspond with practical string teaching, it is possible to draw ideas and parallels from a learning strategy that includes play, dance, and drama.

Edwin E. Gordon (1927–2015): American scholar and music educator, Gordon has contributed to music education with *Musical Aptitude Profile* (1965) and developed a system he called Audiation: "Audation takes place when one hears *and comprehends* music silently, the sound of music no longer being or never having been physically present."[1] His *Music Learning Theory* is implemented in the *Jump Right In: The Instrumental Series for Strings* (GIA: 2000).

Shin'ichi Suzuki (1898–1998): Japanese violinist and educationist best known for his revolutionary Suzuki method, and books *Ability Development from Age Zero* (Athens, OH: Ability Development Associates, 1981) and *Nurtured by Love: The Classic Approach to Talent Education* (Smithtown, NY: Exposition Press, 1983). In 1933 he realized the ability of mother-tongue speech at an early age regardless of intelligence, much like Kodály, and that repetition of stimuli in the form of in-tune repetition of string playing with rote process would produce exceedingly positive results. This ability to follow rote-note method precedes any communication via written music and language by years, therefore it allows string education at a very young age. Suzuki Violin School has ten volumes (books one through eight feature recordings as books nine and ten are standard Mozart concertos), Suzuki Viola School has nine volumes (all books feature recordings), Suzuki Cello School has ten volumes (books one through eight feature recordings), and Suzuki Bass School has five books (books one through three feature recordings).

When taught by well-inculcated Suzuki practitioners who thoroughly comprehend his philosophy, and by conscientious non-Suzuki teachers who understand and follow his principles outlined in detail in abovementioned books, the method generates impeccable results. Indeed, the Suzuki method has been responsible for producing an innumerable number of musicians through the last seven decades including world-renowned soloists, chamber musicians, orchestral musicians, teachers, and non-professional string players alike. The Suzuki method's exceptional success in early string education is not arguable, the question then becomes when to expand it to incorporate sight reading that allows students to improve musical literacy outside the familiar guidance of the Suzuki method, and when to forego it altogether later in string education. It is a controversial question without a definite answer, that string teachers must use their judgment and decide on a case-by-case basis.

Paul Rolland [Reisman] (1911–1978): Hungarian born American violinist, violist, and string educator Rolland is responsible for the Illinois String Research Project (1966–70) that conducted research on motion studies and string playing with a medical and pedagogical consideration.

His research book and accompanying video recordings, titled *The Teaching of Action in String Playing* (University of Urbana, IL: Illinois String Research Project, 1970) [reissued in a single 201-minute DVD and 23 page booklet in 2008], and his collaborative work with Marla Mutschler, titled *The Teaching of Action in String Playing: Developmental and Remedial Techniques [for] Violin and Viola* (1974) [reprinted in 2007] are pioneering and exhaustive studies that make an ironclad case for Rolland's approach in building a solid, free of tension upper strings technique. The involvement of visionary physiologist, physiatrist, and physical medicine and rehabilitation specialist Frances Anna Hellebrandt, MD (1901–1992) in the project under the chapter, titled "Control and Regulation of Voluntary Movement: Application of Newer Knowledge to Violin Pedagogy" (1974) is significant for the fact that she illustrates the neuroscience relationship of Suzuki, Havas and Rolland's approaches in her chapter in prose and diagrams.

Kató Havas OBE (1920–2018): Hungarian born British violinist and teacher Havas has been influential in establishing her "New Approach" as detailed in *A New Approach to Violin Playing* (1961), its continuation of *The Twelve Lesson Course: A New Approach to Violin Playing* (1964) reject the idea of a rigid correct position for the preference of balance and motion, of which Dr Hellebrandt was a resolute proponent. Her influential book, titled *Stage Fright: Its Causes and Cures, with Special Reference to Violin Playing* (1973) is noteworthy of Havas's enduring legacy in removing fears all the way from dropping the violin, trembling bow arm, being out of tune, to the undue stress put upon string students in the pursuit of technical perfection.

Frederick Matthias Alexander (1869–1955): F. M. Alexander, an Australian actor diagnosed with chronic laryngitis, sought to cure the ailment by removing his neck stress and posture concerns. His ability to overcome his health issues and improve performances led to him sharing those techniques with others: first with actors then with the general public through his courses. Today, there are several thousand Alexander teachers who help performers, including string players. The Alexander Technique has been adopted by numerous string professors throughout the world, though any Alexander teacher with proper credentials can help a string player through workshops or private sessions. Both Rolland and Havas's approaches have been likened to Alexander, all three advocate to avoid strain and anxiety in string playing. Incorporated in 1988, The Performing Arts Medicine Association (PAMA) has been instrumental in expanding the discussion further than musculoskeletal concerns to hearing, mental health, nutrition, voice, and occupational health. Furthermore, PAMA makes recommendations to schools of music for health advocacy.[2]

Moving Students between Instruments

In a string program, an ensemble may not have a perfect ratio of instruments all by itself. String educators must work diligently, both in recruiting and in internal moves between sections, to keep a preferred number of strong players in each of the five sections in an ideal string ensemble: sixteen first violins, fourteen second violins, ten violas, ten cellos, and eight basses. In reality, a string teacher may have to start with an ensemble that comprises ten violins, zero violas, eight cellos and zero basses. There may be various reasons for this disproportion: seats of graduating students not having been filled due to inadequacies with feeder programs, an uneven number of students in sections due to shortcomings in school-owned instrument inventory, simple mismanagement, and any other arbitrary cause. Regardless of the cause, and in addition to urgent recruiting, a move between sections must be made in order to alleviate this hypothetical problem.

Transition between instruments is common practice, not just to keep favored proportions in an ensemble, but on account of growth, aptitude, and aspiration of developing string students. Rationale for moving a student between instruments may come from growth of the student and physical aspects of an individual. For example, a taller violin student with long fingers, may be better suited for the viola, or a cellist with particularly large and strong hands is perhaps better suited for the bass (see Instrument Assignment discussion in Lesson 2). However, if the idea of moving between instruments is initiated by the teacher, an in-depth conversation *must* take place with the student to discuss the rationale. Without the student's acceptance and endorsement, a transition is likely to harm the student's self-esteem. A positive way to broach the subject might be the student's potential of growth in the instrument, and leadership qualities of a student to be engaged in a section that is in need. In fact, there are countless examples of plateaued students excelling after a move to a different instrument. However, the unwavering encouragement and support of the teacher is central to keeping the student motivated after the transition. Below are *some* likely permutations, although *all* moves between instruments are possible and occur regularly.

Violin and viola: among the most common transitions between string instruments is the move between violin and viola. American violist of Austrian birth, Paul Doktor (1919–1989) describes a "scratchy and unpleasant" tone quality of a violinist starting on the viola.[3] Indeed, the instrument does require a different approach for the right-hand, as well as the left-hand technique. The bow arm must be adjusted to respond to a larger instrument's resonance, heavier gauge of the C string, and even in spiccato stroke's resonance as Doktor indicates: "All of the spiccato bowings should be played nearer to the string on the viola. The bounce should not be so high up, as the strings will not speak on most violas as quickly as on the violin."[4] Naturally these are only a couple of examples of issues encountered while learning a new instrument. The way strings respond, lower range of viola, vibrato speed and width, reading alto clef along with transition into treble clef are among the challenges a student must overcome. It must be noted that the left-hand technique appreciably differs from the violin by the fact that pivoting is necessary to reach the increased span of four fingers, much like with low string instruments. This way, intonation challenges caused by a larger instrument size are tackled properly. Harvey S. Whistler's forty-eight-page book, titled *From Violin to Viola: A Transitional Method* is an invaluable resource that addresses some of the most common technical issues encountered. In addition to Whistler's book, assigning accessible scales, arpeggios, and technical exercises are crucial in attaining proficiency in viola.

Cello and bass: it is more likely for a student to move from the cello to the bass. Different instrument holds and bow holds, the transition from C-shape to K-shape hand, different fingerings and tuning, vibrato speed and width, and tone production on the thicker gauge strings are all formidable challenges to conquer. Furthermore, understanding how to produce a proper tone with a good bite and not to skid on attacks, particularly on the E string, takes meticulous practice (see Lesson 3, Section G, Tone Production for a "slipping-attack"). For the bow hold there are two approaches: abandon the French, or overhand bow hold altogether and learn German, or underhand bow hold. This approach will start the student afresh on the bow grip and keep from transferring any habits from the cello. The second way would be to keep with the French bow grip and use the similarities between the two instruments' bow holds to benefit from the student's familiarity.

It is quite common for a bass guitar player to take interest in the double bass or upright bass in a string class. In addition to instrument hold, two obvious challenges are the bow-arm and left-hand techniques. The student would be expected to have an uneven proficiency, that bow arm would be at the beginning stages, where the left hand facility would have been developed further along. One prevalent issue with the left hand would be the use of the third finger. The bass guitar uses the third finger in low positions and double bass does not. Therefore, prompt formation of a K-shape left hand, with proper stretch between first and second, and second and fourth fingers is imperative.

Upper strings and low strings: the need to move a student between instruments does not only arise within upper strings and low strings, but also across the upper-strings and low-strings line. Even though, at first, it may appear to be a daunting challenge, given proper attention practice and encouragement, a successful move between any instruments is achievable. To accomplish that, the student must be observed closely and both posture and setup corrected as frequently as necessary. When transitioning between upper and low strings, the position of the left fingers and left hand, left arm slope, and bow grip pronation are most notably different. However, with an attention to establish a proper instrument hold, bow hold and develop rounded tone production, these differences will not endure and the student will progress reliably.

Preparation of Secondary-School String Program Observation

Visit an areas secondary-school's orchestra class. When you arrive at school, sign in at the main office and report to the orchestra teacher. Observe the class using the below form, so that your responses answer the form's questions precisely. Provide additional responses if needed and be as specific as possible on how the observed teacher approached certain technical aspects like instrument hold, bow hold, intonation, and sound production. The form will be due next class.

SECONDARY-SCHOOL STRING PROGRAM OBSERVATION FORM

Your Name: _____
Observed Teacher: _____
School: _____
Grade/Class: _____
Age Range of Students: _____
Technical Studies Covered: _____
Repertoire Rehearsed (if applicable): _____

What was the objective of the class?

How did the observed teacher work on achieving those objectives?

How attentive were the students in their work?

How successfully did the observed teacher attain class objectives?

What was the overall atmosphere of the class?

How was the observed teacher's time management?

What forms of classroom management did the observed teacher use?

Did the observed teacher follow a teaching cycle?

What did you like about the observed teacher?

What would you do differently if you were teaching the observed class?

Additional Observations:

Assignment

1) Provide a list of string pedagogues discussed in this lesson with a brief narrative of their achievements.
2) Practice pizzicato and arco exercises.
3) Prepare for your upcoming secondary-school string program visit and reconfirm your visit with the teacher you are planning to observe.
4) Review today's lesson and read Lesson 18 prior to next class.

Notes

1 Gordon, *A Music Learning Theory for Newborn and Young Children: 2013 Edition*, 25, emphasis in original.
2 https://hpsm.unt.edu (accessed February 2, 2020).
3 Applebaum, *The Way They Play, Book 1*, 228.
4 Ibid., 230–31.

Lesson 18

Contents

This Lesson's Objectives are:

- Student presentations of secondary-school string program visit assignment and a discussion.
- A brief discussion on legato playing and its exercises.

A Presentation and a Discussion on the Secondary-School String Program Visit

Students will present their observation based on the Secondary-School String Program Observation Form, immediately followed by a class discussion facilitated by the instructor. Students should be prepared to answer these follow-up questions:

- Did the observed teacher demonstrate, and if so, in what context?
- How was the observed teacher's rapport with the students, and how do you think it relates to teaching effectiveness?
- How do time management and teaching effectiveness relate?
- How do teaching cycle and teaching effectiveness relate?
- How close was the overall level of students?
- How do you think class size (as in number of students) affected the observed class?
- What technical deficiencies did you observe in the students?

Legato Playing, and Its Exercises

In string playing, legato indicates to play "successive notes in performance, connected without any intervening silence of articulation."[1] The legato bow stroke can be played both with separate and slurred notes: legato and legato slur respectively. As notes within a single slur are naturally connected, both bow changes in between slurs and bow changes between separate legato notes are also played in a connected manner. A nuanced legato playing differs from détaché in that it is *more* connected and requires the movement of the right wrist, hand and fingers. In the early stages of instruction legato playing is not asked of students, however, left-hand exercises that promote smooth motion are necessary in building right-hand technique that enables the execution of the legato bow stroke. The pencil exercises (Lesson 2) and Swimming Octopus exercise (Lesson 3) are vital to preparing the right arm and hand, as legato playing is impossible to execute with a stiff bow hold. There are two factors in executing a legato bow stroke: keeping bow weight into the string during the bow change, and a split-second anticipation of the right wrist.

To build upon pencil and Swimming Octopus, two more advanced exercises are ideal in explaining the abstract notion of "feeling the string resistance" to the student. First, away from the instrument, and second on the instrument.

Finger Dragging exercise: while sitting at a table, students imagine holding a bow and dragging their finger tips on a table allowing the natural arm weight to create friction with the surface. Set the metronome to 60 and move the right arm from left to right, or down bow for four beats, and move right to left, or up bow for four beats (Figures 18.1, 18.2, and 18.3). The right wrist should lead the motion, and utmost attention should be given to keeping the weight in the arm during direction change. First, the instructor will model the exercise for the class, then students will repeat it where the instructor will walk around the room to help students as needed.

Rubber Band exercise: once the students are comfortable with the Finger Dragging exercise, they pick up their instruments, a rubber band is attached through the frog and tip of bow and with one student holding the rubber band taut, the other student plays the above exercise on an open string (Figures 18.4 and 18.5). The right wrist should lead the motion, and utmost attention should be given to keeping the weight of the arm during the direction change. First, the instructor will model the exercise for the class with the assistance of a student, then students will repeat it in pairs as the instructor will walk around the room to observe and help.

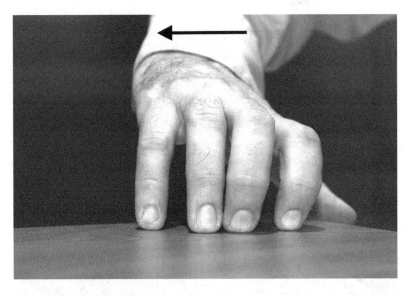

Figure 18.1 "Down bow" Finger Dragging exercise

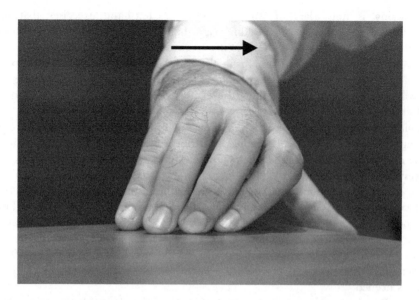

Figure 18.2 "Up bow" Finger Dragging exercise

Figure 18.3 Finger Dragging exercise

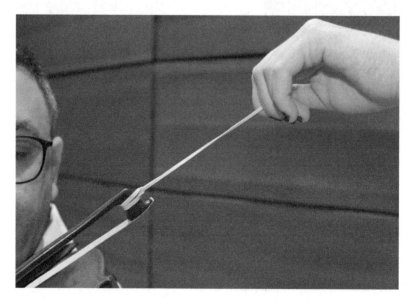

Figure 18.4 Holding the rubber band on down bow

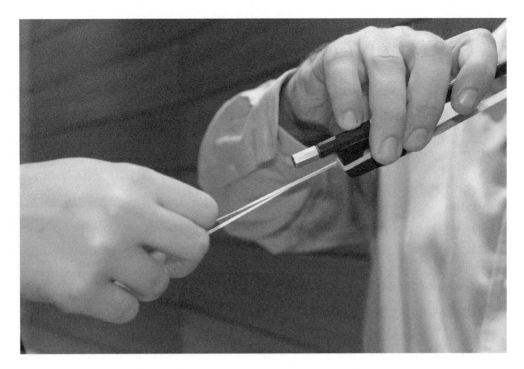

Figure 18.5 Holding the rubber band on up bow

Assignment

1) Write one paragraph reflecting on your visit and today's discussion on it.
2) Practice pizzicato and arco exercises.
3) Review today's lesson and read Lesson 19 prior to next class.

Note

1 Chew, "Legato."

Lesson 19

Contents

This lesson's focus is:

- A discussion on shifting, vibrato, and trill exercises.

Shifting, Vibrato, and Trill Exercises

Teaching Vibrato, and Shifting

In string music education "when to introduce vibrato" is a valid question. The definition of vibrato is the intentional wavering of otherwise perfect pitch in pursuit of a pleasing tone quality. Therefore, students must have a good understanding of, and the ability to play with solid intonation. Furthermore, the student must have a well-developed left-hand technique that is facile, free of tension, with a straight wrist and a perfect mold of fingers. Just because the abovementioned requirements must be met before vibrato is incorporated into one's playing, it does not mean the introduction cannot be made before the students are ready for full implementation of vibrato. On the other hand, even after vibrato and shifting are introduced, both pre-shifting and pre-vibrato exercises may continue concurrently with regular exercises.

1)   Pre-Shifting Exercises

Pre-shifting and pre-vibrato exercises can precede the actual implementation of these techniques by an extended period of time, as a matter of fact, many successful string teachers introduce these exercises quite early in their curriculum. One such exercise is to slide the arm up and down with the first finger and thumb placed on a cylindrical object as a mailing tube, both acting as and positioned as a fingerboard. For upper strings the tube will be placed on top of the student's shoulder, for lower strings it will be positioned above the shoulder. A piece of rolled paper under the hand will ensure smooth shifting motion without squeezing the tube (Figures 19.1 and 19.2). Much like in pre-bowing exercises, the task of achieving a smooth shift is isolated away from the instrument and once students are comfortable with the motion, it is moved onto the fingerboard.

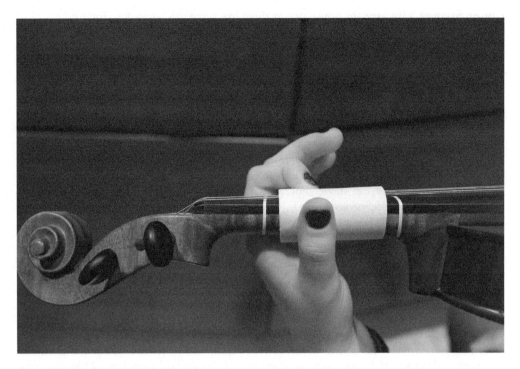

Figure 19.1 Shifting with paper on upper strings

Figure 19.2 Shifting with paper on low strings

Upper Strings Vibrato: for upper strings there are three categories for vibrato:

A)   Finger vibrato signifies the smallest part of the arm associated with the vibrato motion. The most minimal vibrato motion is initiated by the arm, only the first joint appears to move. This is due to the minute amount of vibrato provided, but *not* because the first joint initiates the motion. (Common problems associated with finger vibrato were discussed in Lesson 14.)

B)   Wrist vibrato limits the motion to the wrist and finger joints and excludes the forearm. It is a variety of vibrato that is preferred by some teachers. In a heterogeneous string classroom, it can be omitted as arm vibrato correlates perfectly with shifting and is aligned with the low strings vibrato motion.

C)   Arm vibrato uses the entire arm as active components of the shake motion. The upper arm, forearm, wrist, all three joints of a finger are active participants in the vibrato motion. In a heterogeneous string class, we will focus on arm vibrato, rather than wrist vibrato, as it closely resembles the low strings vibrato.

Low Strings Vibrato: both the cello and double bass share the same motion for the vibrato and it closely resembles that of the arm vibrato of upper strings. When vibrating the entire arm moves, including the upper arm, forearm, wrist, and all three joints of a finger.

1)   Pre-Vibrato Exercises: pre-vibrato exercises are fun activities for the class that often involves percussion instruments. Either a store-bought egg shaker, or a home-made version can be employed for this exercise. Common and inexpensive items like plastic Easter eggs or empty pill bottles can be used as shakers and any seed or grain as corn, rice, or beans as rattle elements (Figure 19.3). Have students hold shakers in the proper position for upper string or a low string instruments. Then have the class shake the instruments rhythmically with a vibrato motion to a metronome beat or a recorded piece of music, first to a slow beat then work up to faster tempos.

Figure 19.3 A homemade vibrato exercise device

Once the students are comfortable with this exercise, move onto the mailing tube, go through the same progressive metronome and recorded music regimens with the matching tempo of the vibrato motion. Once comfortable with the mailing tube, finally move onto instruments to apply the vibrato motion.

Shifting and Vibrato Exercises on the Instrument:

Since both the vibrato and shifting motions share the same attribute of shortening or lengthening the playable span of the string, they can be introduced concurrently in a heterogeneous string class. First, have students start sliding up and down on their fingerboards with inexact pitch, freely on all strings. This free and smooth motion will establish the minimal weight of fingers while in motion and the teacher will ensure the entire arm is engaged for this motion and fingers or wrist will not lead the slide, but the arm moves as a single unit. Once comfortable with the motion, the teacher will ask students to depart from and arrive at two given pitches: move first finger B-natural to D-natural and back to B-natural on the A string. Then, E-natural to G-natural and back to E-natural on the D string. Finally, A-natural to C-natural and back to A-natural on the G string. This shift motion is done without changing the left-hand mold, collapsing distances between fingers, and first-finger and thumb alignment. Lastly, violin and bass move onto the E string and viola and cello move onto the C string (Figure 19.4). This exercise can be practiced with the use of metronome and sound generator as a tuner.

Figure 19.4 Heterogeneous shifting exercises

Alternately, using the adjacent open string is a good reference point as it provides a drone tone during shifting exercises and eliminates the need for a tuner. For instance, when practicing shifting on the D string, the G string provides the perfect drone, as it is a perfect octave below G-natural on the D string.

- As the left hand may impede the vibrato motion for upper strings, because mistakenly the student might be supporting the instrument with the left hand, vibrato exercises may be executed by putting the scroll against a wall. To accomplish that, a piece of cloth is placed between the scroll and the wall, and the student proceeds with the vibrato exercise. Once the student is made aware of the left-hand freedom during this exercise, remove the instrument from the wall.
- Another way to free left-hand tension during vibrato exercises for upper strings is to ask the student to lie down on the floor and execute vibrato exercises. Much like the wall exercise, it should make the student aware of left-hand freedom.

A piece of rolled paper between the student's left hand and the neck/fingerboard can be used to break any unwanted tension while vibrating (refer back to Figures 19.1 and 19.2). Vibrato exercises are repeated on all fingers. Starting with the first finger, moving onto the second, third, and the weakest fourth finger. In all vibrato exercises the teacher must keep a close eye on hand position so that the perfect finger mold is not broken while vibrating. Much like the shifting exercises, it is preferable to optimize class time with heterogeneous vibrato exercises (Figure 19.5).

Teaching Trills

Much like with the vibrato, the constant speed and continuity of the trill are the most vital elements, and a string player must be able to execute trills between second and third, and third and fourth fingers just as well as first and second fingers. Third and fourth fingers are relatively weaker than the first and second fingers and it takes practice to learn, improve, and maintain those trills. Borrowing practice strategies from vibrato exercises, starting trills slowly and building speed and the number of turns and repeating on all fingers and strings is an effective way to build trills (Figure 19.6).

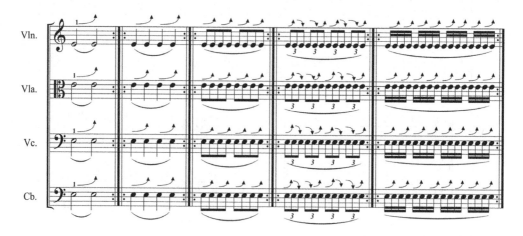

Figure 19.5 A heterogeneous first-finger vibrato exercise

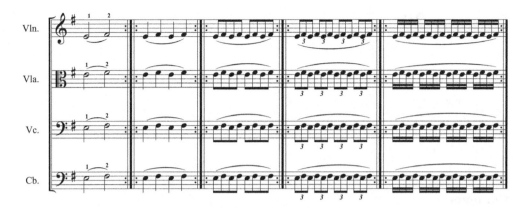

Figure 19.6 A heterogeneous first-and-second-finger trill exercise

Assignment

1) Write a double-spaced one-page essay on vibrato: its variations, when to introduce it, and its relationship with shifting.
2) Practice pizzicato and arco exercises in preparation for the third playing test.
3) Review today's lesson and read Lesson 20 prior to next class.

Lesson 20

Contents

In this lesson students will demonstrate the following:

- Proper posture
- Proper setup
- Good tone production

Videotaping of Third Playing Test

This lesson is dedicated to performing the third playing test. The instructor will be videotaping the playing test and evaluating it on the spot. Each student will play the selections which have been decided by the instructor. Each student will watch the videotape and complete the following Self-Evaluation Form III, using the posture, setup, and tone production guidelines established in class.

Videotaping Number 3

Name:_____**Instrument:**_____**Date:**_____**Grades**____/____

STRING PLAYING TEST RUBRIC III

First watch your video and read your instructor's evaluation of your playing. Afterwards watch your video again and fill out the below rubric. Leave correct items blank, mark any exceptional element by a plus sign and any element in need of improvement by a minus sign. You will receive a grade for full and accurate completion, and timely submission of this form. The form is due at the beginning of next class.

POSTURE—INSTRUMENT HOLD, LEFT HAND, PIZZICATO POSITIONING AND BOW HOLD

VIOLIN AND VIOLA

POSTURE, INSTRUMENT HOLD AND LEFT HAND

_____ torso is square
_____ shoulders are relaxed
_____ feet are positioned correctly
_____ head is not tilted and is free of tension
_____ instrument is supported on the collarbone without tension
_____ instrument is placed parallel relative to the floor and kept with the "nose-scroll-elbow-toe" alignment at all times
_____ wrist is straight from all angles
_____ hand is free of tension
_____ four fingers are curved and tips of fingers are hovering right above strings
_____ thumb is at a proper height and is free of tension

PIZZICATO POSITIONING

_____ hand and arm are at a proper angle to play pizzicato
_____ tip of thumb is placed at the corner of the fingerboard for secure pizzicato anchoring
_____ pizzicato is played with the index finger at a proper distance from the bridge

BOW HOLD

_____ shoulder is relaxed at all times
_____ elbow is relaxed and functioning smoothly
_____ wrist is slightly higher than knuckles
_____ all fingers are properly curved and spaced
_____ thumb's first joint is curved and tip of thumb is wedged against end of frog
_____ pinky finger is on top of stick
_____ forearm and wrist are slightly pronated and index finger is leaning toward the stick
_____ bow is always parallel to the bridge

_____ bow is at proper distance from the bridge with a constant contact point
_____ arm weight and index finger produce a sustained and even tone
_____ bow direction changes are executed smoothly and without stoppage
_____ string crossings are executed smoothly and without disruption

CELLO POSTURE, INSTRUMENT HOLD AND LEFT HAND

_____ seated on front four inches of seat with feet positioned correctly and flat on the floor in a position that can allow the student to stand up at any given time
_____ endpin is at a proper length with cello at a proper angle
_____ C peg is behind left ear, neck is one fist width above left shoulder and cello is tilted slightly to left
_____ cello is not pinched and knees are relaxed with instrument balanced without assistance of arms
_____ wrist is straight from all angles and draws a straight line from elbow to knuckles
_____ elbow height can allow the student to slide up and down on the fingerboard
_____ thumb is behind the second finger and the tip of the thumb is lightly touching the middle of the neck
_____ first joint of thumb is slightly rounded but not straightened
_____ first finger is slightly tilted toward the fingerboard and fourth finger is parallel to the first finger
_____ first to second and second to fourth fingers are equidistant from each other

PIZZICATO POSITIONING

_____ hand and arm are at a proper angle to play pizzicato
_____ tip of thumb is placed at the side of the fingerboard, last three- to four-inches of fingerboard for secure pizzicato anchoring
_____ pizzicato is played with the index finger at a proper distance from the bridge

BOW HOLD

_____ shoulder is relaxed at all times
_____ elbow is relaxed and functioning smoothly
_____ wrist is slightly higher than knuckles
_____ all fingers are properly curved and spaced
_____ thumb's first joint is curved and tip of thumb is wedged against end of frog
_____ forearm and wrist are slightly pronated and index finger is leaning toward the stick
_____ bow is always parallel to the bridge
_____ bow is at proper distance from the bridge with a constant contact point
_____ arm weight and index finger produce a sustained and even tone
_____ bow direction changes are executed smoothly and without stoppage
_____ string crossings are executed smoothly and without disruption

DOUBLE BASS SITTING POSITION

_____ seated tall with left knee behind bass right foot planted firmly on the floor
_____ endpin is at a proper length with bass at a proper angle
_____ instrument is slightly leaning back with the right corner of the instrument in front of the sternum with f-holes facing the conductor

STANDING POSITION

_____　standing tall, shoulders back with a straight spine

_____　endpin is at a proper length with the bass at a proper angle with the right corner of the instrument in front of the sternum

_____　the instrument is positioned diagonally in-front of the player with f-holes facing the conductor

INSTRUMENT HOLD AND LEFT HAND

_____　first finger is at eye level when placed on the first tape

_____　wrist is straight from all angles and draws a straight line from elbow to knuckles

_____　elbow height can allow the student to slide up and down on the fingerboard

_____　thumb is behind the second finger and the tip of the thumb is lightly touching the middle of the fingerboard

_____　first joint of the thumb is slightly rounded but not straightened

_____　first finger is tilted toward the fingerboard and fourth finger is reaching the fourth finger tape with a K-shaped hand

_____　first to second and second to fourth fingers are equidistant from each other

PIZZICATO POSITIONING

_____　hand and arm are at a proper angle to play pizzicato

_____　tip of thumb is placed at the side of the fingerboard, last three- to four-inches of the fingerboard for secure pizzicato anchoring

_____　pizzicato is played with the first joint of the index finger at a proper angle

GERMAN BOW HOLD

_____　shoulder is relaxed at all times

_____　elbow is relaxed and functioning smoothly

_____　thumb, index and middle fingers are joined at the tips

_____　all fingers are properly curved and spaced

_____　thumb's first joint is curved and the tip of the thumb is behind stick, but not on top

_____　forearm and wrist are supinated at a proper angle

_____　bow is always parallel to the bridge

_____　bow is at a proper distance from the bridge with a constant contact point

_____　arm weight and index finger produce a sustained and even tone

_____　bow direction changes are executed smoothly and without stoppage

_____　string crossings are executed smoothly and without disruption

FRENCH BOW HOLD

_____　shoulder is relaxed at all times

_____　elbow is relaxed and functioning smoothly

_____　wrist is slightly higher than knuckles

_____　all fingers are properly curved and spaced

_____　thumb's first joint is curved and the tip of the thumb is wedged against end of frog

_____　forearm and wrist are slightly pronated and index finger is leaning toward the stick

_____　bow is always parallel to the bridge

_____　bow is at proper distance from bridge with a constant contact point

_____　arm weight and index finger produce a sustained and even tone

_____   bow direction changes are executed smoothly and without stoppage
_____   string crossings are executed smoothly and without disruption

Scale: intonation, accuracy, and fingering

Piece: intonation, accuracy, and fingering

Evaluation Summary: provide a summary of your playing test by writing one paragraph on the positive elements of your playing and one paragraph on those elements in need of improvement.

1) A summary of positive elements.

2) A summary of elements in need of improvement.

Assignment

1) Complete Playing Test Rubric III, to be turned in next class.
2) Practice pizzicato and arco exercises.
3) Read Lesson 21 prior to next class.

Lesson 21

Contents

This lesson's objectives are:

- A discussion on the extended left-hand and bow techniques.
- A discussion on heterogeneous string class method books and their selection.

Extended Left-Hand and Bow Techniques

The extended left-hand and bow techniques mentioned in this lesson are not part of the beginning and intermediate string lexicon. Since they are mostly advanced techniques, the following are not likely found in the graded string repertoire.

Artificial Harmonics

Most commonly, artificial harmonics make use of the third partial, a perfect fourth above the fundamental, and create a new fundamental by stopping the string with the first finger and lightly touching the fourth finger in the violin and viola (Figure 21.1), or thumb and third finger for the cello and bass (Figure 21.2), to produce a sounding pitch two octaves above the fundamental. The standard notation for artificial harmonics is regular note head for the stopped fundamental and a diamond note head for the lightly-touched harmonic, although composers may notate the intended pitch in place of, or in addition to the standard notation. Although second and fourth partials are possible to produce in artificial harmonics on all string instruments, they are exceedingly rare in orchestral writing.

Scordatura

It., from *scordare*, "to mistune." Scordatura may be used to indicate any non-standard tuning. The instrument may be called to be "mistuned" ahead, or during the performance. One well-known example is the first violin solo in the opening measures of the symphonic poem, titled *Danse Macabre*, Op. 40 by Saint–Saëns (Figure 21.3). Scordatura may be called for to allow for unusual chords to be played as in *Danse Macabre*, or may be used to brighten the tone quality

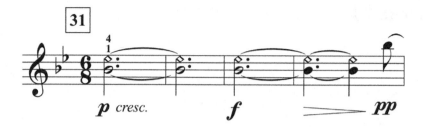

Figure 21.1 Glazunov Symphony No. 4, movement 2, Scherzo, rehearsal 31, first violins, artificial harmonics

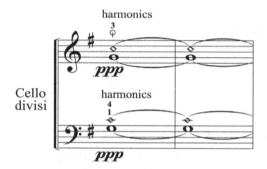

Figure 21.2 Verdi *Aida*, Act 3, mm 3–4, cellos, artificial harmonics

Figure 21.3 Saint–Saëns *Danse Macabre*, Op. 40, mm 25–32, first violin solo, scordatura

of the instrument as in the solo viola's minor-second higher than normal tuning on all strings in Mozart's Sinfonia Concertante, K. 364. Similarly, Paganini employed scordatura in several works of his, including the Concerto No. 1, where all four strings of solo violin may be tuned a minor second higher than normal (a predominantly abandoned version), and Introduction and Variations on "Dal tuo stellato soglio" from Rossini's *Mose in Egitto*, Op. 24, MS 23, "Mosè-Fantasia" for the G string, where the G string is tuned up to a B-flat. For double bass, so called "solo tuning" is used in soloistic repertoire and tunes all four strings a major-second higher than orchestral tuning: F-sharp, B-natural, E-natural, and A-natural (Figure 21.4). As a consequence "solo tuning" necessitates thinner gauge strings that are capable of withstanding this high tension.

Figure 21.4 Double bass solo tuning

Snap Pizzicato

Plucking the string away from the fingerboard in order to produce a snapping tone by striking the fingerboard. Through the string history only a few examples exist, as Bohemian born Austrian violinist composer Heinrich Ignaz Franz von Biber (1644–1704), who, in his programmatic work *Battalia* (Sonata di marche) (1673), asked violone, or double bass viol to execute a snap-like pizzicato to simulate cannon shots. Not until Hungarian composer Béla Bartók (1881–1945) did snap pizzicato become known, so much so that idiomatically the snap pizzicato is referred to as "Bartók pizzicato." Bartók indicates the snap pizzicato with an upside-down cello thumb position symbol, currently a standard notation (Figures 21.5).

Left-hand Pizzicato

Left-hand pizzicato is used to play both open strings and stopped notes. A higher finger number, such as the fourth finger, plucks the string sideways toward the palm of the hand making a lower finger number or open string sound. If the highest string needs to be sounded,

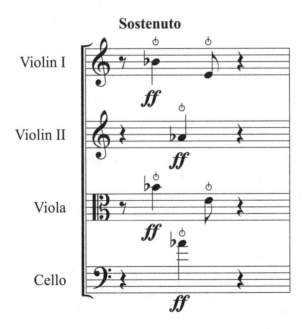

Figure 21.5 Bartók String Quartet No. 4, Sz. 91, movement 4, Allegretto pizzicato, m 119, snap pizzicato

Figure 21.6 Paganini Caprice Op. 1, No. 24, variation no. 9, left-hand pizzicato

Figure 21.7 Rimsky-Korsakov *Capriccio Espagnol*, movement 1, Alborada, mm 15–18, first and second violins, an alternating right- and left-hand pizzicato passage

the bow is struck onto the string toward the tip (Figure 21.6). Currently, the standard notation of left-hand pizzicato is a plus symbol. Primarily, left-hand pizzicato is used in virtuoso solo works as *Zigeunerweisen*, Op. 20 by Spanish violinist and composer Pablo de Sarasate (1844–1908) and Caprice No. 24, Op. 1 by Paganini. However, rarely alternating right and left-hand pizzicatos occur in orchestral writing, as in the first movement of Rimsky-Korsakov's *Capriccio Espagnol*. In Rimsky-Korsakov's example up stems indicate right-hand, low stems indicate left-hand pizzicatos alternating on open E string (Figure 21.7).

Col Legno Battuto *and* Tratto

Col legno (It. "with the wood") can be played both by striking the stick portion of the bow onto the string toward the tip (col legno *battuto*) or drawing it across the string (col legno *tratto*). In Violin Concerto in A Major, No. 5, K 219, "Turkish" (1775) Mozart indicates *coll' arco al rovescio* [with the reverse side of bow], effectively col legno for low strings (Figure 21.8). Another well-known example is the col legno passage of upper strings in *Symphonie Fantastique* by Berlioz (Figure 21.9).

Figure 21.8 Mozart Violin Concerto in A Major, No. 5, K 219, "Turkish," movement 3, mm 227–31, low strings, col legno passage

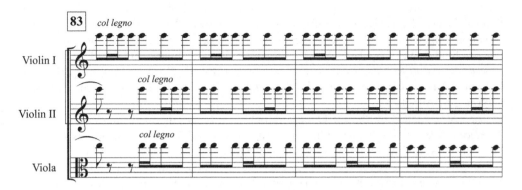

Figure 21.9 Berlioz *Symphonie Fantastique*, Op. 14, movement 5, A witches' sabbath, rehearsal number 83, upper strings, col legno

A Discussion on Heterogeneous String Class Method Books

Method books are among the numerous tools in a string teacher's hypothetical toolbox in the pursuit of imparting solid techniques and good habits in a positive learning environment. A method book should help accomplish fundamental benchmarks in an organized and timely fashion, function seamlessly within a purposeful string curriculum, and philosophically fit with the vision of a string teacher. To determine how a proposed method book would be a good fit, the first year's teaching goals must be established. First year's goals may or may not have been predefined for a teacher. Prudent and achievable goals are listed in *Teaching Stringed Instruments: A Course of Study*, which proposes to cover most of the first book of string method. The following instructional goals that correspond with Grade One level are expected: play with proper posture, instrument hold, left-hand and right-hand positions, keep a steady beat, accurate intonation, perform in the keys of D major and possibly G major, time signatures of 4/4, 3/4, and 2/4, play note and rest values of quarter, half and whole, slurs and ties, unison playing and simple harmonizations.[1]

Furthermore, the method book must work well with academic standards as Common Core, as well as the state or district standards to which the teacher must comply.[2] Some method book series feature repertoire pairings based on the level in the method book. Technology inclusion is another consideration, having started with the addition of accompanying CD recordings and DVDs in the last two decades, SmartMusic compatibility has now become commonplace among recent publications of method books. However convenient technology and text currency are, some old publications still hold their significance among teachers and are presently used and reprinted: *String Builder*, originally published in 1960, and *Müller-Rusch String Method*, published in 1961 are two perfect examples. The below is a list of method and technique books for classroom and ensemble settings.

Method Books

Spotlight on Strings: Level 1, Technique and Program Music for String Orchestra and Individual Instruction (2016) by Doris Gazda & Albert Stoutamire, published by Kjos.

Measures of Success: for String Orchestra (2013), with SmartMusic access, by Gail V. Barnes, Brian Balmages, Carrie Lane Gruselle, and Michael Trowbridge, published by FJH Music.

String Basics: Steps to Success for String Orchestra (2011), with SmartMusic and Interactive Practice Studio access, by Terry Shade and Jeremy Woolstenhulme, published by Kjos.

Sound Innovations for String Orchestra: A Revolutionary Method for Beginning Musicians (2010), with CD and DVD, SmartMusic access, by Bob Phillips, Peter Boonshaft, and Robert Sheldon, published by Alfred.

Simply Strings (2007) by Denese Odegaard, published by Northeastern Music.

Orchestra Expressions (2006), with CD and SmartMusic access, by Kathleen DeBerry Brungard, Michael L. Alexander, Gerald E. Anderson, and Sandra Dackow, published by Alfred.

New Directions for Strings: A Comprehensive String Method (2006) with two CDs and SmartMusic access, by Joanne Erwin, Kathleen Horvath, Robert D. McCashin, and Brenda Mitchell, published by FJH Music.

Introduction to Artistry in Strings (2005), with CD, by Gerald Fischbach, Wendy Barden, and Robert S. Frost, published by Kjos.

Essential Elements 2000 for Strings: A Comprehensive String Method (2004), with CD and DVD, SmartMusic and Essentialelementsinteractive.com access, by Michael Allen, Robert Gillespie, and Pamela Tellejohn Hayes, published by Hal Leonard.

Explorer (2002), with CD and SmartMusic access, Andrew Dabczynski, Richard Meyer, and Bob Phillips, published by Alfred.

All for Strings: Comprehensive String Method (1985) by Gerald E. Anderson and Robert S. Frost, published by Kjos.

Solo Time for Strings, Book 1: for String Class or Individual Instruction (1968) by Forest Etling, published by Alfred.

Müller-Rusch String Method: for Class or Individual Study (1961), by J. Frederick Müller and Harold W. Rusch, published by Kjos.

String Builder: A String Class Method (for Class or Individual Instruction) in Three Volumes (1960) Samuel Applebaum, published by Alfred.

Technical Books

Habits of a Successful String Musician: A Comprehensive Curriculum for Use During Fundamentals Time. (2014) by Christopher Selby, Scott Rush, and Rich Moon, published by GIA.

Daily Warm-Ups for String Orchestra (1993) by Michael Allen, published by Hal Leonard.

A Repertoire Book

The ABCs of String Orchestra (2000) by Janice Tucker Rhoda and Andrew Balent, published by Fischer.

Assignment

1) List extended left-hand and bow techniques and their brief explanations discussed in this lesson, to be turned in next class.
2) List method books discussed in this lesson, to be turned in next class.
3) Practice pizzicato and arco exercises.
4) Read Lesson 22 prior to next class.

Notes

1 Dillon-Krass and Straub, *Establishing a String and Orchestra Program*, 3.
2 Some examples for standards are: NAfME Core Music Standards, https://nafme.org/my-classroom/ standards/core-music-standards/, NAfME Ensemble Standards, https://bit.ly/2EQNAZ5, and ASTA Teacher Standards https://bit.ly/2xMspC9 (accessed February 2, 2020).

Lesson 22

Contents

This lesson's objectives are:

- A discussion on graded orchestra repertoire.
- Ways of avoiding pitfalls of over-programming.
- Spiccato exercises.

Selection of Repertoire: A Discussion on Graded Orchestra Repertoire

Both full and string orchestra repertoire classifications are broken down into six levels: grades one through to six—respectively from the easiest to the most challenging.[1] Separate from state lists, publishers follow their own grade systems which are widely subjective and concerned with, lists of educational publishers. For instance, educational publisher Alfred, under the direction of Bob Phillips, Director of String Publications, in its orchestra catalog meticulously breaks down the first five levels of the system into halves: level 1/2, level 1, level 1-1/2, etc. with precise parameters of key and time signatures, instrumentation, ranges, rhythm, and special considerations. Moreover, audio previews and score samples may be available on publisher websites, which are helpful in familiarizing oneself with a piece of music. Although not all educational publishers are thorough in their catalogs, and coupled with subjectivity of grading systems and profitability pressures those companies face, all level suggestions must be taken with a grain of salt. Additionally, relative strengths and weaknesses of each ensemble cannot be readily accommodated by a simplistic grade and the string teacher is the best person to make any such judgment call.

The most exhaustive study of repertoire in the discipline *Teaching Music Through Performance in Orchestra*, in three volumes, is an invaluable resource. It provides detailed information broken down into units under the Teacher Resource Guide for each composition examined: title of work, date(s) of composer, name of arranger (if applicable), instrumentation, biographical information of composer, biographical information of arranger (if applicable), composition, historical perspective, technical and stylistic considerations, musical elements, form and structure, suggested listening, and additional references and resources.

Although any grade system may be open to argument, the below list is a starting point in venturing into graded string orchestra and full orchestra repertoire. It is based on Florida Orchestra Association's Classification Rubric, which features a corresponding letter system. There is no substitute for knowledge: the more knowledgeable of repertoire string educators are, the better they can reason and positively overcome the fallibility of a simplistic grade system.

Grade 1:

• Only in the keys of D and G major.
• Basic rhythms (eighth, quarter, half and whole notes, minimal dotted notes).
• Written in a moderate tempo.
• Simple or duple meters only.
• Mainly homophonic, without much part independency.
• No tempo changes.
• One or two violin parts, third violin doubles the viola.
• First position only (double basses may encounter 3rd position in D major).
• Short compositions with an average length of one- to two-minutes.
• Basic form, simple repeat signs.
• Terraced dynamics only.

Grade 2:

• Keys of A and F and C major are added.
• More complex rhythms, including some syncopation, triplets and tied notes.
• Minimum changes of meter between 2/4, 3/4, 4/4, 6/8, and 2/2.
• Limited part independency, and some use of polyphony.
• Mostly written in the first position (double basses may encounter the 3rd position more extensively) cellos encounter forward and backward extensions.
• Some chromaticism.
• Slurred notes, staccato, hooked bowing, tremolo and accents.
• Some variation in articulation and bowings.
• More complex repeat markings as D.C., D.S. al fine or al coda.
• Dynamic changes are encountered, more dynamics are added.

Grade 3:

• Keys including three sharps and two flats, including minor keys.
• Some key changes, and mixed meter are encountered.
• More complex rhythms and syncopation.
• More independence between parts, and polyphonic writing.
• Shifting required in all instruments (upper strings up to third position, cello fourth, and double bass fifth).
• All bowings including spiccato and ricochet.
• More complex forms and repeat markings are encountered.
• All dynamics, and dynamic changes.
• Vibrato is appropriate.

Grade 4:

- Keys including four sharps and four flats, including relative minor keys.
- Multiple key changes, and any meter are encountered (including asymmetrical).
- Multiple meter and tempo changes.
- More demanding shifts are required (violins up to fifth position, viola up to third position, both cello and double bass fifth position).
- Faster tempos, and sustained notes in slower tempos.
- More complex and varied bowings and left-hand techniques.
- Vibrato is necessary.

Grade 5:

- All keys and changes.
- Greater stylistic demands.
- All positions are encountered.
- Most complex forms and length of works (including multi-movement compositions).
- Both vibrato and a full command of bow and left-hand techniques are necessary.

Grade 6:

- Essentially equal to, and including non-educational editions of string and symphonic-orchestra repertoire.

How to Avoid the Dreaded Over-Programming

As discussed above the grade system is both subjective and generic and cannot account for unpredictable specifics of an ensemble. In addition, string programs serve students of a wide variety of backgrounds, technical and musical maturity, and an abundance of other variables. Even within a well-matched ensemble, a piece of music may overwhelm one student, while it fails to challenge another. To a great extent, grade systems focus on technical aspects of repertoire, but not musical challenges, with the musical expression seen as the topping of the proverbial cake of technical ability, and not achieved without succeeding in mechanical facility first. James Kjelland's criticism of an arrangement of a Bach chorale's grading that requires sostenuto, or sustained playing is as follows:

> Sustained bowing, such as in an adagio-style piece, for example, can be extremely challenging and may not be taken into consideration in the grade level determination. An arrangement of Bach's chorale, "Come Sweet Death," is marketed as a Grade 3 piece, when in actuality it could challenge a Grade 5 orchestra. For that matter, any advanced orchestra can be challenged musically by a sostenuto piece.[2]

The perceived misclassification is not limited to sostenuto, but is extensive in all technical and musical aspects of repertoire. Therefore, grade in itself is nothing but part of a benchmark, merely a starting point in the repertoire selection process. The string teacher *must* peruse the considered repertoire painstakingly for its musical value, technical benefits, and pedagogical substance. The "go/no-go decision" made by every safe pilot in aviation is analogous to picking string repertoire: part of being a contemplative string teacher is knowing when to accept a certain challenge and when to reject it. Aside from a blatant disregard for the ensemble's capabilities versus the demands of the chosen repertoire, one great misstep in selecting repertoire is underestimating the time it takes to learn a piece of music. In summary, programming conservatively with the "less is more" adage in mind, choosing achievable goals that can be accomplished within a given period, with reserve time for unforeseen events and time left to polish and mature the work is the prudent approach for any new string teacher.

Spiccato Exercises

To execute off-the-string or bouncing notes, spiccato is played at or around the balance point, and the exact location depends on the speed in which it is played: the slower the spiccato, the closer to the frog, the faster, the further toward middle of bow. All of this requires a perfectly supple bow grip, with which a player only guides the springing of bow, but does not "make the bow spring." A perfect analogy to the spiccato stroke is dribbling a ball, in both cases a subtle but defined human interaction with a connected external motion is what makes them work. Therefore, only a measured guidance of the bow spring is necessary, as over controlling will cause tightness of right hand and loss of bow-hold flexibility. It is critical in the early stages of string instruction that the bow grip remains flexible and the entire bow arm is free of tension. Without this solid foundation accomplishing an effective spiccato bow stroke is impossible.

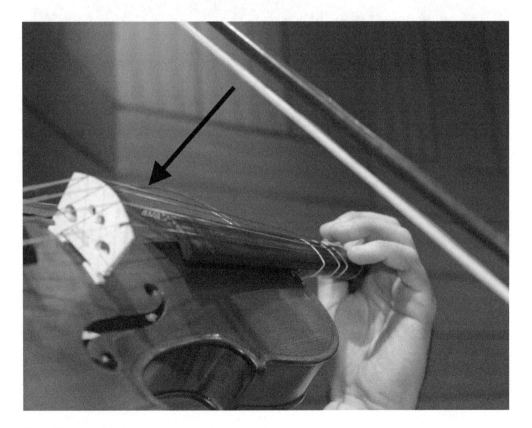

Figure 22.1 Upper strings bow drop

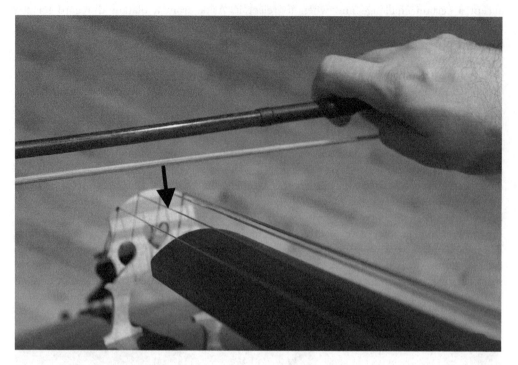

Figure 22.2 Low strings bow drop

Figure 22.3 A spiccato exercise

Figure 22.4 A slow spiccato one-octave D major scale

When it comes to preparing for the spiccato bow stroke, the earlier on-the-string collé exercises prepare the right wrist and fingers for the flexibility it requires. Spiccato will require suppleness of fingers and wrist, however, this diminutive bow stroke will be generated from the forearm. The first step in spiccato is to hover the bow four inches from the string at balance point, around the lower 1/3 of bow, and allow it to drop onto the string as a down bow with no trepidation (Figures 22.1 and 22.2). Repeat this motion numerous times observing the bow grip to make sure the right fingers and wrist are relaxed and a small spiccato motion comes from the forearm. Once comfortable move onto the below spiccato exercise, making sure to observe that the bow grip remains intact and flexible (Figure 22.3). Once pleased with reliability and control of motion, move onto a one-octave D major scale for a slow or artificial spiccato. This bow stroke is executed closer to the frog, at around the lower 1/4 of the bow, with the bow carried, bounced and controlled by the hand (Figure 22.4). As part of the warm-up routine, with the help of a metronome, slow spiccato exercises should become second-nature before speeding up slow spiccato further toward the balance point to a speed where it can spring on its own accord.

Assignment

1) Locate online and peruse the Florida Orchestra Association's Required Music List.
2) Locate online and peruse the Maryland Music Educators Association's String Orchestra List.

3) Locate online and peruse the Maryland Music Educators Association's Full Orchestra List.

4) Locate online and peruse the South Carolina Music Educators Association's String Orchestra List.

5) Locate online and peruse the Georgia Music Educators Association's Combined Orchestra List.

6) Locate online and peruse the New York Music Educators Association's Combined Orchestra List.

7) Locate online and peruse the Texas Music Educators Association's Combined Orchestra List.

8) Locate online and peruse the Florida Orchestra Association's Sight Reading Music Selection Guidelines.

9) Provide a string orchestra contest program at grade one using a state list of your choice from the above.

10) Practice pizzicato and arco exercises.

11) Read Lesson 23 prior to next class.

Notes

1 As this lesson focuses on the strings only, for specific technical requirements of wind and percussion sections in the full orchestra setting, refer to appropriate band music references.

2 Michael Allen, Louis Bergonzi, Jacquelyn Dillon, Robert Gillespie, James Kjelland, and Dorothy Straub. *Teaching Music Through Performance in Orchestra.* (Chicago, IL: GIA, 2001), 11.

Lesson 23

Contents

This lesson's objectives are:

- A brief discussion on what to expect in the first year of teaching and contest preparation.
- Writing lesson plans for individual instruction and classroom teaching.

A Brief Discussion on First Year of Teaching and Contest Preparation

The first year of teaching is among the most exciting and memorable times in a teacher's career. Whether the new string teacher works with other educators in a larger and established program or starts in a smaller one, the expected outcome is just the same: remarkably life-changing. Unbeknownst to the new teacher, the immediate impact on students is real and in return rewards of teaching affects one's life far beyond the power of imagination. Regardless of the exact job description, locale, or any other specifics, the new teacher must be able to adjust quickly to function in this new position that comes complete with its responsibilities. Energy, enthusiasm, and passion for teaching are all exceptionally helpful in overcoming both inherent challenges, and the anxieties of the unknown. Two areas of help are trusted mentors and the ability to draw from one's own experiences in the process of adapting to full-time teaching.

Among the most influential champions of string teaching and heterogeneous string programs, Jacquelyn Dillon-Krass stresses the importance of large classes between eight and twenty-four students in a heterogeneous string orchestra from the very beginning of string instruction. She points out the importance of securing the school administration's support of a string program and to keep string class sizes in those parameters in order to work within a streamlined academic schedule.[1] There are some items in a "to-do list" that are not necessarily apparent from the job responsibilities perspective. It is likely that the new teacher will have colleagues in the immediate region, as teachers of other schools, or feeder programs. It is prudent to establish a schedule of regular visits, promptly establish rapport and trust with teachers in the area, particularly of feeder schools, and collaborate. In the process of building one's program, or expanding an already established program, these are necessary steps.

Contest preparation in the first year of teaching may cause undue anxiety on the part of the new teacher. Preparing an ensemble for a high-stakes outside evaluation with immediate and tangible results is certainly intimidating. The new teacher likely deems the contest outcome an assessment of one's own teaching, and such self-imposed importance of one singular event is simply unjust and unrealistic. In fact, teaching excellence occurs on a day-to-day basis and a high-impact event such as a scheduled concert or contest participation is nothing but a natural extension of routine instruction. Actual preparation for those events occurs in the teacher's early planning and all the rest is implementing those set objectives. For a successful outcome, programming conservatively and challenging students with achievable goals in an organized manner is a prudent approach that has been proven successful. Selecting appropriate repertoire for an ensemble that demonstrates insightful understanding and encompasses diverse styles is the first meaningful step to successful concert and contest performances, as it establishes the priorities of a thoughtful string teacher. Additionally, reading articles written by established educators and adjudicators, such as Dr Mark Laycock's "Here Comes the Judge" is an expedient way to establish those priorities. For instance, scheduling sectionals and implementing seating rotations are among many of his excellent suggestions.[2] In addition to performing the contest repertoire at a preparatory concert, hosting an outside clinician as an adjudicator and performing a mock contest is an excellent "dress rehearsal" for the real event. To familiarize oneself with current contest rules and to prepare for those particular requirements will help eliminate all mysteries. When it comes to the contest itself, it is helpful to remember that adjudicators observe not only musical aspects but also the overall discipline of the ensemble as it relates to musical matters, and the serious approach of the director in extra-auditory details such as delivering well-marked, well-organized scores to judges sets the first positive steps to a successful performance.

Writing a Lesson Plan for Individual and Classroom Teaching

Individual Lesson

In preparation for the Videotaping of Individual Lesson session in Lesson 25, every student should find a student who has not played a string instrument previously, and write a lesson plan. For the purposes of this demonstration, students shall focus solely on the technical facet of their lessons: proper posture and instrument hold. Every aspect of the sample lesson must be accounted for, as adherence to time management is consequential for teaching effectiveness. This individual sample lesson will be dedicated to introducing a string instrument of choice, and both bow hold and right arm will be omitted. By the end of the lesson, the student should be able to hold the instrument properly and make sound by way of plucking. For this short lesson to be successful, the teacher must have a detailed lesson plan that needs to be planned out and practiced.

Teachers should plan for and practice the following:

- Turn to the audience and their students.
- Speak clearly and loudly for everyone to hear.
- Introduce your student to class.
- Speak with your student using age-appropriate vocabulary.
- First, name the parts of the instrument that the student needs to know for this lesson.
- Explain all of the terminology as they go along: "pizzicato means plucking the string."

- Explain and demonstrate the correct posture for the particular instrument, how to hold it, and the left hand/arm position. If the student does not have the accurate position, teachers must verbally and physically correct it.
- Prefer clear directions when offering feedback and avoid inexplicit words as "good" or "great."

Classroom Teaching

For the purposes of Videotaping of Classroom Teaching session in Lesson 25, the classroom teaching will be assigned as per the instructor's prerogative. As tasked by the instructor, every teacher should write a lesson plan, in which students shall focus solely on the classroom material. The lesson plan should spell out all objectives for the selected materials and indicate teacher's methodology.

Teachers should plan for and practice the following:

- Speak clearly and loudly for the entire class to hear.
- Use body and facial expressions to engage your students in a confident manner.
- Model when appropriate.
- Instruct class clearly of the task to be performed.
- Keep speech to less than 15 seconds at a time.
- Keep all ensemble members engaged, whether they are performing at the time or not.
- Recognize and correct all important issues.
- Give clear feedback both in praise and criticism, avoid unconstructive words as "great" or "good."
- Follow a proper teaching cycle pattern as explained in Lesson 10.
- Be prepared to conduct or model as either activity is required.

Assignment

1) Write a paragraph on first-year teaching and contest preparation, to be turned in next class.
2) Find a student for the five-minute sample lesson.
3) Practice pizzicato and arco exercises in preparation to fourth playing test.

Notes

1 Dillon-Krass, "String Class Teaching Philosophy," 1.
2 Laycock, "Here Comes the Judge," 29.

Lesson 24

Contents

In this lesson students will demonstrate the following:

- Proper posture.
- Proper setup.
- Good tone production.

Videotaping of Fourth Playing Test

This lesson is dedicated to performing the fourth playing test. The instructor will be videotaping the playing test and evaluating it on the spot. Each student will play the selections which have been decided by the instructor. Each student will watch the videotape and complete the following Self-Evaluation Form II, using the posture, setup, and tone production guidelines established in class.

Videotaping Number 4

Name:_____Instrument:_____Date:_____Grades____/____

STRING PLAYING TEST RUBRIC IV

First, watch your video and read your instructor's evaluation of your playing. Afterwards watch your video again and fill out the below rubric. Leave correct items blank, mark any exceptional element by a plus sign and any element in need of improvement by a minus sign. You will receive a grade for full and accurate completion, and timely submission of this form. The form is due at the beginning of next class.

POSTURE—INSTRUMENT HOLD, LEFT HAND, PIZZICATO POSITIONING AND BOW HOLD

VIOLIN AND VIOLA

POSTURE, INSTRUMENT HOLD AND LEFT HAND

_____   torso is square
_____   shoulders are relaxed
_____   feet are positioned correctly
_____   head is not tilted and is free of tension
_____   instrument is supported on the collarbone without tension
_____   instrument is placed parallel relative to the floor and kept with the "nose-scroll-elbow-toe" alignment at all times
_____   wrist is straight from all angles
_____   hand is free of tension
_____   all four fingers are curved and tips of fingers are hovering right above strings
_____   thumb is at a proper height and is free of tension

PIZZICATO POSITIONING

_____   hand and arm are at a proper angle to play pizzicato
_____   tip of thumb is placed at the corner of the fingerboard for secure pizzicato anchoring
_____   pizzicato is played with the index finger at a proper distance from the bridge

BOW HOLD

_____   shoulder is relaxed at all times
_____   elbow is relaxed and functioning smoothly
_____   wrist is slightly higher than knuckles
_____   all fingers are properly curved and spaced
_____   thumb's first joint is curved and the tip of the thumb is wedged against end of frog
_____   pinky finger is on top of stick

_____ forearm and wrist are slightly pronated and index finger is leaning toward the stick
_____ bow is always parallel to the bridge
_____ bow is at proper distance from the bridge with a constant contact point
_____ arm weight and index finger produce a sustained and even tone
_____ bow direction changes are executed smoothly and without stoppage
_____ string crossings are executed smoothly and without disruption

CELLO

POSTURE, INSTRUMENT HOLD AND LEFT HAND

_____ seated on front four inches of seat with feet positioned correctly and flat on the floor in a position that can allow the student to stand up at any given time
_____ endpin is at a proper length with cello at a proper angle
_____ C peg is behind left ear, neck is one fist width above left shoulder and cello is tilted slightly to the left
_____ cello is not pinched and knees are relaxed with instrument balanced without assistance of arms
_____ wrist is straight from all angles and draws a straight line from elbow to knuckles
_____ elbow height can allow the student to slide up and down on the fingerboard
_____ thumb is behind the second finger and the tip of thumb is lightly touching the middle of neck
_____ first joint of thumb is slightly rounded but not straightened
_____ first finger is slightly tilted toward the fingerboard and fourth finger is parallel to the first finger
_____ first to second and second to fourth fingers are equidistant from each other

PIZZICATO POSITIONING

_____ hand and arm are at a proper angle to play pizzicato
_____ tip of thumb is placed at the side of the fingerboard, last three- to four-inches of the fingerboard for secure pizzicato anchoring
_____ pizzicato is played with the index finger at a proper distance from the bridge

BOW HOLD

_____ shoulder is relaxed at all times
_____ elbow is relaxed and functioning smoothly
_____ wrist is slightly higher than knuckles
_____ all fingers are properly curved and spaced
_____ thumb's first joint is curved and the tip of the thumb is wedged against end of frog
_____ forearm and wrist are slightly pronated and index finger is leaning toward the stick
_____ bow is always parallel to the bridge
_____ bow is at a proper distance from the bridge with a constant contact point
_____ arm weight and index finger produce a sustained and even tone
_____ bow direction changes are executed smoothly and without stoppage
_____ string crossings are executed smoothly and without disruption

DOUBLE BASS

SITTING POSITION

_____ seated tall with left knee behind bass right foot planted firmly on the floor
_____ endpin is at a proper length with bass at a proper angle
_____ instrument is slightly leaning back with the right corner of the instrument in front of the sternum with f-holes facing the conductor

STANDING POSITION

_____ standing tall, shoulders back with a straight spine
_____ endpin is at a proper length with bass at a proper angle with the right corner of instrument in front of the sternum
_____ the instrument is positioned diagonally in-front of the player with f-holes facing the conductor

INSTRUMENT HOLD AND LEFT HAND

_____ first finger is at eye level when placed on the first tape
_____ wrist is straight from all angles and draws a straight line from elbow to knuckles
_____ elbow height can allow the student to slide up and down on the fingerboard
_____ thumb is behind the second finger and the tip of the thumb is lightly touching the middle of the fingerboard
_____ first joint of thumb is slightly rounded but not straightened
_____ first finger is tilted toward the fingerboard and fourth finger is reaching the fourth finger tape with a K-shaped hand
_____ first to second and second to fourth fingers are equidistant from each other

PIZZICATO POSITIONING

_____ hand and arm are at a proper angle to play pizzicato
_____ tip of thumb is placed at the side of the fingerboard, last three- to four-inches of the fingerboard for secure pizzicato anchoring
_____ pizzicato is played with the first joint of index finger at a proper angle

GERMAN BOW HOLD

_____ shoulder is relaxed at all times
_____ elbow is relaxed and functioning smoothly
_____ thumb, index and middle fingers are joined at the tips
_____ all fingers are properly curved and spaced
_____ thumb's first joint is curved and tip of thumb is behind stick, but not on top
_____ forearm and wrist are supinated at a proper angle
_____ bow is always parallel to the bridge
_____ bow is at proper distance from bridge with a constant contact point
_____ arm weight and index finger produce a sustained and even tone
_____ bow direction changes are executed smoothly and without stoppage
_____ string crossings are executed smoothly and without disruption

FRENCH BOW HOLD

_____   shoulder is relaxed at all times
_____   elbow is relaxed and functioning smoothly
_____   wrist is slightly higher than knuckles
_____   all fingers are properly curved and spaced
_____   thumb's first joint is curved and the tip of the thumb is wedged against end of frog
_____   forearm and wrist are slightly pronated and index finger is leaning toward the stick
_____   bow is always parallel to the bridge
_____   bow is at a proper distance from the bridge with a constant contact point
_____   arm weight and index finger produce a sustained and even tone
_____   bow direction changes are executed smoothly and without stoppage
_____   string crossings are executed smoothly and without disruption

Scale: intonation, accuracy, and fingering.

Piece: intonation, accuracy, and fingering.

Evaluation Summary: provide a summary of your playing test by writing one paragraph on the positive elements of your playing and one paragraph on those elements in need of improvement.

1)   A summary of positive elements.

2)   A summary of elements in need of improvement.

Assignment

1)   Complete String Playing Test Rubric VI, to be turned in next class.
2)   Write your individual lesson plan and classroom lesson plan to be turned in next class.

Lesson 25

Contents

In this lesson students will demonstrate the following:

- Proper teaching traits as discussed in Lesson 23.
- Good tone production.

Videotaping of Individual Lesson and Classroom Teaching

This lesson is dedicated to teaching a mini individual lesson to a student who does not have any prior string instruction, and a brief classroom teaching session. The instructor will be videotaping your teaching and evaluating it on the spot. Each student will teach the class a specific section which has been selected by the instructor. Each student will watch the videotape and complete the following Self-Evaluation Forms, using the guidelines established in Lesson 23.

Name:_____**Instrument:**_____**Date:**_____**Grades**____/____

INDIVIDUAL LESSON RUBRIC

First, watch your video and read your instructor's evaluation of your teaching. Afterwards watch your video again and fill out the below rubric. Leave correct items blank, mark any exceptional element by a plus sign and any element in need of improvement by a minus sign. You will receive a grade for full and accurate completion, and timely submission of this form. The form is due as per your instructor's directions.

_____   speech clarity and volume
_____   demonstration of correct posture
_____   model as needed
_____   proper and timely use of terminology
_____   interaction and rapport with the student
_____   teaching effectiveness
_____   clear instruction of the task to be performed
_____   use of age-appropriate vocabulary
_____   appropriately and timely naming of the parts of the instrument
_____   recognize and correct all important issues
_____   provide clear directions when offering feedback

Evaluation Summary: provide a summary of your individual lesson by writing one paragraph of the positive elements of your teaching and one paragraph on those elements in need of improvement.

1) A summary of positive elements.

2) A summary of elements in need of improvement.

Name:_____**Instrument:**_____**Date:**_____**Grades**____/____

CLASSROOM TEACHING RUBRIC

First, watch your video and read your instructor's evaluation of your playing. Afterwards watch your video again and fill out the below rubric. Leave correct items blank, mark any exceptional element by a plus sign and any element in need of improvement by a minus sign. You will receive a grade for full and accurate completion, and timely submission of this form. The form is due as per your instructor's directions.

_____ speech clarity and volume
_____ use of body and facial expressions to engage students in a confident manner
_____ model as required
_____ proper use of terminology
_____ interaction and rapport with students
_____ clear instruction of the task to be performed
_____ speech is kept to less than 15 seconds at a time
_____ all ensemble members are engaged, whether they are performing at the time or not
_____ recognize and correct all important issues
_____ follow proper teaching cycle pattern
_____ clear directions both in praise and criticism when offering feedback

Evaluation Summary: provide a summary of your classroom teaching by writing one paragraph of the positive elements of your teaching and one paragraph on those elements in need of improvement.

1) A summary of positive elements.

2) A summary of elements in need of improvement.

Assignment

1) Complete Individual Lesson Rubric and Classroom Teaching Rubric, to be turned in next class.

2) Review final test preparation prior to next class.

Conclusion

Having completed this textbook, every student should have a basic understanding of all four orchestral string instruments and be conversant in matters related to teaching strings at the secondary level. Each student shall consider this experience as a "license to learn" as study of string teaching is a never-ending pursuit. It is most beneficial for string teachers to take lessons on all string instruments as part of their continuing education efforts, as gaining deeper knowledge in every aspect of strings, the craft of conducting, and keeping up with the latest research in pedagogy affords the teacher to be a more effective educator.

Whether a person sets out to become a string teacher from the very beginning, or has found one's calling later in one's education, or was called upon to teach strings after having started a career in a different discipline, the gift of teaching strings is a truly unique experience. It is undoubtedly among the most rewarding careers, helping students make discoveries on these instruments that allow them to "sing" and express themselves. In the words of master luthier Anton Krutz, "the uniqueness of the violin family is that even though they are wood boxes with synthetic strings the sound produced, at least on the very top level instruments, resembles a voice quality more than any other type of instrument."[1]

When it comes to building a string program and to be relevant in a community, wisdom Jacquelyn Dillon-Krass imparts is as follows:

> Basically, a good string program needs two very important ingredients — quantity and quality. Strong programs need to have many students at many levels, and high-quality teaching and playing are a must. There also needs to be much visibility of the program in the community. The director needs to do much more than having students play concerts for their parents. You need to get groups out into the local area to play for civic events, and have them play music that appeals to the average taxpayer. If there are lots of students playing well and loving it, your program will be on fairly solid ground.[2]

Finally, in the words of Shin'ichi Suzuki, "[t]alent is no accident of birth,"[3] and as string teachers we make a difference in the lives of students every day. In some cases orchestra class is the *only* motivation for an at-risk student to come to school, the *only* band of friends the student has, and the string teacher is the *only* person who facilitates this connection. There is no greater joy, official recognition, or monetary compensation that could eclipse that knowledge. Perhaps the true mission of a string teacher is to work tirelessly to foster string education in the pursuit of providing the greatest positive influence on students to last a lifetime.

Notes

1 Anton Krutz, email message to author, July 15, 2018.
2 Wilcox, "Music is Key," 10.
3 Suzuki, *Nurtured by Love*, ix.

Appendix A

Instrument Sizing Chart

Arm length to be measured from base of neck to middle of palm while the arm is fully stretched out. As a rule of thumb, a slightly smaller instrument is preferred to a too-large instrument for the student. The below chart is provided as a starting point or an approximation guide, since proper fitting of an instrument will require an instructor's scrutiny in the pursuit of student's comfort.

Violin Size	Instrument's Body Length[1]	Student's Arm Length	Student's Likely Age
1/4	11"	18–20"	6–7
1/2	12-1/2"	20–22"	8–10
3/4	13-1/4"	22–23"	10–13
4/4	14"	24"–up	14–up

Viola Size (Body Length)	Student's Arm Length	Student's Likely Age
12"	20"	7–9
13"	21"	9–11
14"	23"	11–14
15"	24"	12–up
15-1/2"	26"	12–up
16"	26"	12–up
16-1/2"	27"–up	12–up

Cello Size	Instrument's Body Length	Student's Arm Length	Student's Likely Age
1/4	22-7/8"	18–20"	6–7
1/2	25-1/2"	20–22"	8–10
3/4	27-5/16	22–24"	10–13
4/4	29-5/8"	24"–up	14–up

Bass Size	Instrument's Body Length	Student's Arm Length	Student's Likely Age
¼	37-1/2"	20–22"	8–10
½	41-1/4"	22–24"	10–13
¾	43-1/4–44-1/2"	24"–up	13–up

Figure A.1 Instrument Sizing Chart

Note

1 Knilling MENC instrument measurements from "Average Body Length in Instruments" table in *Knilling String Reference Guide*, 22.

Appendix B

One and Two Octave Scales in D Major, G Major, and C Major for a String Ensemble

Figure B.1 One octave D major scale for a string ensemble

Figure B.2 One octave G major scale for a string ensemble

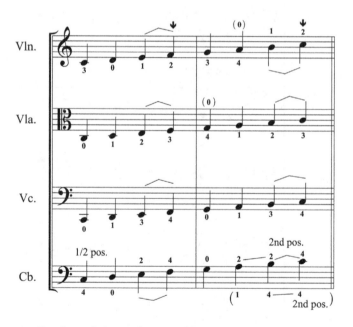

Figure B.3 One octave C major scale for a string ensemble

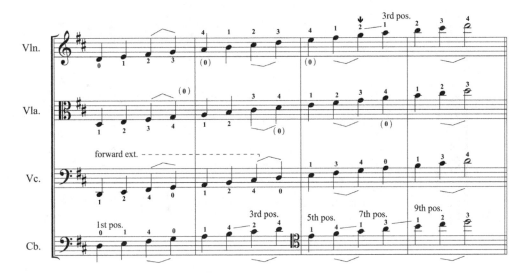

Figure B.4 Two octave D major scale for a string ensemble

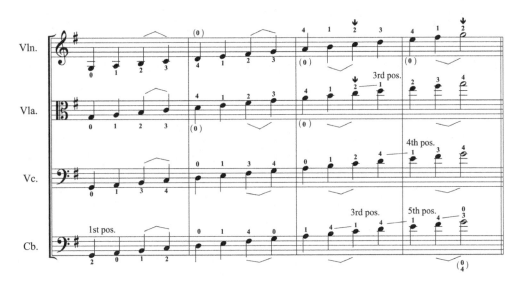

Figure B.5 Two octave G major scale for a string ensemble

Figure B.6 Two octave C major scale for a string ensemble

Bibliography

Adler, Samuel. *The Study of Orchestration*. 3rd ed. New York: Norton, 2002.

Applebaum, Samuel and Applebaum, Sada, "Paul Doktor," in *The Way They Play, Book 1: Illustrated Discussions with Famous Artists and Teachers*. Neptune City, NJ: Paganiniana, 1972, 228.

Bachmann, Werner, Robert E. Seletsky, David D. Boyden, Jaak Liivoja-Lorius, Peter Walls and Peter Cooke. "Bow." *Grove Music Online*. 2001; Accessed December 24, 2019. https://doi.org/10.1093/gmo/9781561592630.article.03753

Boyden, David D. and Peter Walls. "Spiccato." Grove Music Online. 2001. Accessed August 7, 2019. www.oxfordmusiconline.com/grovemusic/view/10.1093/gmo/9781561592630.001.0001/omo-9781561592630-e-0000026404.

Bugaj, Kasia and Selim Giray. "The Many Sides of Setup, Part I: Rehearsal Room Related Issues," *American String Teacher* 66, no. 3 (August 2016): 42–45. doi: 10.1177/000313131606600309.

Chew, Geoffrey. "Legato." *Grove Music Online*. 2001. Accessed July 7, 2019. www-oxfordmusiconline-com.umiss.idm.oclc.org/grovemusic/view/10.1093/gmo/9781561592630.001.0001/omo-9781561592630-e-0000016290.

Coelho, Victor and Keith Polk. *Instrumentalists and Renaissance Culture, 1420–1600: Players of Function and Fantasy*. Cambridge, UK: Cambridge University Press, 2016.

Colucci, Karen. "The Continuous Teaching Cycle." University of South Florida, College of Education. Accessed November 8, 2019. www.coedu.usf.edu/colucci/documents/thecontinuousteachingcyclerevised.pdf.

Dakon, Jacob M. and Selim Giray. "Collé Action: An Alternative Perspective on Right-Hand Finger and Wrist Mobility," *American String Teacher* 65, no. 3 (August 2015): 32–35. doi: 10.1177/000313131506500304.

Dillon-Krass, Jacquelyn and Dorothy A. Straub. *Establishing a String and Orchestra Program*. Reston, VA: Music Educators National Conference, 1991.

Dillon-Krass, Jacquelyn. "String Class Teaching Philosophy." *No Strings Attached*, 1999.

Flesch, Carl. *Problems of Tone Production in Violin Playing*. Translated by Gustav Saenger. New York: Fischer, 1931.

Flesch, Carl. *The Art of Violin Playing*. 2 vols. Translated and edited by Eric Rosenblith. New York: Fischer, 2000.

Gearhart, Fritz. "The Use of "Tartini tones" in Teaching." *American String Teacher* 57, no. 3 (2007): 32–34.

Geminiani, Francesco. *The Art of Playing on the Violin: Containing All the Rules Necessary to Attain to a Perfection on that Instrument, with Great Variety of Compositions, Which Will Also Be Very Useful to Those Who Study the Violoncello, Harpsichord &c. Composed by J. Geminiani Opera IX*. London, 1751.

Giray, Selim and Steve Oare. "Common Core to Common Score: Implementing the Common Core State Standards in Orchestra Classes." *American String Teacher* 68, no. 1 (February 2018): 30–34. doi: 10.1177/0003131317742342.

Gordon, Edwin E. *A Music Learning Theory for Newborn and Young Children: 2013 Edition*. Chicago, IL: GIA, 2013.

Guettler, Knut. "Some Physical Properties of the Modern Violin Bow." *Semantic Scholar.* 2006. Accessed December 24, 2019. www.semanticscholar.org/paper/Some-Physical-Properties-of-the-Modern-Violin-Bow-Guettler/2369b786635d1cf400cc5920b23812aa7183f1c9.

Heron-Allen, Edward. *Violin-Making, as It Was and Is: Being a Historical, Theoretical, and Practical Treatise on the Science and Art of Violin-Making, for the Use of Violin Makers and Players, Amateur and Professional.* London: Ward, Lock & Co, 1884.

Hodgson, Percival. *Motion Study and Violin Bowing.* Urbana, IL: American String Teachers Association, 1958.

Hogwood, Christopher. *Handel: Water Music and Music for the Royal Fireworks.* Cambridge, UK: Cambridge University Press, 2005.

Kjelland, James. "But What about the Sound? Toward Greater Musical Integrity in the Orchestra Program." In *Teaching Music through Performance in Orchestra*, Vol 1, compiled and edited by David Littrell and Laura Reed Racin, 6–13. Chicago, IL: GIA, 2001.

Knilling String Reference Guide. Saint Louis, MO: Knilling, 1996.

Koury, Daniel J. *Orchestral Performance Practices in the Nineteenth Century: Size, Proportions, and Seating.* Ann Arbor, MI: UMI Research, 1986.

Laycock, Mark. "Here Comes the Judge." *American String Teacher* 62, no. 3 (August 2012): 28–32. doi: 10.1177/000313131206200305.

MENC Task Force on String Education Course of Study. *Teaching Stringed Instruments: A Course of Study.* Reston, VA: The National Association for Music Education, 1991.

Meyer, Jürgen. "Seating Arrangement in the Concert Hall." In *Acoustics and the Performance of Music: Manual for Acousticians, Audio Engineers, Musicians, Architects and Musical Instruments Makers*, Translated by Uwe Hansen, 263–346, 5th ed. New York: Springer, 2010.

Nanny, Edouard. *Méthode Complète Pour La Contrebasse À Quatre Et Cinq Cordes [Complete Method for Double bass].* Paris: Alphonse Leduc, 1920.

Rolland, Paul and Marla Mutschler. *The Teaching of Action in String Playing: Developmental and Remedial Techniques [For] Violin and Viola.* Urbana, IL: Illinois Research Associates, 1974.

Rolland, Paul. *The Teaching of Action in String Playing.* Urbana, IL: Rolland String Research Associates, 1970.

Schmidt, Rodney. "Contours, Images, and the Bow." *Journal of the Violin Society of America* 7, no. 4 (1986): 102–113.

Shin'ichi, Suzuki. *Nurtured by Love: The Classic Approach to Talent Education.* Smithtown, NY: Exposition Press, 1983.

Simandl, Franz. *New Method for String Bass.* New York: International Music Company, 1968.

Spohr, Louis. *Violinschule.* Vienna: T. Haslinger, 1832.

Stahura, Mark W. "Handel and the Orchestra." In *The Cambridge Companion to Handel*, edited by Donald Burrows, 238–248. Cambridge, UK: Cambridge University Press, 1997.

Terry, Charles Sanford. *Bach's Orchestra.* London: Oxford University Press, 1932.

Thrasher, Alan R. and Jonathan P. J Stock. "Huqin." *Grove Music Online.* 2001. Accessed November 6, 2019. 10.1093/gmo/9781561592630.article.45369.

Wilcox, Ella. "Music Is Key: Training Tomorrow's Teachers." *Music Educators Journal* 82, no. 5 (1996), 10. doi: 10.2307/3398926.

Wilkinson, Scott R. *Tuning In: Microtonality in Electronic Music: A Basic Guide to Alternate Scales, Temperaments, and Microtuning Using Synthesizers.* Milwaukee, WI: Hal Leonard Books, 1988.

Wollny, Peter. "Bach and the Violin." In *The Violin*, edited by Robert Riggs, 95–122. Rochester, NY: University of Rochester Press, 2016.

Zaslaw, Neal. "Toward the Revival of the Classical Orchestra." *Proceedings of the Royal Musical Association* 103 (1976): 158–187. www.jstor.org/stable/765891.

Index